INFRAPOLITICS

Infrapolitics
A HANDBOOK

Alberto Moreiras

FORDHAM UNIVERSITY PRESS   NEW YORK 2021

Fordham University Press gratefully acknowledges financial assistance and support provided for the publication of this book by Texas A&M University.

Copyright © 2021 Fordham University Press

This book first appeared in Spanish as Alberto Moreiras, *Infrapolítica: Instrucciones de uso*, published by La Oficina, 2020.

All rights reserved. No part of this publication may be reproduced, stored in a retrieval system, or transmitted in any form or by any means—electronic, mechanical, photocopy, recording, or any other—except for brief quotations in printed reviews, without the prior permission of the publisher.

Fordham University Press has no responsibility for the persistence or accuracy of URLs for external or third-party Internet websites referred to in this publication and does not guarantee that any content on such websites is, or will remain, accurate or appropriate.

Fordham University Press also publishes its books in a variety of electronic formats. Some content that appears in print may not be available in electronic books.

Visit us online at www.fordhampress.com.

Library of Congress Cataloging-in-Publication Data available online at https://catalog.loc.gov.

Printed in the United States of America

23 22 21   5 4 3 2 1

First edition

To my friends

Contents

Preface to the English-Language Edition ix

Exergue. On Jacques Derrida's *Glas*:
A Possible Second Moment in Deconstruction 1

1. The Last God: María Zambrano's Life without Texture 9
2. The Wolf's Hide: Ontotheological Militancies 25
3. Infrapolitical Distance: A Second Note on the Concept of Distance in Felipe Martínez Marzoa 50
4. Infrapolitics and the Politics of Infrapolitics 63
5. The Absolute Difference between Life and Politics 85
6. A Politics of Separation: An Alternative Politicity 114
7. Infrapolitical Derrida: The Ontic Determination of Politics beyond Empiricism 152
8. A Negation of the Anarchy Principle 170
9. On the Illegal Condition in the State of Extraction: How Not to Be an Informant 183

NOTES 197

WORKS CITED 213

INDEX 223

Preface to the English-Language Edition

I first started using the term *infrapolitics* and reflecting on what it might mean in the early 2000s, which was a very different period in my life, not to mention my academic career. At the time I was preparing an earlier book, *Línea de sombra: El no sujeto de lo político*, which appeared in English only in the form of a few articles dispersed in various places. It is easy, retrospectively, to state that *Línea* already included some intuitions that would lead me down the path of thinking more consistently about infrapolitics, but an interruption in my life, and a general change in my approach to things, caused a number of delays, as well as disenchantment, even boredom, with the idea of writing books, particularly books that would validate my presence in the field of Latin American studies, which is all I had attempted to do up until that period, with uneven success.

I started experimenting with a different sort of writing, on social networks and blogs, while keeping up the work of preparing conference papers to keep in touch with colleagues. I suppose the curious reader could check out the blog called Infraphilosophy (http://www.infraphilosophy.com) to see, if not the progress of my thinking, at the very least the problems into which I decided to immerse myself. There are other texts even the curious reader may not see. But I make no grand claims. As Reiner Schürmann says, in order to think about certain things, "a certain way of life is required" (*Heidegger on Being and Acting*, 287). To engage (intimately) in that alternative way of life, in that alternative understanding of time and work, which I have found hard to do, has been my main preoccupation over the last ten years. And counting. Infrapolitics is nothing if it does not lead to a change in form of life, and for the better, of course. But it is a long path, and for the most part a silent one as well.

Eventually I came around to the decision that writing a few more books could be good for me, if not necessarily for others. This is inevitably one of them. A certain curiosity developed among a narrow circle of friends, together with a generous insistence that I write this book, which was easier said than done. In fact, I can date the beginnings of a plan to a precise moment in the summer of 2014, at a hotel bar in Madrid, when Angel Octavio Alvarez Solís told me in no uncertain terms that he expected me to do it. But first I needed to finish off a number of projects that had been worrying me, which have been coming out over the last few years.[1] Arturo Leyte had invited me early on to publish a short book on infrapolitics with his publishing house, La Oficina, but in the meantime I had committed to sending Miguel Valderrama, a Chilean editor, a very short book as well, finally published as *Infrapolítica*, which includes chapters 5 and 6 of *Infrapolítica: Instrucciones de uso*. Arturo got stuck with a longer text than he had bargained for, and which is, except for this preface and a few revisions, the Spanish version of what you hold in your hands.

I suppose it is fair to say that the idea of infrapolitics developed as an obscure consequence of my engagement with what was called "subaltern studies" in the 1990s. For many of my colleagues (not all), subaltern studies was nothing but political thinking, but some of us started wondering at a fairly early point if politics, or at any rate political talk, was all subaltern studies could do. The problem for those of us engaged in the discipline known as Latin American studies, especially within the humanities, was compounded by the field's radical resistance to theory. I have discussed elsewhere some of the problems the Latin American Subaltern Studies group had (see my *Against Abstraction*, 22–29, 115–17), and I do not wish to repeat myself. Let me just say that the group was partially committed to good old leftist work in the political sense, more or less in the radical leftist style of post-1968 social democracy, which was all right with the rest of us, of course, as far as it went. Or else to what later came to be known as decoloniality, an exercise in cultural critique from a range of extreme particularisms that was perhaps not as all right, given some of the claims that were made.

When we started to insinuate, timidly, that perhaps politics was not all there was to it, we did not mean that we should all therefore exclusively engage in culture or the study of culture or claim infinite decolonization as the ultimate goal of our work. This was the time of the dominance of the cultural studies paradigm, you must remember, which had its own problems, and from which we wanted to achieve some distance. Rather, we wanted to think about subaltern existence, and that meant not just the cultural existence of those confined to disenfranchised sectors of the population, but also everything in the experience of existence that could be deemed to have been subalternized by hegemony in any of its forms. Yes, we knew, there is also an existential form of hegemony, not merely political, not merely cultural, poignant and most unrecognized, even though it absolutely determines our everyday life through its imposed regime of constitutive exclusion, which is always to our experiential and existential detriment. But rejecting hegemonic forms of discourse, even those that thought of themselves as directly counterhegemonic (which we had some tangible reasons to doubt), and doing it from a marginal field like Latin American studies could not happen without a price. Some of us have paid the price through soft marginalization, silencing, a relative social exclusion from the field, which is ironic to the extent those are the very things we fought against when we fought hegemony. We should be at peace from now on, though who knows what the future will bring.

The Anglo-American reader might be hard put to care about what a small group of mostly expat Spanish-speaking academics, with some choice accomplices from elsewhere, might have to say. Their intellectual commitments vary, certainly, but their search beyond subaltern studies finds parcels of common ground in post-Marxism, deconstruction, and an interest in Lacanian analysis. And of course there is our common primary language, in some cases the only language of our professional commitment, with its vast if somewhat theory-deficient archive. In any case—I no longer remember the exact date, but I remember very well the Texas night, on the back porch of our house by the lake—Sergio Villalobos-Ruminott suggested that we create a study group on infrapolitics. After he said it—in the presence of others who were in Texas for a conference I had organized: Gareth Williams and Jaime Rodríguez Matos, Gerardo Muñoz and Maddalena Cerrato, Peter Baker, Michela Russo, Teresa Vilarós, Ronald Mendoza de Jesús—it became the obvious thing to do. So we did it: we created the Infrapolitical Deconstruction Collective, and others—Jorge Alvarez Yágüez, Humberto González Núñez, Benjamín Mayer Foulkes, Gabriela Méndez Cota, Jon Beasley-Murray, Angel Octavio Alvarez Solís—joined. We had a lot of fun with it during the few years that it lasted, but it ended, fortunately without conflicts, which is not always the case with these adventures. In the meantime, people were thinking of infrapolitics, and deconstruction, and deconstructive infrapolitics and infrapolitical deconstruction, in any way the devil led them. A number of publications followed, including, just a few months ago, the first full book in English, Gareth Williams's *Infrapolitical Passages: Global Turmoil, Narco-Accumulation, and the Post-Sovereign State*. Other books and dissertations and articles are being prepared, though, so there will be discussion of infrapolitics for a while to come.

This book, my book, is mine only. I do not pretend to represent anyone, although I am indebted to all of my comrades, to whom this book is dedicated. Its "exergue" devotes a perhaps exorbitant interest to claiming the legacy of deconstruction for infrapolitical thought, provided that deconstruction can be deemed to carry in itself a move away from writing as such and into existence and existential predicaments, which I believe to be the case. The chapters are then arranged to offer an indirect, if partial, genealogy of my own development. Again, I make no grand claims. Chapter 1 is about María Zambrano, whose book *El hombre y lo divino* seemed to me, and still does seem to me, a fundamental book in Spanish philosophy, and one in which I was able to locate two concepts I take to be at the core of the infrapolitical endeavor. I will only name them rather than rehearse them here: "degrounded relation" and "life without texture." These concepts are a crucial precondition for the development of the thought of infrapolitics, since they allow us to understand that life is other than being, different from it, but it remains ungrounded from itself as a result of an immemorial forgetting it is now our job to compensate for. But they still do not name infrapolitics.

Chapters 2 and 3 are also markers on the way to infrapolitics. Chapter 2 is an attempt to indicate the necessity of drawing a third way in the wake of the two main conceptualizations, the reactionary and the progressive, of political subjectivity that developed with full force in the nineteenth century and became hegemonic in the twentieth century. I deal with mostly Spanish thinkers and writers, including Juan Donoso Cortés and Ramón María del Valle-Inclán, so-called reactionary subjects, as a way into defining the progressive subject on their reverse side. My contention—namely, that it is, even politically, important to step out of the path of those two figures of modern consciousness—is certainly based on work I began when preparing *Línea de sombra*, and it still does not directly name infrapolitics, but it constitutes its precondition. Chapter 3 returns to the work of another Spanish thinker already studied in Chapter 2, Felipe Martínez Marzoa, whose engagement with the works of Karl Marx and Martin Heidegger in particular is essential to my own intellectual development. Martínez Marzoa complements a certain inversion of Heideggerianism that, I try to show, María Zambrano foreshadowed, and his notion of double distance, the distance from distance, gives us both a way to find a direction away from progressive and reactionary figures of subjectivity and a way of penetrating into the enigmatic world of Antigone, an infrapolitical figure if there is one, by way of Heidegger's 1942 seminar on Hölderlin, especially the lectures dealing with the choral ode in Sophocles's *Antigone*.

The central chapters of the book, Chapters 4 through 6, name and develop the notion of infrapolitics more precisely. These chapters draw a conceptual map that I hope will allow the reader to place infrapolitics within contemporary thought. In Chapter 4 I draw on Derridean deconstruction, try to indicate the particular position infrapolitics wants to occupy vis-à-vis a general conception of politics and the political, and show how the Argentinian philosopher Oscar del Barco and the French anthropologist Pierre Clastres provide examples of infrapolitical practice. Chapters 5 and 6 continue attempting to present infrapolitics directly by exploring the notion of an absolute difference between life and politics, which is also a difference between being and thinking. In Chapter 5, I engage with Jean-Luc Nancy's critique of the principle of general equivalence and more critically with Etienne Balibar's attempt to develop a philosophical anthropology based on the equivalence of the human and the political. I also discuss some aspects of the work of Alain Badiou that I find particularly fascinating in the infrapolitical context. In Chapter 6, I endeavor to distinguish the notion of infrapolitics from the notion of the impolitical developed in contemporary Italian thought, and particularly in the work of Massimo Cacciari and Roberto Esposito. I try to show how infrapolitics is impolitical with a twist, and how that twist makes all the difference. This leads me to Esposito's more recent renunciation of the impolitical, which he has come to see as a not sufficiently political neutralization and literaturization, as he puts it, and to Derrida's politics of separation, which is for me a variation on infrapolitics or moves in its direction.

Chapter 7 engages Derrida's early work on Lévinas, and Chapter 8 visits the Levinasian oeuvre as such, along with the thought of another revisionist Heideggerian that has been determinant for my own itinerary, namely the aforementioned Reiner Schürmann. I signal my differences with his understanding of the anarchy principle. Finally, Chapter 9 tries to present a last infrapolitical example, centered on the study of the figure of the informant in surveillance or expository society. I return to the notion of subaltern life, or rather, subaltern existence, and I draw on Werner Hamacher's notion of the "protopolitical" as my last claim for an infrapolitical differentiation.

I want to express my deep appreciation to Gareth Williams, Jaime Rodríguez Matos, and Teresa Vilarós for reading drafts of this book, and for their encouragement and kindness.

El lobo es una cosa incognoscible, he said. Lo que se tiene en la trampa no es mas que dientes y forro. El lobo propio no se puede conocer. Lobo o lo que sabe el lobo. Tan como preguntar lo que saben las piedras. Los arboles. El mundo. Dijo que el lobo es un ser de gran orden y que sabe lo que los hombres no saben: que no hay orden en el mundo excepto el que la muerte ha puesto allí. Si pudieras respirar un aliento tan fuerte como para poder apagar al lobo. Como se sopla un copo o como apagas el fuego de una candela. El lobo está hecho de la manera en que el mundo está hecho. No puedes tocar el mundo. No puedes aguantarlo en la mano porque está hecho solo de aliento.
— CORMAC MCCARTHY, *The Crossing*

Exergue: On Jacques Derrida's *Glas*
A Possible Second Moment in Deconstruction

In the fall of 1987, I had just arrived in Madison, Wisconsin, for my first job as an assistant professor. At a local bookstore I bought a book in French, surprised they would have it there: it was the two-volume edition of Jacques Derrida's *Glas*, published by Denoël-Gonthier in Paris in 1981. The volumes had what seemed to be a subtitle, *Que reste-t-il du savoir absolu?* (What Remains of Absolute Knowledge?), but that subtitle was missing from the first edition of the work, published by Galilée in 1974. Subsequent translations and editions have not included it. While it would be strange if it were done without the author's consent, the subtitle was possibly an editorial decision by Denoël-Gonthier that, as such, conditioned or determined many readings.

What was at stake? Between 1981, when Denoël-Gonthier published a second edition of *Glas*, and 1987, when it came to my hands, Derrida had become famous in the United States. He was already an assiduous visitor; his fame was radiating from Johns Hopkins, Cornell, Yale, and it was the fame of a revolutionary thinker who would have come to subvert contemporary thought by, among other things, breaking its ties from philosophy departments. There was a welcome reception accorded to deconstruction by institutional sectors in academic philosophy connected to phenomenology and hermeneutics that would soon begin to be called "continental philosophy," but Derrida's first reception in the United States happened in departments of comparative literature, later in departments of French and English, still later in German and Spanish departments and in other areas of the humanities and the social sciences. It was the moment of the irruption of what was quickly ceasing to be merely "literary theory" and became "theory" as such. It was a challenge to disciplinary philosophy, which in the United States, despite the continental philosophy niche, and at least as perceived from literature departments, was buried in the deep and rather servile boredom of analytic philosophy, dominant then as well as now.

The impression for a relatively recent immigrant like myself was that in the United States free thinking, insofar as it existed, had moved to literature departments, and it was projecting some considerable influence toward other fields of knowledge (an influence that no longer exists). But this meant that literature, understood not in the strict sense of the creative writing of novelists and poets and dramatists, but in the academic sense of literary studies and the production of writing about literature, had a new generative capacity, a potency of inscription, some power for the mobilization of thought. It amounted to a change, serious and effective, in the conditions of production of university discourse. That was our reality or our mirage in 1987, even if retrospectively it has become all too clear that the dividing line between reality and the phantom is hard to gauge. *There is* one, but *it is not*, to echo a distinction Derrida proposes several times in his book. In the wake of that mirage or reality I prepared to read *Glas* in French in 1987, because the English translation, published in hardcover in 1986, was already out of print, and I could not find it. The paperback in English would not be published until 1990.

In the meantime, what was happening in the Spanish-speaking countries that were still my main referent and focus of professional attention? Outside the early attempts by Cristina de Peretti and the attention Derrida's work had elicited in some academic corners in Chile or Mexico, Derrida was not yet a strong presence in the philosophical discussion, certainly not in Spain. Translations of his work into Spanish in those years, the end of the 1980s and the early 1990s, existed; they were being published, but they were dispersed and nonsystematic, and they were not always good, the options taken sometimes whimsical. Between 1986, say, when the English translation of *Glas* became accessible, and 2016, when La Oficina published its first Spanish translation, entitled *Clamor*, there is a thirty-year lapse, which is not nothing. With so many years separating the English and Spanish translations, is it the same book, in the sense that it prompts the same effects, the same reading expectations? I think it is not, and consequently I would like to offer the idea that *Clamor*, the Spanish version of *Glas*, is already a book to be read (or ignored) from the perspective that elsewhere I called (I know, controversially—how did I dare?) a "second turn of deconstruction."

We may take a look at a text that was written as a necrological offering, in the event of Derrida's death, in 2004, by one of the first-hour North American Derrideans, one of the members of the Yale group—the Gang of Four, as they were called—a good friend of Derrida's, Geoffrey Hartman. Hartman published an "Homage to *Glas*" in *Critical Inquiry* in 2007 that is also an homage to the dead friend and a celebration of the thirtieth anniversary of the original French publication. We can trace in Hartman, perhaps somewhat partially and arbitrarily, symptomatically, the reading expectations of the first generation of Derrideans and what became of them. For Hartman it was a matter of leaving "a mark in the history of the French language" (345). This is the intention Hartman, a scholarly philologist, assigns to Derrida, but it is worth mentioning that he does it immediately after saying, "Since *Glas* played a special role in my own thought, what I have to say is necessarily about myself as well as about Derrida" (345). The celebration concerns, therefore, "a linguist's treat" to which Hartman assigns political and geopolitical effects of several kinds: "A Mallarméan sense of *la glu de l'aléa*, the glue of the aleatory, makes a cornucopia of philosophic and literary themes cohere better than any telic (end-oriented) argument" (347). But what is the function of such an avant-garde "better"? What does or can that "better" mean beyond being a matter of Hartman's personal preference?

For Hartman everything hinges on *écriture* as a form of work, and in work as an access to experience: "The concept of *écriture* invokes an interminable effort to achieve experience. Learning to write one's life is also learning to discover or stay with a difference, to abide a labor of the negative in oneself" (348). This experience of writing, however, would be an experience of difference in the sense that it would open experience to the impossibility of *pleroma*, to the impossibility of accessing any "fullness of time:" "as in Hegel's dialectic, the passage of time reveals at every turn an alienating force producing absence and duality, even if history is thought to be slouching toward the presence of the present, a Parousia-closure viewed as the end of history" (349). This is enough: for Hartman, writing, the writing that Derrida performs in *Glas*, and more specifically in the Genet column, is what destroys the possibility of any metaphysics of presence at the level of experience, and what finds in itself the possibility of a remainder of absolute knowledge. By so doing, writing saves and restitutes, taking an exception against every return, every *Aufhebung* as a name of being. This is the pretension, and this is the leap. Writing, as the infinite displacement of the signifier, offers the possibility of a return without return, a gift without redress, an experience that cannot be subsumed and is thus irreducible to any fullness in the present, or any fullness of presence. In a nutshell, North American deconstructionism, at the time of its relative dominance in the critical scene, in the mid-1980s, swears by that conceit.

Are we still there? Would Hartman himself still be there? If Hegel offers us a "supersubject" at the end of history, via his monumental absorption of the world into the dialectical *Aufhebung* that concludes in absolute knowledge, *parousia* of *parousias* and final phantom, for Hartman Derrida would have solved the problem "opening philosophy (or I should say, more precisely, thought) to literature and literature to thought" (361). He would have given us, continues Hartman, "the courage to envisage a commentary without bounds, yet as precisely attentive to existing texts as the nowadays more or less abandoned tradition of meditative religious exegesis" (361). I am not sure that is what we once wanted or still want: to break ontotheology in favor of a now newly interminable meditative religious exegesis, even if no longer based on a sacred text but rather on the general sacrality of the text. Hartman does not present *Glas* as a new sacred text and does not quite say that deconstruction is an initiation into a new form of totality under erasure. What does he say? He leaves in his text the trace of a fallen thought when he states, "a strange thing happened. *Glas*, as a *discours de la folie*, nourished by an inky humor or melancholy milk, took its toll and convinced me of the foolishness" of the ambition of an idea of totality, or a total work (359). Against the idea of the book as absolute writing there emerges the idea that the "limits of textuality are the limits of the reader; it is we who stabilize the meanings of significant works by following their formal solicitation or imposing bounds of our own. Verbal thinking, as it questions itself, as it engages with and reflects on its medium, finds only provisional boundaries between a particular work (*ergon*) and texts outside of or offside to that work (*parergon*)" (360). In my opinion, the essential conservatism of the first reception of Derrida in the United States becomes clear, perhaps counterintentionally, in that drift toward conventional subjectivism. There is no total work, only an infinite commentary regarding which any limit will only be a function of the subjectivity of the particular reader. Is that the conclusion of the first turn of deconstruction? Is that what remains of Hegelian absolute knowledge? And, above all, is that a just adjudication of the promise and the limits of deconstruction? I do not think so.

Glas requires a new interpretation that should not limit itself to establishing the conditions for a new meditative-religious exegesis. It should reject it both on the basis of an understanding of reading in general and on the basis of an understanding of Derrida's own text. The book, monumental as it is, makes interpretation difficult, but we can start from the notion already indicated in the false subtitle of the second French edition: it is not necessary to proceed on a strategy that seeks completion in the name of an interpretative *Aufhebung* culminating in absolute knowledge and the final resolution of critical substance into a subject and of the critical subject into a substance. If there is a remainder of absolute knowledge, if Derrida's work, even through its own unworking, seeks to perform the remainder, then no interpretative strategy can be conclusive or look for a conclusion. We ought to change the terms of the question regarding *Glas* and from there move on to change the terms under which we have understood deconstruction. This book is an attempt to begin such a change. It posits that the second moment of deconstruction is an infrapolitical one, and it looks for a rereading of the Derridean corpus in an infrapolitical key. It simultaneously proposes more and less than that: more, because infrapolitics has no interest in presenting itself as yet another modality of textual exegesis, and less, because Derridean exegesis quite exceeds it. But we have to start somewhere. Others have of course already done it, in their own way.[1]

In the spirit not of exhausting that challenge but of opening it up beyond the presupposition of a dissemination of the signifier, which has served so many times as an alibi for the deployment of an infantile and ultimately narcissistic relationship with the Derridean text, I can propose something else. Yes, there is a parergonic overflow in the Derridean text, or there may be one, or so it is believed. But we should overflow the overflow, move beyond it, and I think we should do it starting from the enigmatic *hapax legomenon* that is the subtitle of the second French edition in 1981: What remains of absolute knowledge? Toward the end of the Hegel column, at the moment when Derrida would seem to be reaching the possibility of a direct answer to that question, Derrida talks about an undefined phantom that finds a counterpart at the beginning of the Genet column. Two phantoms, then: the philosophic phantom, the phantom of absolute knowledge, and the literary phantom, the phantom (an angelic one) of the immaculate conception, the phantom of the origin, the phantom of a petrified sphynx that raises a question that is also an impossible gift. There are two phantoms, two angels, two ghostly possibilities, but they remain undefined.

Glas places itself, to my mind, antiphantasmatically, outside one or the other, away from both. If we can understand the Genet column as an attempt to find an exodus from Hegel, and more specifically away from the *Aufhebung* as the last name of being, and if we can understand the Hegel column as an attempt to find in Hegel himself an autographic inversion that would be presenting a nonsublatable singularity (a singularity resistant to any *Aufhebung*), then it would seem as if the work on language that is common to both columns were seeking the production of a nonreturnable gift, a gift without an equivalent, a gift beyond any reciprocity. That gift would break away from the ghost; it would be the annihilation of the ghost.

We could offer direct but inconclusive quotations from the end of *Glas*, but then anybody can find them there. The point is rather that the gift cannot be captured, not even through quotations, and it is the remainder itself of any capture. From it, thinking is exercised as the very process of eluding *Aufhebung* as the name of Being. I will present, however, a quotation from what is for me one of the central sites in *Glas*. Derrida, consistent with his strategy in the Hegel column, seems to be producing nothing but a description. He is neither passing judgment nor critique. He is just saying, and what he says is what Hegel says and that Hegel says it. Derrida is talking about the master-slave dialectic, and he is glossing the fact that, even in Hegel, life cannot endure in the ceaseless imminence of death, neither from the perspective of the slave nor from that of the master. In both cases, Derrida says, I lose. Life loses.

> I lose every time, with every blow, with every throw, on both registers. To recognize, with a light-hearted cruelty, with all the enjoyment possible, that nothing of all this is in effect viable, that all this will end in a very bad way, and that yet, on the cutting edge of this blade (*sur le fil coupant de cette lame*), more fleeting and thinner than everything, a limit so taut in its inexistence that no dialectical concept can grasp or master or state it, a desire stirs itself. Dances, loses its name. A desire and a pleasure that have no sense. No philosopheme is attired or prepared to make its bed there. Above all not that of desire, of pleasure, or of sense in the Hegelian onto-logic. Nor, besides, is any concept. What here must be put into play without amortization is the concept that always wants to seize on something. There is on this edge (*fil*), on this blade, the instant before the fall or the cut (*coupe*), no philosophical statement possible that does not lose what it tries to retain and that does not lose it precisely by retaining it. Nothing else to say about this than what is said about it at Jena. The blow (*coup*) to the other is the fatal contradiction of a suicide. "When I go for his death, I expose myself to death, I put in play my own proper life. I perpetrate the contradiction of wanting to affirm (*behaupten*) the singularity of my being and my possession; and this affirmation passes over into its contrary, that I sacrifice (*aufopfere*) everything I possess, and the very possibility of all possession and enjoyment, my life itself. In that I posit myself as totality of singularity, I relieve myself as totality of singularity." (139–40)

Consciousness, which is always murder, is always also a suicide. This is a perhaps enigmatic but also classically Hegelian conclusion. It is also aporetic. It hides, or reveals, Derrida says, a strange desire without sense, a desire and a *jouissance* away from any possibility of ontological redress. Derrida is still not naming the secret pleasure, the *jouissance* that would subtract from the path to absolute knowledge as it would resist any *Aufhebung*, perhaps because it would be an unnameable *jouissance*, resistant to its own concept and to any concept. The text then informs us that Hegel solves the problem of the master-slave dialectic, which is the problem of the blow to the other, and the problem that every murder is also a suicide, by recourse to politics, that is, by way of the constitution of the community into the people, breaking the aporia. And it is only then that the figure of Antigone emerges into the Derridean text as a step back from the political resolution, as a rejection of the human law and the law of *Sittlichkeit*, as a rupture of the logic that links family and community and unleashes interminable war. The question is, "Where does Antigone's desire lead?" (145). Antigone's desire is inassimilable by dialectics. Derrida insists then that Hegel himself recognizes and affirms the inassimilability. "And what if what cannot be assimilated, the absolute indigestible, played a fundamental role in the system, an abyssal role rather, the abyss playing an almost transcendental role and allowing to be formed about it, as a kind of effluvium, a dream of appeasement? Isn't there always an element excluded from the system that assures the system's space of possibility? The transcendental has always been, strictly, a transcategorial, what could be received, formed, terminated in none of the categories intrinsic to the system. The system's vomit" (151 and 162).

I will claim that this strange affair, which by the way only confirms one of the key positions of deconstruction upon referring to the necessary destructuration of any structure as a condition of the structure itself, is determinant for what I am calling the second turn of deconstruction, which is certainly well beyond Hartman's meditative hermeneutics and has left them far behind. It depends not on a critique of Hegel, but rather on a determination regarding the Hegelian text. I claim, running a risk I know well, that infrapolitics is also there, in that destructuring non-place that is a condition of every structure, an unnamable *jouissance*. In any case, that is the intuition on which this book is based. Take my word for it.

Antigone's desire is the unlikely desire that interrupts the death exchange and presents itself to dialectics as its irreducible quasi-transcendental. Derrida finds in Antigone "an end of history without *Sa*" (166) (without absolute knowledge, that is, but also without that *ça* beyond the subject, included the subject of the unconscious).[2] Antigone, or rather Antigone's relationship to history, is literally the remainder of absolute knowledge, what subtracts itself, what overflows, what stays behind. Something in Antigone, in her character or existence, responds to the question of absolute knowledge by opening a path toward infrapolitics.

In another passage Derrida speaks in the first person singular, which is rare, not frequent, perhaps the only time in the Hegel column, another *hapax legomenon*, a kind of interruption or off-voice through which Derrida says: "Like Hegel, we have been fascinated by Antigone, by this unbelievable relationship, this powerful liaison without desire, this immense impossible desire that could not live, capable only of overturning, paralyzing, or exceeding any system and history, of interrupting the life of the concept, of cutting off its breath, or better, what comes down to the same thing, of supporting it from outside or underneath a crypt" (166). It is a feminine desire, and not any desire, and not any feminine desire. Antigone's desire destroys the ghost and demetaphorizes the system and takes absolute knowledge to its ruin. The phantom is the endless metaphor of *Aufhebung* as a name of Being, which Antigone belies. Antigone appears in *Glas* as the site or the figure for a second (or third, or fourth: other people, Derrida himself, have already intervened in this story and they have claimed their stakes) turn of deconstruction, anti-phantasmatic and infrapolitical. From it there is no passage to any meditative religious or quasi-religious hermeneutics on the sacrality of the text; or not without a certain ridicule. Antigone, who is not writing, not writing in general, not the writing of the exegete, takes a step back from any commentary; her silence encrypts her tongue, or her tongue encrypts her silence. Hesycastic rhythm, we can start again.

1
The Last God
María Zambrano's Life without Texture

María Zambrano (1904–1991) studied with José Ortega y Gasset at the University of Madrid in the 1920s and was intimately connected to the intellectual events surrounding the Second Spanish Republic. She was at the time something like a radical liberal, in the complicated Spanish tradition, a deep thinker whose early work already contains hints of the poetic and the religious veins that would mark her later work. She was forced into exile during the Spanish Civil War and initiated a pilgrimage through various countries in Latin America (Cuba, Mexico), then Europe (Italy and France), until her return to Spain in the 1980s. During those long years of defeat, poverty, and intense commitment to the tasks of thinking as she saw them, she produced an idiosyncratic oeuvre that is perhaps one of the most important instances of Spanish thought or Spanish philosophy.

This chapter is an attempt to read María Zambrano's major 1955 book, *El hombre y lo divino*, as a subdued but significant critical engagement with the thought of Martin Heidegger, or rather with the political implications of Heidegger's work, particularly *Being and Time* (1927).[1] I am interested in examining two of the conceptual structures that Zambrano offers in *El hombre y lo divino* against a dual background: the definition of democracy she provides in *Persona y democracia: La historia sacrificial* (1958) as renunciation and abandonment of the sacrificial structuration of history, and the notion of epochal dissolution of the identity of being and thinking in *El hombre y lo divino*. The first of those conceptual structures she calls *"relación abismada,"* which I will translate as "degrounded relation," and the second is *"vida sin textura,"* or "life without texture."

For Zambrano, a democratic politics is bound to the precise determination of the abandonment of "sacrificial history." If the abandonment of the sacrificial structuration of history defines democratic politics, similarly the practice of democracy defines an antisacrificial perspective on action. A democratic politics, regardless of what politics could be in itself, is always bent on the suppression of the divide between what Zambrano called "idols" on the one hand and "victims" on the other (*Persona*, 42). Beyond the search for power or the search for recognition, if politics is understood as the practice of abandonment of the sacrificial structuration of history, then politics appears as specifically democratic politics. This is what Zambrano proposes. But there can be no abandonment of the sacrificial structuration of history insofar as there is no abandonment of the understanding of politics as primarily subjective militancy. If subjective militancy is at the same time a condition and a result of ontology, to go beyond ontology, beyond the subjectivity of the subject, beyond an understanding of world as the domination of the object by the subject, is the condition and result of an ethical (or, rather, infrapolitical) position that has refused sacrificial politics. Zambrano follows here an intuition that Emmanuel Lévinas would have clearly articulated for twentieth-century thought. In the deeper layers of *El hombre y lo divino*, Zambrano hears a form of Levinasian saying at the heart of ethico-political articulation.

In the identity of thinking and being—an old notion of philosophy, one of its very first words in the poem of Parmenides—the very principle of sovereign subjectivity that has marked modernity itself is ciphered, perhaps deceitfully (as the Parmenidean phrase requires more than a literal translation). There is in effect no sovereignty without subjectivity, in the same way that there is no subjectivity without sovereignty. To paraphrase Juan Donoso Cortés or Carl Schmitt, every relevant concept of political thought in modernity is anchored in transcendental subjectivity, which turns subjectivity into the matrix of everything that is thinkable on the basis of the identification of subject and substance. Zambrano, in her sustained meditation on the necessary deidentification of thinking and being, is already pointing toward an alternative, nonmodern conception of the political. Only from that alternative conceptualization is it possible to formulate a project for political life based on the abandonment of the sacrificial structuration of history. But to abandon the sacrificial structuration of history is also to abandon every attempt at a politics of sovereignty, every attempt at establishing the political on the basis and ground of an experience or practice of sovereignty. María Zambrano as a thinker of the political thinks the possibility of politics beyond (modern, conventional) subjectivity and beyond sovereignty. The concepts of degrounded relationship and life without texture, which I will attempt to determine in what follows, are essential to this endeavor.

The Nonprimacy of Politics in Democratic Politics

In terms of the political as the practice of sovereignty, could any possible primacy of politics over history (including economic history) be considered absolute or relative? If the autonomy of the political is relative, then politics would still be subordinate to history in the last instance. If it is absolute, then politics would be the norm of action. But an absolutely primary politics, that is, an absolutely sovereign politics, would have to rely on the total immanence of its own conditions and would in fact be normless: that is, it would provide something like a normless norm for action. A politics without a norm, that is, a politics that would itself be the normative standard, without recourse to alterity or to a heterogeneous grounding, can only be a politics of force, and it would have become an ontology (as in the Nietzschean case, where the will to power is the ontological principle of Nietzsche's "grand politics").

Or is it possible that a norm for politics can be found outside history itself, and thus also outside force? That norm beyond history would not be an ontology, but it would register at some infraontological level, at the level of desire perhaps, a normative affect regulating something like Walter Benjamin's hatred of mythic violence, what Jacques Derrida refers to as the final indeconstructibility of the call for justice, or Alain Badiou's communist invariant. If something like that transhistorical or transpolitical norm were to exist, if politics can emerge through it as heteronormative, that is, always dependent upon an affect that would be exterior to itself, then it would be necessary to conclude that politics is always a partisan politics precisely to the very extent that it will not let itself be reduced to force or to an ontology of force. Can politics be thought without partisanship? Is partisanship, as expression of an affect that is only secondarily or derivatively political, an unconditional, irreducible determinant of any theory of the political? Partisanship, understood as the heteronomous recourse of every political positioning (I love my people, which is why I side politically with them, not the other way around), would therefore be the negation of the autonomy of the political, or autonomy's limit.

Zambrano, as mentioned, states in *Persona y democracia* that a democratic politics is bound to the abandonment of "sacrificial history." If the abandonment of the sacrificial structuration of history defines democratic politics, the practice of democracy defines an antisacrificial perspective on action. A democratic politics is always bent on the suppression of the divide between "idols" on the one hand, and "victims," on the other; it is based on the refusal of the fact that the existence of idols must always feed off the existence of victims. Only democracy, Zambrano says, among all the political systems, can shelter the possibility of marching toward an abandonment of sacrificial history.

There is no possibility of social justice without an abandonment of sacrificial history. The abandonment of sacrifice and the accomplishment of social justice, premised on equality, are then the goals of democracy, and they define the promise of politics from a democratic perspective. This cuts across other divisions of the political field, such as Carl Schmitt's friend/enemy division, or the division of the social between the part of the whole and the part of no-part proposed by Jacques Ranciére.

If politics is exhaustively contained in the friend/enemy division, then politics is defined by power: politics seeks power—its acquisition or its continued possession—as the power of one group over other groups, even if the need for group alliance is already a partisanship and introduces elements themselves alien to power. If politics marks the fundamental act of appearance of a claim to existence by the part of no-part, that is, of those who are negated by the ideological articulation of social totality, then politics is defined by recognition: the part of no-part wants to be recognized as such by the social totality, or it wants to be recognized as the social totality (the proletariat as universal class, or the people as general will). If politics is understood as the practice of abandonment of the sacrificial structuration of history, then politics appears as specifically democratic politics. Through each of those determinations there emerges the thought, only superficially paradoxical, that the only possible nonpartisan understanding of the political is precisely the understanding of the political as always already partisan. How can we link those three definitions of the political? We can imagine a complex interaction between demands for power, demands for recognition, and demands for the end of sacrifice in any concrete situation. At their limit, however, the three definitions are incompatible. The demand for power must subordinate one group to another group, since its limit is the existence of the enemy, and the enemy must be kept in check, which reveals this practice of the political as profoundly sacrificial, and thus antidemocratic; the demand for a democratic end of sacrificial history must give up power, insofar as it can only absorb the radical power of the nonapplication of power; and the demand for recognition is never just either a demand for power or a demand for democracy and social justice. The three definitions exceed each other, and, in their mutual excess, they organize something like an aporia of the political. Politics would finally be the infinite negotiation between those three ultimately incompatible demands: for power, for recognition, and for an end to social sacrifice.

But, if so, then only democracy can organize, even if aporetically, the simultaneous pursuit of the three demands, since no other system can countenance the end of the sacrificial structuration of history. Democracy can authorize, however, unconditional demands for power and recognition—not any demands for power and recognition, of course, just some: the absolute power of the people, for instance; or the total recognition of the proletariat as class, which is the political abolition of class; or the total recognition of gender, which is the political abolition of gender. Only in the horizon of democracy is it possible to think of the total subsumption of power, recognition, and the end of sacrifice. But this would be the end of the political, and thus necessarily also the end of democracy, and the end of the end of sacrifice: hence the aporetic character of democratic politics and, a fortiori, of any politics. As aporetic, the political instance appears as always already heteronormative, never sovereign, not self-contained. Zambrano will make it depend on an experience of the "pure sacred," of the *fondo oscuro*, of a contact with a last god that is to be understood as the very void of any *pleroma* or compact fullness.

Zambrano and Heidegger on Forgetting

Zambrano thinks of subalternity as the possibility of an understanding of the political beyond transcendental subjectivity, beyond the sovereignty of the subject of politics (or of history), beyond the conditions under which we have thought of the political in modernity and through modernity. Zambrano's notion of democratic politics as the abandonment of the sacrificial structuration of history shows that such an understanding forces us to determine the heteronomy of the political in favor of a partisan stance, that is, in favor of an always already previous ethical engagement. *El hombre y lo divino* can be comprehensively understood as a book that wants to narrate, impossibly, the history of a forgetting. I would now like to move toward the exposition of the two conceptual structures that I mentioned as particularly relevant to understand Zambrano's contribution to political thinking, namely, "degrounded relation" and "life without texture," as presented in *El hombre y lo divino*.

In twentieth-century philosophy the thematization of forgetting is intimately linked to Heidegger's *Being and Time*. But for Heidegger what is at stake in the history of philosophy is the history of the forgetting of being. Zambrano, roughly thirty years later, does not concern herself with being. What she is interested in is the forgetting of God, and with it the forgetting of the dimension of the sacred, the forgetting of the dimension of the divine as such. For Zambrano, as for Lévinas, God is beyond being. God, the sacred, the divine—such is for Zambrano the constellation of an epochal forgetting, the register of a radical insufficiency in the philosophical and spiritual experience of her historical time. Zambrano wrote her book, or finished it, during the years she spent in Rome. The repeated mention in her book of a white Pythagorean chapel, then recently excavated by archaeologists in a neighborhood close to her place of residence, is far from being incidental—just as her references to the Roman Empire's universalism are also not incidental. Zambrano wonders if the "fortunes of the [Pythagorean] white chapel" are ready to declare, in 1955, their *"oculto sentido,"* or "hidden sense" (116–17). Would it be a counterimperial sense? What is the secret that Rome preserves, on the side of the vanquished? And why thematize the forgetting of God to think, not even democracy, but the possibility of a radically antisovereign, antisacrificial politics? Hasn't God been precisely the ultimate guarantor of ontotheology? Hence the very ground of sovereignty? Is there something like a god without sovereignty?

How does one deal with forgetting? To the very extent that the forgetting is such, that is, that it is a true forgetting, it is inaccessible to the memory of the thinker. At most one could rescue traces, if there remains a memory of the forgetting itself, rather than a memory of its object. To think the trace of the forgetting of the divine, is that a theological or a philosophic enterprise? Is one to think theologically or to think philosophically the forgetting of the divine, not as forgetting of the *divine* but as *forgetting* as such? What could be the point of a treatise on the forgetting of the divine historically and politically? In 1955, in Rome, at the heart of Latin, Christian, Catholic Europe? To think about the forgetting of the divine is a task different from the task Heidegger had indicated as essential: to think through the forgetting of being. The forgetting of the divine is also immediately the forgetting of the transpolitical sovereignty of the ontotheological god. Must we go back to the source of secularization to reestablish a proper ontotheological norm? Or is ontotheology, which is absolutely founded on the notion of sovereign presence, itself already a forgetting of the divine in Zambrano's sense? If politics in modernity results from the secularization of ontotheological postulates, a politics based on the critique of ontotheology as a forgetting of the divine does not presuppose the return to any notion of transpolitical sovereignty. Rather, it seeks the destruction of the concept of a secularized sovereignty.

To think the forgetting of the divine defines for Zambrano a task very different from the one Heidegger would have determined as the philosophical necessity of his time: to think the forgetting of being. In his 1942–43 lectures on Parmenides, Heidegger came to link the thought of the forgetting of being with the destruction of an imperial thinking of the political, which for him exhausted the European thinking of the political, and which he associated with the curialization of the Greek legacy through the Latin translation of the fundamental concepts of the first beginning of philosophy in Greece (*Parmenides*, 43, 46). Western politics, in other words, is for Heidegger predetermined by the ecclesiastical internalization of the Roman concept of imperial hegemony. For Heidegger, in 1942–43, as the battle of Stalingrad was coming to an end, and with it the might of the Wehrmacht and of Nazi power, the enterprise of thinking about the forgetting of being, by now tragic for him, had become the enterprise of thinking through a nonimperial configuration of the political. Thinking the forgetting of being was for Heidegger in a very precise form—after he himself had taken the issue to catastrophic extremes through his Nazi commitments—thinking a nonimperial possibility of the political. Zambrano, a few years later, may have been attempting something similar, but at the same time radically different, from the thought of the forgetting of God. She wanted to think that nonimperial possibility, which for Zambrano has a name that remained alien to Heideggerian thought, namely, democracy, beyond its metaphysical and sacrificial theorizations rooted in the history of the West. Zambrano's fundamental category is the category of degrounded relation: for Zambrano, the forgetting of God can be thought only starting from the historical understanding of a degrounded relation to the divine.

El hombre y lo divino contains some hidden references to Heidegger's 1947 "Letter on Humanism." As is well known, "Letter on Humanism" attempts an account of the present—not just any present, since the essay was written in 1946—through "a thinking that abandons subjectivity" (207). This might sound faintly ridiculous today, when everywhere a vague and at the same time precise notion of subjectivity, suffering but triumphant, rules as the unthought in our presuppositions. Its critique is a constant motive in Heidegger, linked as it is for him to the moment of consummation and exhaustion of the history of metaphysics. In contemporary political thinking—a genuine and faithful descendant of metaphysical thought—subjectivity rules explicitly as the impassable horizon of any possible thinking of the political, and it is no exaggeration to say that, against Heidegger, most contemporary thinking thinks of subjectivity as the true house of Being, as the home where contemporary humanity might find refuge against the onset of homelessness, understood as that which is "coming to be the destiny of the world" (219). But subjectivity is for Heidegger homelessness itself and the site for the most devastating effects of technical thought. Take, for instance, nationalism, still fundamentally important in 1946, or expand it to any identity ideology: "Every nationalism is metaphysically an anthropologism, and as such subjectivism. Nationalism is not overcome through mere internationalism; it is rather expanded and elevated thereby into a system. Nationalism is as little brought and raised to *humanitas* by internationalism as individualism is by an ahistorical collectivism. The latter is the subjectivity of man in totality. It completes subjectivity's unconditioned self-assertion, which refuses to yield" (221). Man, the human, conceived from subjectivity, remains caught up in "essential homelessness"

(221). Is that true also for Zambrano? It certainly is true. But Zambrano takes her path in divergence from Heidegger's.

In "The Question Concerning Technology" (1954), a text strictly contemporary of *El hombre y lo divino*, Heidegger quotes Friedrich Nietzsche on the political importance of philosophy: "The time is coming when the struggle for dominion over the earth will be carried on. It will be carried on in the name of fundamental philosophical doctrines" (Nietzsche quoted by Heidegger, "Question," 101). Heidegger adds: "'Fundamental philosophical doctrines' does not mean the doctrines of scholars but the language of the truth of what is as such, which truth metaphysics itself is in the form of the metaphysics of the unconditional subjectness of the will to power" ("Question," 101). Both the Nietzschean will to power and the Hegelian-Marxist kind of transcendental subjectivity ("The essence of materialism [consists] . . . in a metaphysical determination according to which every being appears as the material of labor. The modern metaphysical essence of labor is anticipated in Hegel . . . as the self-establishing process of unconditioned production, which is the objectification of the actual through man experienced as subjectivity" ["Letter," 220]) are what Heidegger has in mind as fundamental doctrines when he says "the danger into which Europe as it has hitherto existed is ever more clearly forced consists presumably in the fact above all that its thinking—once its glory—is falling behind in the essential course of a dawning world destiny which nevertheless in the basic traits of its essential provenance remains European by definition" (220–21). Carl Schmitt's influence on Heidegger is here as notorious as it is unconfessed. These are to some extent enigmatic words. In them the displacement of European thought, its lag to itself, seems to take on the guilt for a coming (or perhaps just ongoing) world conflagration.

What, then, is this dawning world destiny in 1946? Nazi Germany having been destroyed, what is present as world-historical can be conceived in terms of only either communism or Americanism. Heidegger's recollective thinking of the history of Being aims at something else, but it must be reached in what he calls a "productive dialogue" with both communism and Americanism, understood as world-historical options that are themselves produced by the history of metaphysics: "Whoever takes 'communism' only as a 'party' or a '*Weltanschauung*' is thinking too shallowly, just as those who by the term 'Americanism' mean, and mean derogatorily, nothing more than a particular lifestyle" (220), as "an elemental experience of what is world-historical speaks out in" them (220). The lag in European thinking, the lag of European thinking with itself, as it makes Europe unable to confront the pincers of Americanism and Sovietism, asks for Europe to assume the guilt of a world conflagration. Europe cannot think its own epoch, and it is because of that

that Europe seems to be moving toward a hecatomb that will be presumably larger than the one that was still smoldering in southern Germany around 1947. In 1947 Heidegger is still anticipating disaster, never mind his claim that there is a saving power in thinking, in his thinking, that might perhaps avert its consummation. If there is to be a salvation, it is only because there will be more disaster.

Is Zambrano, during her Rome years, searching for the establishment of an option for thinking that would be simultaneously anti-Nietzschean, anti-materialist, and endowed with saving power? Yes, without a doubt. Zambrano is, in a sense, repeating the Heideggerian project. Her thematization of the God—of God, of the sacred, of the divine—attempts to offer such an alternative to European thinking. There is a specific will in Zambrano to think another beginning, and that will is consubstantial to the establishment of a historico-political project for Europe. To think of Europe, from Rome, even from the white Pythagorean chapel, and from her condition as a Spanish Republican exile, from her condition as a political victim of a world conflagration, to think of Europe from mourning, and from the mourning for the forgetting of the God, is certainly to think of the future of the world in its degrounded relation with the unknown god, with the last god: with a god, presumably, no longer ontotheological. Ontotheology is for Zambrano, as it was for Heidegger, the very name, the proper name, of the forgetting of the divine.

Authentic Historicity and the Repetition of a (Non)heritage

In paragraph 74 of *Being and Time*, which finally brings the work's entire existential analytic to rest on the notion of authentic historicity, Heidegger had notoriously sustained that "the resoluteness in which Da-sein comes back to itself discloses the actual factual possibilities of authentic existing in terms of the heritage which that resoluteness takes over as thrown. Resolute coming back to thrownness involves handing oneself over to traditional possibilities, although not necessarily as traditional ones. If everything good is a matter of heritage and if the character of goodness lies in making authentic existence possible, then handing down a heritage is always constituted in resoluteness" (*Being and Time*, 351). That heritage is very specifically the German heritage, precisely to the extent that, for Heidegger, the Germanic constitutes the periphery of Imperial Rome and therefore preserves the possibility of another beginning—other, that is, than the thinking of a corrupt legacy: a noncurialized legacy, a legacy not automatically translated into the rules of Roman hegemony, as it was the case, in Heidegger's opinion, for Latinized countries. The thought of that communitarian or transcommunitarian heritage or legacy, which later work will make it possible to understand as an anti-Roman legacy, is perhaps the most explicitly political contribution of *Being and Time*. But the hypostasis of this Germanic reworking of the legacy as the instrument of a new politics ruins the possibility of thinking politics outside a constituting subjectivity, and as constituting also exclusive. A politics of subjectivity, into which Heidegger necessarily falls as a consequence of the positing of a *völkisch* communitarianism understood as the resolute possibility of the affirmation of a new understanding of the legacy, like every culturalist politics, cannot subtract itself from its sacrificial condition. The idols of the tribe would always claim their rights.

There is a genuinely alternative understanding of the political in Zambrano's sense. For her, only a thinking of "un-legacy" can eventually abandon the sacrificial structuration of history in favor of a democratic possibility. A legacy, even in its radical, or "authentic," sense as the giver of a certain simplicity of destiny, creates sacrifice as it enthrones idols. From the legacy, from the necessary finitude of every legacy, the world can only be divided between idols and victims, and the victims are those for whom access to the legacy is constitutively restricted and denied. The simplicity of historical destiny, assumed in resolution, in the anticipation of death, and in the repetition of a legacy, where the establishment of the possibility of an authentic historico-political community lies for Heidegger, ignores the terrible facticity of what we would have to call dis-heritage, disinheritance, or un-legacy. Regarding a historical legacy, the denial of legacy constitutes the outside. In the forgetting of the facticity of un-legacy, the Heideggerian critique of subjectivity cannot avoid falling into the repetition of a subjectivizing communitarianism, since it is based on the response to the interpellation of a historical memory. The repetition of a legacy, whether intact or corrupted, excludes un-legacy, unlearns it, hides it. The disinherited is the one who cannot repeat a legacy and falls into forgetting. The abandonment of subjectivity, the accomplishment of a thinking that abandons subjectivity, is not possible in the wake of the resolute acceptance of a historical legacy—rather, it fundamentally presupposes a thought of un-legacy, a thought of disinheritance, of disheritage, a thinking of the forgetting of that which will not be remembered. The forgetting, or dismissal, of un-legacy is also a closure of the *Da-* of Dasein, since there is un-legacy, and not just experienced as inauthenticity. The repetition of a legacy, authentic or not, excludes un-legacy, un-thinks it. But thinking un-legacy is to my mind Zambrano's political project as formulated in *El hombre y lo divino*.

Because there is a different possibility: what if repetition could repeat the disheritage as such? If repetition, in the name of historico-political action, could repeat the nameless as such? Isn't this the only possible form of thinking about a forgetting? This open search for the nameless and the unnamable is the most relevant and poignant tension in Zambrano's text. In *El hombre y lo divino* Zambrano turns the conditions that regulate the difference between theology and philosophy around to the extent that, if philosophy were to remain as ontological knowledge, knowledge of being as such, the knowledge Zambrano seeks is not any kind of positive knowledge of a being, even if that being were to be the being of beings, or the maximum being. Zambrano does not seek the restitution of ontotheology. Rather, the science of the divine and the sacred, the science of God or of the last god, is in Zambrano a science of nonbeing, and thus not a theological science, rather an a-theology whose emphasis on the ontological excess, in what is beyond philosophical vision, reaches the rank of political a-theology.

Is *El hombre y lo divino* a political atheology? Does it at least give us a formal indication of a possible political atheology? Zambrano's word is always at the margins or in excess of any attempt to name representationally or calculatively regional being. It moves in a region that could be considered nonregional, since it is beyond any ontological horizon: the nonregional region of the god, of the last god. Zambrano's text on the forgetting of the god, on the disheritage, un-legacy of the thought of the god in our times, can offer the possibility of both a political and an a-theological thinking beyond subjectivity. Perhaps that unknown possibility of thinking finds its source in what Zambrano calls "the historical reserve that the vanquished always already form," and as such the site of "whatever is imperceptible in whole epochs, what was defeated, what never made it to reason or what went beyond reason, the seed of future reason" (*Hombre*, 115). That unknown possibility is then the possibility of subalternity, of subaltern thought. This is for her the possibility of another beginning of thought, and of another beginning of political thought.

The notion of degrounded relation appears in Zambrano's text at the beginning of the chapter called "God Is Dead," which is of course a sustained reflection on Nietzsche's doctrine. For Zambrano, "contemporary man" embodies, as contemporary, "all the condensed religious history of humanity . . . all the conflicts that have occurred in the decisive moments of history" (127). There is thus also a strong thinking of the legacy in Zambrano, but the legacy she refers to is anonymous and coextensive to humanity and its history. Thus, for her the Nietzschean expression "God is dead" is not the announcement of a liberation, is not the announcement of the beginning of another history, but rather marks for Zambrano precisely the moment of the degrounding or "*abismamiento*" of the history of the present: the moment when the forgetting of the god becomes official, to put it that way, and is forgotten as forgetting. Zambrano says: "One could divide things in life into two categories: those that disappear when we disavow them and those of a mysterious reality that, even disavowed, leave our relation to them intact. The latter is the case with that which is hidden in what is today the almost unutterable word, God" (126). She goes on: "The more the object remains outside our horizon, the larger and deeper our relation to it, until it invades the entire area of our life, until it stops being a relation in the strict sense of the term. . . . When one of the two [terms of a relation] . . . disappears, the relation becomes de-grounded. And then it simply happens that the other term, the one that cannot disappear—in this case, us, our human life—is thrown into an indefinable situation, is, in turn, de-grounded" (126).[2]

Contemporary humanity lives in a degrounded relation—god has disappeared, is dead, or has been disavowed, but in such a way that our relationship to it has come, through its very forgetting, to occupy the entire area of our life. To live in a degrounded relation means to live in the forgetting of forgetting, in degrounded memory. Forgetting does not therefore mean the end of a relationship, not even in the case of a radical forgetting. The trace of forgetting is structural: the more the forgetting, the more degrounded the relation to the forgotten object, but to deground the relation is not to erase it. A degrounded relation signals a coextension: what is degrounded invades "the entire area of our life." And then, on degrounding, life itself is degrounded and no longer has access to the rescue of a legacy, can no longer become resolute regarding the repetition of an inheritance for the sake of any simplicity of destiny. Except that, paradoxically, forgetting is the legacy, un-legacy is the legacy. If we embody every conflict in history, the entire history of religious humanity, that is, the entire history of the relation of the human to the divine, and if we do it abysmally, degroundedly, our heritage is disinheritance itself, but to the precise extent that there is no disinheritance without a legacy. Disinheritance, the lot of the subaltern, of the defeated, degrounds the heritage. Disinheritance is the abyss of our time for Zambrano—something the Spanish Republican exiles were in a much better position to understand than Heidegger ever could. In the concept of a degrounded relation to the divine, Zambrano inverts the communitarian and culturalist sign of paragraph 74 in *Being and Time* and she announces the possibility of a thinking of the political based upon the experience of radical un-legacy. But, if disinheritance degrounds the heritage, how are we to extract political relevance from this strange Zambranian figure, which amounts to a radical rereading of the concept of authentic historicity in *Being and Time*? What concept of the political can attend to the impossible memory of un-legacy?

Nothingness beyond Being, and the Last God

I set out to do two things: the first one was to elucidate Zambrano's understanding of democratic politics as the push toward the abandonment of the sacrificial structuration of history. On this issue, it seemed important to proceed to establish how Zambrano's *El hombre y lo divino* radicalizes the Heideggerian project for "a thought that abandons subjectivity" and, through a silent critique of *Being and Time*'s notion of authentic historicity based on the notion of *relación abismada* or "de-grounded relation," sets the ground for the democratic repetition of subalternity, for the endless repetition of a legacy of un-legacy upon which the very possibility of the abandonment of sacrifice rests. This is in itself a major accomplishment, even if largely unrecognized, and perhaps still unequalled in post-Heideggerian political philosophy.

But the second thing was to articulate Zambrano's conception of the political beyond subjectivity and sovereignty and beyond the identification of subjectivity and sovereignty that has produced political modernity as such. The identity of thinking and being, an old Parmenidean word (*to gar auto noein estin te kai einai*, for thinking and being are the same; Kirk, Raven, and Schofield, 246, 292), is metaphysically interpreted in the sense of the equivalence between subject and world. It marks in that sense the discourse of historical metaphysics which informs at its end the thought of transcendental subjectivity in both Hegelian and Husserlian philosophy. But transcendental subjectivity also marks the triumph of the totalitarian state-form in the twentieth century. Zambrano, who fought for the Spanish Republic, who became an expatriate and an exile for many years at deep personal cost, produces in the notion of *vida sin textura*, "life without texture," the very possibility of a radically democratic, antisacrificial conception of the political against subjective militancy, which is one of the political forms of transcendental subjectivity.

Subjective militancy is ontotheological militancy. There are two primary ways of it in modernity. In the first way, the militant—formal subject of a practice of the will—seeks the exhaustive exploitation of being, the thorough appropriation of being to militant practice. The subject, as a singular absolute, works on the remainder of its autistic immanence, thinks of the world as the infinitely reducible, and affirms its own apotheosis in the closure of world into subject and subject into world. This is the figure of the liberal subject, which is also the communist subject, and ultimately the neoliberal subject: a progressive subject, a subject beyond the shadow of its own impossibility, a subject who relies on the march of history from the explicit subsumption of the world as subjective project. In the second way of ontotheological militancy, the militant emphasizes distance, dwells on the loss through which the subject finds its bliss through open, painful deconstitution. The subject is here pierced by its own insufficiency, and must affirm a blind transcendence from that which, upon giving itself, is lost: from that which gives itself as loss. This is the reactionary subject, which is also the subject of personal identity.

In both cases, through both ways, the ontotheological ground of militancy is ground because the world appears as an entity regarding which one must either insist or resist. Through the first militancy, insistence is a will for saturation: the world will reach proper totality, will be the One-All as it coalesces with a subject only upon which a world is possible. In the second militancy, resistance is a will to distance. The world is always already One-All, and the subject experiences it as it experiences its own expulsion toward nothingness. The world is experienced as possible through its very withdrawal, appears as an always vanishing horizon, and it is through this very vanishing that the subject can exercise its own overwhelming presence: the subject is nothing but a resistance against nothing, hence the subject is all. In both cases un-legacy is not radical, it is only the ground for insistence or resistance. For the two subjects of ontotheological militancy—so many times subjects that are as doubled as they are empty: they hollow themselves out through the double claim—un-legacy does not fold into a degrounded relation but constitutes itself, precisely, in the open disavowal of degrounded relation.

What possibilities remain beyond ontotheological, subjective militancy? Beyond progressivism and reaction? This was, in a way, Heidegger's political question, and it was also, from a very different perspective, Zambrano's question. In *Heidegger y su tiempo*, Felipe Martínez Marzoa speaks about a distance from distance, a double distance, which would be the minimal distance provided by the very fact of understanding the game of appropriating presence and appropriating absence. But, Martínez Marzoa says, there is no "minimization" in that notion of minimal distance. Double distance—a distance from reactionary militancy, and a distance from progressive militancy, a distance from the insistence of subject/world and the resistance to its loss—is rather "enormous, immeasurable" (*Heidegger*, 45, 46). This double distance cannot form a new subject of the political, but it is the site for the appearance of that which dwells in the unthought of modern subjectivity. It is the promise of another constitution of the political. If progressivism is in political terms the form of the first militancy, and reaction is the form of the second, the double distance from both is the promise of another constituting gesture for politics, at its very limit, which is the limit where politics discovers with perplexity an instance that precedes and conditions it, and which I call infrapolitics.

Zambrano's concept of life without texture in *El hombre y lo divino* seeks the dissolution of every subjective insistence and of every subjective resistance. It seeks a possibility of experience beyond the autistic experience of ontotheological militancy. Starting from her radicalization of the notion of legacy, that is, from the experience of the legacy of un-legacy, Zambrano says: "[The action of nothingness] is a living action. One could call it life without texture, without consistency. Life with texture is already being, even though in life there is always more than texture, and so in man life is in excess of what it is in those for whom life is only texture. In man, life shows that it is more than being, being, that is, in the way of things, of objects. That is why in man, as being grows, so grows nothingness. And then nothingness works as a possibility. Nothingness *hace nacer*,[3] brings into the world" (169).

There is a textured life, and a texture of life, which can be articulated, or woven, through an experience of the legacy. But nothingness is precisely "what cannot be thought as a function of being" (165). It is the consequence of the degrounded relation, of the forgetting of every legacy. It is the dissolution of the thinking/being identity. Nothingness propitiates nihilism only for philosophical consciousness, and more properly for philosophy understood as a philosophy of consciousness, as a philosophy of subjectivity. But, in Zambrano, nothingness does not announce nihilism. On the contrary, *"la nada hace nacer,"* nothingness brings into the world, and what it brings is the *"fondo sagrado"* or sacred ground: "The sacred ground from which man went on slowly awakening as if from the initial dream reappears now in the nothingness" (173). Nothingness is for Zambrano the excess of subjectivity, the absolute resistance to—as double resistance, as double distance—subjectivity, "a resistance that is not being, since the thinking subject knows nothing about any being that is not itself" (174). And that which is not being is nothing, *"mas es todo; es el fondo innominado que no es idea"* ("but it is everything; it is the nameless ground that is not idea," 174). To think through to this nameless ground, nothingness, since not-being, not-idea, is for Zambrano to think "the last appearance of the sacred" (162), the last god. This is for Zambrano the philosophical task of the present, understood as a "conversion" (164), insofar as it requires a renunciation. In fact, it requires a renunciation to the renunciation of the excess of being, it requires to give up having given up nonbeing, hell, or nothingness. Only in that renunciation to renunciation, which is a welcoming of what dwells beyond subjectivity and its militancies, in that double renunciation and double distance the totality of thought opens up. Zambrano speaks of a *"desmoronamiento,"* a "falling apart of what is texture, of what is being in human life" 169) as an essential condition of that possibility of experience. This falling apart, this emptying out of being will open the space for the harsh but redeeming unthought. Here is a translation of Zambrano's words: "Nothingness is like the shadow of an All that cannot come into understanding, the void of such a compact fullness that it becomes its equivalent, the mute, unarticulated negation of all revelation. It is the pure sacred without any indication that it will allow itself to be unconcealed" (175).

How is the possibility of thinking the pure sacred, then, political, or how does it announce a new constitution of the political? A politics of untextured life is a politics of the end of the sacrificial structuration of history. The thinking of untextured life connects with the thinking of subaltern un-legacy. Something other than life shows up in untextured life, as life is not the limit of the thinkable. Beyond life there is a pure sacredness that remains close to the nakedness of nothing. The task today is to think or to undergo the experience of the pure sacred, to pass the test of the last god, that god that always already occupies the "entire area" of our life through our forgetting, and through our forgetting of forgetting. In life without texture, life without being, life without *bios*, accessible only through the experience of degrounding, in itself a consequence of the revelation of the death of God, the possibility and hence the necessity of an encounter with the last god—as the void of compact fullness—opens up. It is a remembering, but it is a remembering of what remains unlegated, and thus not the object of communitarian property. To remember life beyond life, against biopolitical subjectivation—that is the historical reserve of the vanquished as vanquished, and hence the promise of an altogether different politics, the infrapolitical beginning of another politics, of another beginning: the other side of sacrificial politics. Zambrano gives us, against the sovereignty of ontotheological subjectivity, an antisovereign political atheology. Is that the last or present sense of the Pythagorean white chapel at the heart of a thoroughly declined empire? But its promise for the abandonment of sacrificial history must still be thought out. For sacrificial history is always a history of the legacy, and of the life that is legated.

2
The Wolf's Hide
Ontotheological Militancies

Let us imagine that the foundational word of philosophy and political thought in the West or for the West, the Parmenides fragment that reads that "thinking and being are the same," is an error and a grievous misunderstanding. Let us posit, rather, a scission, a split, a dissymmetry, an alterity or allergy between thinking and being, a nonrelation deeper than any relation. To start from that hypothesis is to risk the collapse of language, but not to do it is to wage on the possibility of a thought exhausted in an unendurable legacy. The scission is the condition of possibility for the rupture of the well-rounded sphere of ontotheological truth. But the scission risks what should not be risked: if thinking and being are not the same, if their relation is canceled out in a nonrelation, language must be divided between a sacred language, accessible only from grace, and an idiot language, common to all. Unless there is another language, a third language. A third language means: a language subtracted from either the affirmation or the negation of the nonrelation, an infrapolitical language.

In *Heidegger y su tiempo*, Felipe Martínez Marzoa presents ontotheological militancy as the autism of the subject. The autistic structure of subjective practice in modernity has to do with the ontotheological determination of being as One-All or *ens unicum*. Thought in modernity must determine the conditions of subjective certainty for the world to offer itself. But "only at first sight every certainty is one regarding its own theme or affair, since the fact that this or that detail is like this or like that is finally an option that is referred not to the detail itself but to the all, in such a way that what is being posited as inherent to the very notion of certainty or validity or of thing is only the unicity of the 'about what,' the *ens unicum*" (9). Given the unicity of being, the *subjectum*, that is, what is talked about when one talks, that about which we say that it is something or other, is irrevocably marked by it and becomes "a kind of absolute singular" (10). But the *subjectum* as *ens unicum* opens the way to the establishment of a minimal distance through which the question itself is not absolutely identical to the answer—there is a residual uncertainty in the question about the certainty, and it is not an uncertainty that can be absolutely taken care of by the answer. That remainder is what Martínez Marzoa calls "distance," and about distance he says: "There is the thing itself because there is distance. The question of the thing itself goes from each thing to the totality of things, but the very question is only possible because there is something like a break with things, there is a distance from things or a sinking of the thing" (11). There is the thing and there is distance, and from the distance we obtain that the thing is sunk "in an inert and unlimited quantitative continuum" (12) which is already the result of the loss of the thing in the distance and through the distance. This is tragic.

First Militancy, Second Militancy, and the Distance from Distance

It is also the reason why ontotheological militancy becomes the only possible game for the unique subject of modernity, since the subject, always already fallen into the unicity of being, can do nothing except to affirm itself through a capture that is distance or through a distance that is capture. "It is not a matter of any duality of meanings in the word 'being,' rather the only meaning of that word happens in the hinge of that whose relevance is loss, in the fact that the distance or the play takes place insofar as it simultaneously vanishes. In other words, 'being' means always at the same time and inseparably 'being' and that which in 'being' has always been left behind" (14–15). The hinge indicates a fundamental choice. You look at the unlimited continuum and you privilege a rootedness that is unrootedness, or you look at the distance and you privilege an unrootedness that is rootedness. Either way, you have become a militant in the autistic game of the subject/One-All. Martínez Marzoa concludes his intricate presentation with the following words:

> The only truly new thing that remains possible is to understand, not to propose some "new" formula. But that means, already, completely to exclude . . . anything resembling even remotely "taking up a position," which would be the same as thinking we could appeal to some other-place-from-which in order to proceed from there to refer to things like what we have called . . . the unlimited continuum. . . . Understanding

is the distance, and it is so in the fact of being understanding, that is to say, precisely no longer as being any "new proposal"; the character of distance in understanding will become manifest, but only if it is effectively distance, that is, if it is no more and no less than understanding. (48)

The equivalence of being and thinking—an equivalence that Martínez Marzoa's formulation destabilizes through its absolute intensification and then breaks through the notion of distance, which is therefore an alternative option for thought and at the same time an alternative option for existence—ciphers the very principle of sovereign subjectivity constitutive of modernity. There is no sovereignty without subjectivity, but there is no subjectivity without sovereignty. In transcendental subjectivity, which turns subjectivity into the matrix of everything thinkable from the identification of subject and substance, all our relevant concepts regarding the political meet. This is why their outside, or their anteriority, which as such may generate other forms of politics, another beginning for politics, can be named infrapolitics.

In "The End of Temporality" Fredric Jameson mentions the by now old film *Speed*, where time, subjected to libidinal reduction, shows up as the multitudinous explosion of the present, as an ideological allegory of the vanishing of historicity, therefore of the full temporality of the subject. There is no longer a subject of time, or the subject is, like the present, an empty totality. The compulsive ideology of subjective action, such a frequent pretension in thrillers, which are without a doubt the most symptomatic narrative genre for our conditions of experience, that is, the pretension that the subject always acts, reveals on its reverse side the radical penury of subjectivity. For Jameson, *Speed* becomes historically "true" in its revelation of the contrast between the penurious subjectivity of work and the abstract wealth of finance capital. In the film the city of Los Angeles appears as the deterritorialized and desertic landscape of alien property, that is, of total expropriation. Full globalization is alien property, total expropriation of experience. The vertigo of speed, the ceaseless vanishing of the fullness of the phenomenological present, is the figural moment of a literality that can only be conceived as the empty place of the subject of history.

How are we to deal with empty literality? Some contemporary thinkers—Gilles Deleuze and Felix Guattari, Alain Badiou, Antonio Negri—have sought to invent a logic of singularity that, at its limit, reinstitutes metaphysics through an ontology of creation whose cruelty is not based on the oppression of the figural by the literal, but in the oppression of the literal by the figural in the indifferent quantification of a plane of immanence. Others—Michel Foucault,

Jacques Derrida, Jean-Luc Nancy, Ernesto Laclau, Giorgio Agamben—accept the Heideggerian critique of transcendental subjectivity in Hegel and Husserl and seek a reconceptualization of the place of the subject beyond the subject through various theories of political decision. And there is a third way, the more popular, which is followed by neo-Hegelians such as Jameson, Slavoj Žižek, Judith Butler, Wendy Brown, Luce Irigaray, or by the crypto-neo-Hegelian branch of postcolonial theory (Stuart Hall, Homi Bhabha, Enrique Dussel), which is committed to the retheorization of specific subjectivities as the central category of the political.

Singularity, decision, and cultural specificity, respectively, are useful to draw a homely map of contemporary determinations of the political subject. Under such determinations the subject is still a metaphor, therefore crossed by the literal/figural split. The path of the nonsubject (the nonsubject of history, the nonsubject of politics, which is an aporetic and impossible concept and which only wishes to mark the nonviability of its opposite number, the properly so-called subject) was perhaps announced by Gayatri Spivak's formulation of the subaltern position as the limit-place or the non-place where political and social histories are narrativized as logic.[1] The nonsubject is therefore in every case a formal indication of historical denarrativization, but it is a denarrativization that precedes all narrativization—the necessarily disavowed and covered-up instance where all political narratives find their spectral or negative counterpart. If Saint Paul, in Alain Badiou's work, offers us, for the first time in our history, in a form of theoretical caesura, since it is delinked from any explicit doctrinal content, the narrative of the structural conditions of the militant subject of politics (*Ethics*, 115), then the aporetic place of the nonsubject draws the destructuring conditions of nonmilitancy. If the Pauline subject is the subject of the so-called theological virtues, faith, hope and charity, a faithless, hopeless, and loveless constitution for the nonsubject determines a curious (de)structuration that is previous to any subjectivation.[2] The potential effects of all this on contemporary political reflection show up to what point the latter is sealed by a metaphoricity that is already dead as metaphoricity, already reified: the metaphoricity of the militant subject of ontotheology.

In the previous chapter, I proposed two primary or dominant forms of ontotheological militancy in modernity. In the first one, the militant, the formal subject of a practice of the will, seeks the exhaustive exploitation of being, the identification of being with militant practice. The subject as singular absolute reduces the residue of its autistic immanence, conceives of the world as the infinitely reducible, and affirms its own apotheosis in the closure of the world into the subject and of the subject into the world. In the second one, the militant places his or her emphasis on distance, in the loss concerning which the subject is constituted in open deconstruction, traversed by its own resistance, affirming a blind transcendence from that which on giving itself withdraws itself as such. In both cases the ontotheological foundation is foundation because the world appears as an entity in the face of which only insistence or resistance are possible.[3] In the first militancy insistence is a will for saturation: the world will be One-All in its coalescence with a subject that conditions the self-giving of the world. In the second militancy resistance is a will to distance: the world is always already One-All, but the subject lives in its expulsion toward nothingness, and the world appears in its withdrawal, as an always vanishing horizon, and precisely not in any other way.

Martínez Marzoa's "distance" is a distance from distance, "only the distance that is given through the mere fact of understanding" the play of distance and its negation. But he adds that the "only" has nothing to do with minimization. The distance from distance, which is a distance from the second militancy (distance) and from the first militancy (negation of distance), is, rather than minimal, "enormous, unmeasurable." In that distance, double distance, an existential position opens up that happens in the infrapolitical region. A distance from distance and from its negation, a distance from the subject-world insistence and from the loss of the world in the resistance to its loss: an inconspicuous (but unmeasurable) presencing, a happening, "a coming-into-presence only through subtraction" (*Heidegger*, 45, 46). That subtractive presencing, what presences upon subtraction, is not the subject of any politics, but that which subceeds and dwells in the unthought of modern subjectivism. In politics, progressivism is the form of the first militancy. Reaction is the form of the second one. The distance from distance is the promise of another gesture at the same time constitutive and destitutive of politics, perhaps barely thinkable but in whose possibility this book seeks its place.

Progressivism and Reaction

The pair progressivism/reaction, Arturo Leyte says, is constitutive of modernity along a line of mediations symptomatized, for instance, in Galilean mathematical physics, and in Galileo's postulation of "a law of movement as a principle of inertia, which presumes an antagonistic duality between an unlimited trajectory and a resistance" ("Naturaleza," 167); in Baroque painting, where "a movement and progression are presumed that goes from darkness and shadows, generally at the bottom of the painting . . . to the plenitude of the light that is laboriously accomplished in the upper parts of it" (164); in Baroque architecture, "wrapped up in a fragility that highlights the difference between the clarity toward which it rises and the darkness from which it departs" (168); and in the Cartesian opposition between *cogito* and nature, or between clear and distinct ideas and dark and confused ones (168). But in the Baroque age the triumphant possibility of the spiritual element is still not presupposed or taken for granted. It is rather Absolute Idealism, and its transcendental subjectivity, that consummates the full entry of Martínez Marzoa's unlimited continuum under the sign of a lineal temporality aiming for progress (*Heidegger*, 12). With Schelling and Hegel, "if reason is absolute, nothing can be left outside and no difference can be established beyond it. . . . If it is possible to speak of nature and spirit as separate it is because they are part of the same. And 'the same' is the very constitution of reason, which is nothing but the process itself that leads from nature to spirit. . . . Reason, understood as process, is its own history, whose origin is to be found in the shadows (of nature) and whose end is the clarity (of spirit) that knows itself. Reason is its history" (Leyte, "Naturaleza," 169).[4] That being the case, "in the horizon of the infinite line of history, which is also the infinite line of reason that can conceive of everything, any resistance immediately becomes a reaction to the progress of reason. It immediately becomes reactionary" (170). The pair progressivism/reaction is essential to a world understood as the structuring triumph of transcendental subjectivity.

Friedrich Nietzsche's philosophy, the last historical non-epigonal manifestation of such a structure, will take the full historicization of reason to its inversion into will to power, which fundamentally affirms the reactive character of any truth in order to posit its overcoming. What is active in Nietzsche, which is the instance where Gilles Deleuze will cipher his own endless progressivism, is absolutely bound to the reactive, without which it could not function.[5] The very pretension that will to power, and its corollary the eternal return of the same, will begin another history and will undo the ascetic ideal of European metaphysics hides a terminal nihilism in which the very notion of progress becomes indifferently replaced by the infinite intensification of a power that needs, in order to produce itself, an equally infinite resistance. Dionysus incessantly repeats his fight against The Crucified, and that is perhaps the clearest and most exhausting image of the progressivist/reactionary nature of philosophy through modernity. But that is also the image of its ontotheological militancy.

With Nietzsche, however, ontotheological militancy gets dissolved as a possibility, and reaches its putative end. If will to power undoes the distance between reactionary and progressive subjectivity, it is because subjectivism reaches its apogee and apotheosis in the substitution of *cogito* by *volo*. Everything is now within *volo*, I will, because everything finds its place in a hierarchical distribution of force starting from force as ontological principle. The unlimited continuum, which is now a continuum of ontological force, finds its consummation in Nietzsche, which is also its (putative) historical end. In Martínez Marzoa's words,

> the fact that the One-All project comes to full formulation can only mean the sacrifice of the One-All. It means, in effect, that the One-All, precisely because it is what it is, no longer has anything opposing it and keeping it from being what it is, leaves nothing outside, not even as some modality of presence or of knowledge that could be thought of as irreducibly different. And if it leaves nothing outside and is opposed to nothing, then it simply has no place. In other words: the task of the One-All ends up being the task of refusing to recognize it in any way, of keeping oneself from giving it acknowledgment; this is what the "let us guard ourselves" in paragraph 109 of *The Gay Science*, where the eternal return and the will to power are contained, is about. (*Heidegger*, 37)

Ontotheological militancy comes into its modern end through the Nietzschean "let us guard ourselves," which is also its undifferentiated formulation.

There is therefore no possible critique of reactionary reason that should not at the same time be formulated as a critique of the progressivist reason that is its necessary counterpart, in the same way that there is no possible critique of progressivist reason that is not at the same time a critique of reactionary reason. But the suspicion or the fear that we will not be able to get rid of reactionary/progressivist reason without risking through it a total loss of historicity, which would also be a total loss of politics if we insist on the militant equivalence of politics and subjectivity, should not lead us to the decision of becoming, in disavowal, secret agents of reaction, or of progressivism. It is rather a matter of moving toward an alternative determination of politics, of displacing the ontotheology of subjectivity in the underground of the Western conception of politics to a place other than ontotheological. Opposing progressivism, however, in the context of opposing the larger historical configuration of the co-implicated pair progressivism/reaction as a delimitation of politics, is not in any way to oppose the political claims of those oppressed by any given situation of domination and inequality. Rather, on the contrary. The analytical attempt that follows, even though centered upon ideologemes more proper to reactionary reason, has a subalternist and infrapolitical intentionality and thinks the end of sacrificial history, as it was announced in the previous chapter.[6]

The strict content of the notion of reactionary thinking is framed by the historical cycle that goes from the French Revolution of 1789 to the fall of the Soviet regime, consummated in 1991. Another history begins to open there for which we still have no adequate categories. It is barely useful, for instance, to think about North American imperial politics after 1991 and until September 2001 as reducible to criteria based on the traditional play of progressivism and reaction, to which it is largely heterogeneous perhaps even in spite of itself.[7] The alternative conceptual pair "subalternity/hegemony" might help a little more in order to understand the fundamental coordinates of politics in our long present. There is no proper symmetry between progressivism/reaction and hegemony/subalternity. The subaltern is neither immediately nor even mediately progressive or reactionary—nor is the hegemonic. So hegemony/subalternity are largely deprived of properly political valences, which means that it would be difficult or impossible to establish a legitimate political practice on the basis of the second conceptual pair: at the political level, and beyond general partisanship, which can only be tendential, one cannot be unconditionally in favor of the hegemonic or the subaltern without stupidity or blindness. And stupidity and blindness are usually paid for, by others for the most part.

I will begin therefore in a different place: in the critique of the second militancy, which is reactionary militancy. Let us imagine the possibility of establishing the notion of reactionary thought as a concept in the context of a general theory of thought or of theoretical practice, understanding theoretical practice as a resistance to processes of formal reification, whether aesthetic forms, forms of valuation, or conceptual forms. If a productive determination of a critique of reactionary reason were possible, we would count on at least three paradigms: following Carl Schmitt, reactionary thought is post-Enlightenment resistance to the advancement of the secularization process through political practice. For him, reactionary thought is (re)theologizing and pro-sovereign as well as antidemocratic. For Althusserian Marxism, reactionary thought is a resistance to the rise of a new mode of production from a previously dominant one (feudal or absolutist at the time of dominance of the bourgeois mode of production, bourgeois at the time of late capitalism). And for neo-Spinozianism reactionary thought is constituted power facing the constituent power of the multitude. What is common to all three of them is a definition of the reactionary as that which functions against the grain of every emergent or dominant mode of production or social organization, that is, that which symbolically results from a social residue, but which reaffirms itself, through reactionary militancy, through the radical negation of its residual character. If we can call any production of sense thought, reactionary thought is a production of sense that is formulated in the context of a residual/

antiresidual understanding of the political. It lives in the residue in the negation of the residue, of the residual quality of the residue. It consummates itself through resistance and disavowal.

Juan Donoso Cortés's "Discurso sobre la dictadura" (Discourse on Dictatorship), which he prepared in 1849, is a reaction to the revolutionary events of 1848 that had shaken several European cities through the production of the specter of communism. By 1849 Europe had lived in revolutionary and counterrevolutionary times for sixty years, and things only seemed to become more complicated. Donoso, and with him European reaction in general, knew that there was no simple return to the past. But Donoso is particularly lucid and understands the postulate of a renewed Catholic unity in the context of a restored absolute monarchy as an impossible dream. He knows, in other words, that "God, the Fatherland, the King!" will hardly trump even in the European south the countercry "liberty, equality, fraternity!" Even so, Donoso's political solution is still a negation of the residual quality of the old theologico-political principles of the ancien régime, which politically meant the affirmation of a necessary violence regarding the containment or the restraining of the future.

For Donoso, the future is a terrible monster. A passage that is extraordinary for its rhetorical force in his *Essay on Catholicism, Liberalism, and Socialism* expresses the Donosian conception of the temporality of politics. He says:

> Do not tell me you do not want to fight, because at the very instant you tell me you are already fighting; or that you do not know what side to take, because, at the very moment you say that, you have already taken sides; and do not affirm you want to be neutral, because when you deem yourself so you are neutral no longer; do not assure me that you will remain indifferent, because I will mock you, since the minute you pronounce that word you have become a partisan. Do not tire yourself seeking a secure shelter against the hazards of war, because you tire yourself in vain; that war will expand as much as space and will prolong itself as much as time. Only in eternity, the fatherland of the just, will you be able to find rest; because only there there is no combat; do not however assume that the doors of eternity will open for you if you are unable to show first the scars you carry; those doors do not open except for those who fought here gloriously the fights of the Lord, and for those who, like the Lord, arrive crucified. (*Ensayo*, 79, my translation)

These words translate an ominous political truth of modernity, after the fall of the ancien régime and its protective network against the necessity of decision. They may have found a new resonance today. In his *Ethics of Psycho-*

analysis Jacques Lacan says that the European nineteenth century, not only Donoso's historical horizon but also the century for the general conflagration between progressives and reactionaries that would end up acquiring global dimensions, is a witness to "a radical decline in the function of the master" (*Ethics*, 11). The latter would explain the growing irrelevance of the notion of the sovereign Good, which is so determinant for previous European political history. The decadence of the function of the master is no doubt a decline in the faith that makes ontotheological God the warrant of the supreme transformation, understood as the acquisition of the sovereign Good: the faith in the eschatological promise. Under the domination of the master, the political path was simply a facilitator, a path to transformation: political action might not touch the infinite promise, but it could lead toward it or anticipate it through obedience, patriotism, respect for authority, and other civic virtues. The postrevolutionary decline of the master function in nineteenth-century Europe turns politics into a tool for the secularization of the promise and makes it accessible to all as citizens, and not as immortal souls. The first ontotheological militancy seeks its goal in modernity through the secularization of the promise of the infinite identification of the subject and its foundation, the supreme substance. For Donoso the maintenance of the promise of the sovereign Good, even if now immanent to the social even for him, was at the same time a condition of the new role of politics and a reminder of the deep theological compromise of political modernity, including its disavowal and repression. Today the residue of such a disavowal has become a sinister symptom. The return of the repressed *in theologicis* hits the world and reorganizes it in "degrounded relation," in Zambrano's sense, not just through the various neopatriarchal fundamentalisms in non-Western countries but also through the Western fundamentalisms that the current US administration, or its British counterpart, push against the ambiguous and impotent consternation of the European political establishment. Not to mention the various so-called *soberanismos*.

Lacan says that "in Hegel . . . we find expressed an extreme devalorization of the position of the master, since Hegel turns him into the great dupe, the magnificent cuckold of historical development, given that the virtue of progress passes by way of the vanquished, which is to say, of the slave, and his work. Originally, when he existed in his plenitude in Aristotle's time, the master was something very different from the Hegelian fiction, which is nothing more than his obverse, his negation, the sign of his disappearance" (*Ethics*, 11–12).[8] For Lacan, Hegel is already a thinker of the decline of the master function, which is why Hegel can only think its negation. The Hegelian negation will come to experience in postrevolutionary modernity in general through the possibility of what Lacan calls "the naturalist liberation of desire" (3). It is precisely because we are no longer subjected to the rule of the master that we can prepare ourselves for a practice beyond ostensible rule, which would be the consummation of the first ontotheological militancy. But, Lacan says,

> Now the naturalist liberation of desire has failed. The more the theory, the more the work of social criticism, the more the sieve of that experience, which tended to limit obligation to certain precise functions in the social order, have raised in us the hope of relativizing the imperative, the contrary, or, in a word, conflictual character of moral experience, the more we have, in fact, witnessed a growth in the incidence of genuine pathologies. The naturalist liberation of desire has failed historically. We do not find ourselves in the presence of a man less weighed down with laws and duties than before the great critical experience of so-called libertine thought. (3–4)

Our experience, in other words, is still subjected to a master, in spite of the decline of the master function. How is this possible? Could the decline in the master function have been but a mirage? Can the great critical experience of libertine thought have meant nothing? Is man, or is woman, as Kant said somewhere in his anthropology book, an animal that needs a master? But these are Donoso's questions, to which he opposed his crucial doctrine in the "Discourse on Dictatorship."

The Donosian doctrine of repressive equilibrium is one of the most notorious nineteenth-century formulations concerning the historical failure of the naturalist liberation of desire. It is also as good a place as any to cipher the irruption of the second ontotheological militancy. For Donoso, who is not so far in this from Lacan or from Lacan's master, Freud, the liberation of desire leads to evil. The decline in the function of the master is a political as well as a moral disaster. Theological decline demands political action, demands a political decision. The latter is therefore a fundamentally post-theological political decision. Once we have lost the illusion that the theological kingdom can be restored, a just politics of force finds its measure in its capacity to contain the advancement of post-theological evil. For Donoso the imminent presence of post-theological evil requires in reply the affirmation of the right to sovereign exception, the dictatorship of the friend. But who is the friend?

"Gentlemen, there are but two possible repressions: an interior and an exterior one, religious and political. These are of such a nature that, when the religious thermometer is high, the thermometer of repression is low, and when the religious thermometer is low, the political thermometer, political repression, tyranny, is high. This is a law of humanity, a law of history" ("Discurso,"

253–54). The zero degree of political repression was, therefore, the highest moment of religious repression: "with Jesus Christ, where religious repression is born, political repression completely disappears. This is so true that, Jesus Christ having founded a society with his disciples, it was the only society that has ever existed without a government. Between Jesus and his disciples there was no government other than the love of the Master for his disciples and the love of the disciples for the Master. That is to say, when interior repression was complete, freedom was absolute" (254). Since then, through the Conversion of Constantine, feudalism, the Renaissance, the Reformation and the Counter-Reformation, the Enlightenment, interior repression diminishes and political repression increases. In modernity the degrees of such an increase are ciphered for Donoso in four epochal events, which are the creation of permanent armies, the creation of the police, the creation of a centralized state administration, and the invention of the telegraph. All of them raise the political-repression temperature, which means they are all symptoms of a prior liberation of desire, a prior revolt against the master, hence a descent in the temperature of the religious thermometer. "Gentlemen: such was the state of Europe and the world when the first explosion of the last revolution came to tell us all that there still wasn't enough despotism in the world: because the religious thermometer was below zero" (256). This moment of maximum danger, which foretells in 1849 the potentially imminent triumph of a communist revolution, understood by Donoso as the night of the world in the full plenitude of political despotism, marks the need for a decision. "Therefore, one of two" (256): "Either religious reaction happens, or it does not" (256).

The stakes of that decision are the very future of the world: "the paths are ready for a gigantic, colossal, universal, immense tyrant" (257). Only a religious reaction can "avoid the catastrophe; that and nothing else" (257). And yet: even if it were in our hands to provoke a religious reaction, even if that were our most pressing duty, "I have seen, gentlemen, and I have known many individuals that exited their faith and have returned to it; unfortunately, gentlemen, I have never seen a people return to the faith after having lost it" (257–58). A religious reaction will not come. There is no hope. How, then, to avoid the catastrophe?

The die has been cast. There is no return. Donoso is not calling for a restoration; he is not looking for a restorative form of first militancy. If Donoso is a reactionary thinker, and we should harbor little doubt as to it, it is because he reacts to the future as the terrible monster of the colossal, gigantic, immense, and universal tyranny. The old times will not come back, certainly not in our current historical cycle. The option is not between religious reaction and inaction, but rather between the despotic tyranny of absolute political repression and a dictatorship of order: "it is a matter of choosing between the dictatorship from below and the dictatorship from above; I choose the one from above . . . it is a matter of choosing . . . between the dictatorship of the dagger and the dictatorship of the saber; I choose the dictatorship of the saber" (261). The die has been cast, and you must choose. To contain evil is better than achieving the sovereign Good, since in post-theological times the sovereign Good is indistinguishable from sovereign Evil. Who takes up the knife and who takes up the saber today?

Donoso is a reactionary among reactionaries, and he is definitely to blame, together with any number of kind-hearted progressives, to tell the truth, for the numerous catastrophes that have besieged the history of Europe and of the world between 1850 and the present. But it is important to understand the structure of his notion of politics, which to my mind is sustained on four theses to a large extent contrary to the ones the sorry critical tradition assigns to him: first, Donoso is a post-theological thinker of the political; second, he affirms the absolute primacy of politics over history; third, his lucidity enables him to posit a notion of dictatorship whose main intent is the cancellation of hegemonic politics in the name of the universal protection of social rights; and, fourth, he abandons the pretension of a politics of the Good in favor of a politics of the real. Even from a nonreactionary position it is possible to benefit from Donoso's lesson in his four arguments.

Lacan says that Jeremy Bentham took a decisive post-Hegelian step when he established the distinction between the real and the fictional, "in the sense that every truth has the structure of fiction" (*Ethics*, 12). Since the fictitious is the symbolic, fictionalization is crucial to history and to truth, whereas the real is their interruption. A few years later, Louis Althusser developed his notion of ideology as "the representation of the imaginary relationship of individuals to their real conditions of existence" (Althusser, "Ideology," 162). Ideology is fictional, in the Benthamian sense according to Lacan. Or, as Althusser puts it, "ideology has no outside . . . but at the same time . . . it is nothing but outside" (175). From a certain perspective, Donoso must be considered a fundamentally ideological thinker, even an ideologue rather than a thinker. His ideology is Catholicism understood as a total system: there is nothing substantial outside the Catholic good, and everything that is not Catholic is merely accidental or modal. Accidents and modes, insofar as they may be non-Catholic, are evil properly so-called. Donoso is a theological ideologue. He resolutely places himself outside politics, that is, within a history whose substantiality is so absolute that it can only be sacred or divine history. Donoso's struggle is the struggle of the Catholic residue against postrevolutionary Europe, therefore it is a hegemonic struggle on the side of the aristocracy and clergy and their petit-bourgeois allies, particularly in a country like Spain, where the liberal revolution had not yet properly succeeded. Far from having abandoned the thought of the sovereign Good in order to embrace the real, Donoso lived in stubborn denegation of the real and in an essential nostalgia for the master. This would seem to counter the four theses I presented earlier, but there is a different reading.

Catholicism was Donoso's fiction, a fiction of fictions, anchored in an understanding of freedom as a total identification with the master. If the eternal truth of the Catholic dogma is the unity of God and humanity as universal substance, that truth would have been stated and would have been left behind at the zero point of repressive equilibrium. History, as site of the real, is only errancy, a drifting movement in the wake of fictionalizations and ideologies whose lie is total. History is therefore itself the decline of the function of the master, and the only reasonable way of dealing with it is through radical skepticism, a radical challenge that, far from accepting any of the premises of the notion of a progress-based liberation of desire, would at the same time make a mockery of and fear the residual projection of the discourse of the master into its negation, political repression, which is the very name of evil. The dictatorship of the friend, opposed to the dictatorship of evil, and there is no third option, is the only possible procedure against despotism, the lesser evil, happening not in the name of a return to ideology, but rather in the name of a suspension of ideology; not in the name of a new theology of praxis, but in the name of the post-theological interruption of fallen theologies; not in the name of the Good, but in the name of the restraining of evil: an apotropaic relation to evil, the second militancy.

Concerning the apotropaic relation Lacan says that man must defend himself against *das Ding*, la Cosa, the good/evil object that "presents itself at the level of unconscious experience as that which already makes the law" (*Ethics*, 73). "Human defense takes place by means of something that has a name, and which is, to be precise, lying about evil. At the level of the unconscious, the subject lies. And this lying is his way of telling the truth of the matter. The *orthos logos* of the unconscious at this level . . . is expressed as *proton pseudos*, the first lie" (73). Donoso's Catholic fiction is his first lie: an apotropaic defense against the despotic. Hence Donoso's word: "I believe laws have been made for society, not society for laws . . . There are two things that are impossible for me: to condemn dictatorship and to put it into practice . . . I am incapable of governing" ("Discurso," 243). To be incapable of governing: the aporetic dream of an antidespotic revolution, already itself a revolution. But here, who are the friends and who are the enemies?

Between freedom and dictatorship, Donoso says, he would always choose freedom ("Discurso," 260–61). But the option does not exist. The world is not marching toward freedom but toward catastrophe. The open way is not a path to the future but to its very absence. The necessity of a political decision in the sense of a suspension of the constitutional order and the declaration of a state of exception does not seek a restoration, it only seeks an interruption of what is coming. What is coming is the other dictatorship, the dictatorship of the dagger, full despotism, perhaps today to be understood as the chaos that will follow climatic change, of which we can already experience a few glimpses. The interruption of catastrophic constituent power in the name of the theoretical force and of the essential goodness of the old principles, in the name of the restraining of evil—that is reactionary thinking, second militancy, in a definition that is consistent with the three paradigms mentioned earlier.

If this is so, then reactionary thinking could be understood as something other than a thinking of the residue, a thinking of the negation of the residual quality of the residue. Progressivism—no doubt today equally subjected to harsh theoretical difficulties—is the idea that there is an open history under a promise of increasing freedom. But the understanding of freedom as consistent with whatever is constituent, with whatever adjusts itself to the emerging mode of production and of social organization, with an increasing secularization and effective immanentization of the social—well, it is about as arbitrary as fallen reactionary thinking. There is an antireactionary militancy in progressivism and there is an antiprogressive militancy in reaction that ends up turning both options interdependent, exposing them to a radical mutual contamination. To understand politics today goes through a destruction of the ideologeme of a lineal temporality of history, of history as the simple conflict between an exhausted and residual temporality and an emerging and potentially full temporality, of history as the replacement of the constituted by the constituent. It is therefore not only a matter of establishing a critique of reactionary thinking. We must move beyond in order to understand, beyond said critique, what the very category of reaction conceals—and, upon concealing, reveals—regarding a new possibility for thinking politics. Of course it is also a matter of proceeding to an understanding of what progressivism conceals and thus reveals. It is a matter of letting what subtracts itself come into presence through its very subtraction, infrapolitically or deconstructively.

The Wolf's Hide

Karl Marx introduces into the writing of history the decisive notion of noncontemporaneity, of a conflict of temporalities for any concrete political experience. In the 1867 Preface to *Capital* he will say: "Alongside the modern evils, a whole series of inherited evils oppress us, arising from the passive survival of antiquated modes of production, with their inevitable train of social and political anachronisms. We suffer not only from the living, but from the dead" (Marx quoted by Bensaïd, *Marx*, 22). Daniel Bensaïd is basically glossing Marx—both of them are thinkers of the first militancy—when he says that the present always puts on clothes of another time, lives under old names, with words that come from the mother tongue until the new idiom ends up throwing the old one into oblivion. And politics is precisely the place where those discordant times meet (22). Politics is therefore the aporia of time, and to dwell on the understanding of politics as aporia of time is already to be beyond any simple determination of the conflictive but eminently solvable temporality of politics. Progressive thought is under the impression of undoing the aporia, but so is reactionary thought. Aporias have however a way of not letting themselves be solved, and they remain at the heart of a process that they secretly undo. In any case, in the meantime politics, pragmatic as it may be, is crossed by utopian and reactionary elements in its very structure.

The weapons of utopian reason are narrativization and conceptualization. Reactionary reason, however, denarrativizes in its constant recourse to the affect of times past, to ineffable, and insofar as ineffable also inarticulable, historicity. Walter Benjamin's "The Story Teller" links the disappearance of the art of telling a story to the vanishing of experience, hence binding storytelling and affect, against the conceptual work of the novel and of Enlightened reason in general. Storytelling then, paradoxically, even scandalously, emerges as an instance of reactionary reason, which connects to the Benjaminian insistence on repetition as the primary element of storytelling. What is primary in storytelling is not the narrative itself (narrative can be separated from storytelling, which is why narrative can become hegemonic with the rise of the novel), but rather repetition (the ciphered repetition, Benjamin says, of deep structures of experience, temporal substances, affects, and troubles in temporality). What is primary in the novel is the narrative, and never repetition. This is why the novel form is teleological, proleptic, and utopian, more proper to modernity than to its end.

While narrative may or may not be utopian—the narrative element in traditional storytelling is not utopian—utopian reason always narrativizes. While the mobilization of affect is not inherently reactionary, what is reactionary is always a mobilization of affect. The notion of aura in Benjamin's essay on the artwork at the time of mechanical reproduction can be very precisely related to a reactionary affect, as Schmitt would have confirmed, since for him all the relevant concepts of political philosophy are secularizations of theological thought.[9] The (aesthetic) aura is already a secularization of reactionary affect. While any utopia affirms historicity, any utopia at the same time cancels out, suspends, brackets historicity. Every narrativization (every periodization, including the periodization known as the time of the crisis of the ancien régime, or the periodization known as postmodernity) reduces truth and operates through the symbolization of truth though abstraction. Abstraction—the move toward the concept—is truth production in the Lacanian sense, which means that it is also at the same time a reductive subtraction of truth (a fictionalization, a lie). If I say "cat" I kill the cat, but the cat lives on. The necessary thesis is that we cannot get rid of reactionary reason—or of storytelling—without risking through it a loss of historicity.

The civil wars known as Carlist in nineteenth-century Spain emblematically exemplify the struggle between progress and reaction. The Carlists, who were partisans of an antiliberal and absolutist Bourbon faction, sought the restoration of a legitimist monarchy along ancien régime presuppositions and principles. Liberal regimes would have brought to Spain, according to the Carlists, nothing but sin and corruption: the political present was nothing but sin and corruption. In absolutist irredentism, a paradigm of the second militancy, there lurked the promise of a utopian future, an antimodern happiness, in a context where modernity was synonymous with decadence and the decomposition of social relations. When the Marquis of Bradomín, at the beginning of the first novel in Ramón del Valle-Inclán's Carlist trilogy, *Los cruzados de la causa* (The Crusaders of the Cause), announces his intention of selling the Viana del Prior palace and all the entailed estates associated to his person in order to be able to contribute financially to the raising of partisan militias for Charles VII, we witness the manifestation of a Carlist sublime. Bradomín emerges as a properly modern hero upon declaring his disposition to sacrifice everything for the cause, including that which makes a cause of the cause. After all, without his entailed inheritances, without his "old stones" that one should never sell, as the Abbess Isabel de Montenegro reminds him, the old and one-armed marquis will enter subjective destitution: he will have sacrificed Carlism to Carlism itself, his own libidinal investment in Carlism, his desire, the treasure that is worth more than he himself. Having in such a way traversed his own constitutive fantasy, what will remain? Above all, can he still be considered a reactionary subject?

Toward the end of *Los gerifaltes de antaño* (The Bigwigs of Yesteryear), the shepherd Ciro Cernín discovers in a ravine the corpse of the guerrilla chief Miquelo Egoscué, just about to be devoured by a wolf. Egoscué had been vilely betrayed by the priest Santa Cruz. Cernín manages to kill the wolf, and he puts on the wolf's hide, thus managing metonymically an apotropaic strategy that saves, from Carlism, the best of Carlism—the strength and cunning of the wolf, but not the wolf's evil.[10] Cernín reverses Bradomín's action upon engaging in an ethico-political act that also sacrifices Carlism to Carlism (he kills the wolf), but at the same time resubjectivizes Carlism in the partial object of the wolf's hide. The act of the Marquis denarrativizes, and it opens that way Valle-Inclán's Carlist trilogy to the very hole of its impossible resolution. But Cernín's act renarrativizes, and it closes the trilogy in at least one sense: the hide of the wolf becomes the emblem of reactionary utopia, the itself aporetic resolution of Marquis de Bradomín's aporetic act. The wolf's hide sets into question the exhaustion of the political in terms of the endless confrontation (three civil wars in seventy years) between liberalism and legitimism, progressivism and reaction, first and second militancy. Valle-Inclán is referring to something that reveals itself through its subtraction.

We do not know how Valle-Inclán would have continued to develop his Carlist tropology if he could have finished his saga with an intended fourth volume. Valle-Inclán's Carlism, crossed by an aesthetic or archi-aesthetic Nietzscheanism, is the *apotrope* of liberal evil. Valle-Inclán thinks of himself as a posthumous reactionary, as postreactionary, a kind of negator of the negation. Against the liberal state, against its Kantian moral infinite based on the tendential accomplishment of a full mediation of nature and freedom, against the secular labor of the concept, which is represented in the trilogy by the veteran of the republican army, Captain García ("I fought for my ideas . . . the ideas of liberty and progress!" [764]), Valle-Inclán offers a nonconceptual, affective, irredentist, and melancholy writing. Carlist utopia is anticonceptual and denarrativizing and takes on the Kantian fragment about man being an animal who needs a master. But the place of the master is empty. The symptom of Carlism is the Lord of Montenegro, don Juan Manuel, who tells the Marquis: "Nephew, when I raise a faction it won't be for a king or an emperor. . . . If I were not so old, I would have already raised it, but it would be to make justice in this land, where foxes and martens have spread their litters. I call thus the mob of clergy, police, *indianos* and purchasers of national real estate. That riffraff of servants that have become masters! I would raise a faction to bring justice to all of them, burn their houses, hang them all in my Lantañón oak forest" (714). The messianic and radically anticonceptual position of Lord Montenegro becomes explicit in his sovereign declaration: "If with a good law there are bad sentences, we could have good sentences with bad laws, because virtue is not in the law, but in the man who applies it. That is why I rely so little on the law, even less on the judges, because I have always seen their justice as smaller than mine" (720).

But don Juan Manuel is too old. He cannot or will not enter his own militancy, which he symbolically delegates in his son Cara de Plata. Reactionary militancy may hate itself, may give itself up, as it must always conclude it is forced to act against a loss whose object cannot be recovered. If the lost object were recoverable, a militancy looking for it would be active or progressive; it would move toward a properly futural goal; it would not be reactionary. To the extent reactionary militancy impossibly desires a return, or desires the return of the impossible, reactionary militancy essentially incorporates a longing for nonmilitancy. Reactionary militancy only seeks, finally, the impossible moment of its self-dissolution in the return of an immemorial past, in the return of an old justice, an inaccessible one—which to that extent must be consigned to the endless future.

The subject of reactionary militancy is radically split between thought and action. He is not a subject of thought, since his only possible thought is the impossible thought of the loss of thought, including the thought of loss. And he is not a subject of action, since his only possible action is the impossible action of recovering an unretrievable loss. I do not mean that a reactionary subject, say, don Juan Manuel, does not have access to thoughts or actions; clearly he does. It is rather that thought and actions are not constitutive of him as subject. If he is not a subject of thought or a subject of action, then the subject of reactionary militancy is a subject of desire. But what he desires—the *thing*—is by definition erased. The hole of denarrativization, its apotheosic accomplishment in the Lantañón oak forest, the point or *punctum* of inarticulable longing, contains the desire, or it so attempts. But the desire escapes. Reactionary desire desires the unnameable and unreachable remainder.

The reactionary, whether he knows it or not, is he who has abandoned, in his constitution as obscure subject of desire, every pretension of canceling desire out. He therefore gives himself, through the second militancy, subjectively to terror and death, to treason (he will betray a desire that betrays him or will not betray a desire that betrays him, but he still lives in the betrayal of desire), and to disaster (he thinks there is no unnamable beyond the unnamable of a desire outside which there can exist no name). For Alain Badiou there is a fundamental question to any ethics of truth: "How could I continue to think?" (*Ethics*, 50). For Badiou that is a question that has to do with sustaining the immortality of truth through my singular and finite being upon my constitution as a subject of truth. The principle of subjectivity for him is the maintenance of the Immortal. Can reactionary militancy maintain the Immortal? Or is the obscure reactionary subjectivity precisely the impossible and mortal attempt to survive, in militancy, against every militancy; in death, against every death; in desire, against every desire? But, if this is so, then all progressivism, to the extent that it triumphs as progressivism, that is, politically, will inevitably fall into reactionary affect, looking for its own precarious survival. This draws an unlivable line in the political conjuncture of any present, hence also of our present. Denying it can only bring about punctual and always deficient compensations.

If reactionary affect, including the reactionary affect of progressives, like every historical subalternity, is irreducible, if we cannot abandon the immemorial affect without losing historicity itself, if politics is in effect an aporia of temporality, then there is no possible constitution of a Kantian state; there is no possible full mediation of nature and freedom. What remains is a messianic process whose very condition is the abandonment of militancy. The subject of politics is no longer the militant subject. The militant subject of politics is just another figure of utopian technics. What reactionary reason seeks, against reaction itself, is the return to the scene of a discourse of the master that annihilates the master, that is, a politics without a subject, a politics of the nonsubject, or a headless subjectivation. We may call it the politics, or the infrapolitics, of the wolf's hide. What is the difference between radical reactionary thought and subaltern thought? Can the subaltern be conceived as the index of a subtracting appearance, an alternative to the two ontotheological militancies? The index of an existential variation that implies a step back regarding politics itself? Is the subaltern the proper name of infrapolitics?

Subalternism and Recoil

Subalternity produces an experience of the limit. Gayatri Spivak defines it as the absolute limit of the place where history is narrativized, and Ranajit Guha glosses it in Wittgensteinian terms: if, in order to find a limit for thought, we would need to think both sides of the limit, that means we would have to be able to think the unthinkable (8). But the unthinkable remains unthought for the most part. Spivak's notion places the subaltern at the precise limit of (un)thinkability, beyond which the subaltern is unthought and perpetually unthinkable (but not less pressing as a consequence). If thinking the subaltern is at the same time necessary and impossible, it announces the constitutive aporia for the theoretical subject. The latter is not the subaltern subject, if such a thing could exist, but rather the subject of subalternity, the subject constituted in deconstitution, the subject that gains the possibility of history at the same time it cancels it out. We cannot get rid of the notion of subalternity without risking through it a total loss of historicity. At the same time, the subaltern is the limit of historicity, since its affirmation is the condition of possibility of historiographical logic.

Guha, in his *History at the Limits of World History*, seeks a deconstruction of Hegelianism in favor of a restitution of a notion of full historicity, which he calls "a historicity beyond world-history." World-history translates the Hegelian concept of *Weltgeschichte*. Its intention is conceptual rather than descriptive, since for Hegel *Weltgeschichte*, in a way thoroughly consistent with the first ontotheological militancy, is "reason in history" (2). The notion of a historicity beyond world-history can only be restituted, perhaps, through a deconstruction of Hegelianism, and in particular of Hegelian panlogicism. Guha shows how the notion of the state, far from being a solid ground on which to base the notion of world-history, takes on in Hegel the function of an empty signifier. The state becomes, in Hegel, a hegemonic tool on which to set the notion of spirit as the motor of world-history. But world-history, its concept, far from opening up, closes the possibility of a full historicity of the world. This is not a simple error in Hegelian panlogicism, but rather something that fundamentally threatens Hegel's entire construction. If the end of the progress of spirit through world-history is the full conciliation of humanity with itself, which would make it the culmination of the first ontotheological militancy, the final erasure of the gap between thinking and being, and the very end of subalternity in general, Guha shows—in full agreement with Ernesto Laclau's critique of Hegel—that Hegelian universality "exists only incarnated in, and subverting, some particularity" ("Identity," 56). The signifying particularity happens to be of course the Eurocentric universality of the Germanic state, that is, in Hegel's expansive definition, of the modern European world, which is a state-world. Universalization can only happen as a consequence of the fact that a particular segment of the social, for Hegel the imperialist West, achieves general domination. Hegel's progressivism is absolutely linked to the utopian construction of the universal triumph of the European form of state, and it reveals on its reverse side the impossibility, constitutive for all progressivism, of subtracting itself from a concrete ideological incarnation regarding which everything else—such as, in the Hegelian philosophy of history, the Orient— is both reactionary and vanquished by history. In Hegelian philosophy the subaltern and the reactionary are both on the side of the infinite resistance to the labor of the concept understood as *Weltgeschichte*. Hegel himself is the incarnation of progressive reason, foam of the infinite.

For Laclau, as for Guha, Hegelian dialectics claims "to rethink, in terms of its own logical transitions, the totality of the ontological distinctions that the philosophical tradition had discerned within the real" ("Identity," 61). And there is a parallel between the political postulate of a full universalization of the social and the philosophical postulate of a full rationalization of the real. But what Guha's analysis enables us to see in concrete detail is that "if Reason, on the one hand, has hegemonized the whole realm of differences [upon reducing, as Guha shows, the full historicity of the world to *Weltgeschichte* understood as the history of the state], the latter, on the other, could not avoid contaminating the former" (62). Difference contaminates reason by denying the necessity of the dialectical transition. The differential remainder, the fact that reason cannot show that it fully absorbs and exhausts difference, which is comparable to the fact that domination cannot be *total* domination at the risk of disappearing as domination in pure identity, deorganizes dialectical necessity and reconfigures it as contingency. Once there, having established the substitution of necessity by contingency, Hegelianism will have been destroyed: the possibility of a full restitution of the historicity of the world is now open at the expense of the Hegelian conception of world-history. Would that possibility of full historicity constitute the moment of a subtractive manifestation of appearance of a non-ontotheological character? Or would it be the very opposite? Is Guha correct in his contention that we can righteously conceive of an unsequestered, not doomed to lack, full historicity of the world?

Additionally, is the contingent and destabilizing remainder all one needs to destroy Hegelian progressivism? To be sure, contingency is a necessary condition of subalternism, but is it a sufficient condition? Once the notion of contingency, as the revenge of the realm of differences, is introduced as the foundation of the very possibility of the restitution of full historicity, in the perception that world-history is only a hegemonic hypostasis that cannot account for total history as such, subalternism may have broken away from Hegelianism, but at the cost of becoming subjected to the embrace of hegemony theory. Against the old hegemony of liberal progressivism, which Hegel articulates in relation to world-history, subalternism uses hegemony theory in order to dismantle the hegemonic project of world-history. But can the restitution of historicity accomplish the possibility of an end of subalternity? Can full historicity dismantle the unthinkability of the destitutive place at the limit of which history gets narrativized as logic? I think Guha's adaptation of hegemony theory flies in the face of Spivak's position, from which there can be no historical *pleroma* and no end of subalternity. Hegemony theory is incompatible with a radical understanding of the subaltern position, which it attempts to tame and domesticate.

The question of the restitution of history is equivalent to the more general question of the possibility of a social and political end of subalternity. The anti-Hegelian (as such, also antiprogressivist) turn toward hegemony theory brings to the surface the question whether subalternity can be eliminated, which is in principle the very stuff of the liberal dream. Can subalternity be erased from the social without remainder? Or is the ceaseless presence of subalternity—or, *mutatis mutandis*, of the reactionary—the condition of production not only of any hegemonic subjectivation but also of any counterhegemonic subjectivation? Subalternity is not eliminable because hegemony needs it to produce itself. Subalternity is the necessary and sufficient condition of hegemony. If so the restitution of the right to subaltern historicity by way of an appeal to hegemony theory, which Guha aims to establish through his deconstruction of the Eurocentric and state-centric Hegelian progressivism, is far from being sufficient to establish the possibility of a hypothetic end of subalternity. Nor can it mobilize political thought away from the first onto-theological militancy, since the latter must find its point of departure by fixing parameters that would relegate what is not itself to the dark side of the limit where history is narrativized as logic. The understanding of the subaltern as the very limit of narrativization implies, to start with, the refusal of any renarrativization that will reproduce subalternity, since any ambiguities there would pay the price of the bypassing of the aporetic structure of historical temporality. Renarrativizing in counterhegemony is always necessarily a recoil, since it fosters resubalternization.[11]

Martin Heidegger used the notion of recoil in the context of his own critique of Hegelianism. What was at stake for Heidegger was also the restitution of the plenitude of temporality against its hijacking by Transcendental Idealism. Heidegger's critique of Hegel was undertaken first, obliquely, as a critique of Kant. In the third section of *Kant and the Problem of Metaphysics* he showed that, in his terms, the first edition of Kant's *Critique of Pure Reason* must be essentially preferred to the second edition, and that the first edition contains a revelation of the true nature of temporality that would have altered the course of the history of philosophy if Kant had not immediately covered it up through his second edition. According to Heidegger, Kant saw that temporality is the ground of transcendental imagination and that, therefore, it is also the basis of the (thinking, imagining) ego. Transcendental imagination, as the foundation of pure knowledge, should determine, or should have determined, the essential constitution of the human in philosophical terms. The problem was to understand why the transcendental imagination became for Kant so dangerous a device that it led him to recoil from his earlier discovery and to suppress, in the second edition of the first *Critique*, the passages that elaborated on it as fundamental faculty of the soul. Heidegger concludes that the transcendental imagination itself led Kant to take his distance from it (*Kant*, 117).

Heidegger offers two possible reasons: in traditional philosophical anthropology imagination was considered a minor faculty. Could it be tolerated that a minor faculty determine reason? If the answer is affirmative, the primacy of logic in scientific discourse disappears and the very architectonics of Western culture is ruined. The intuition of the transcendental essence of imagination takes thought to an abyss: "In the radicalism of his questions, Kant brought the 'possibility' of metaphysics to this abyss. He saw the unknown. He had to shrink back" (*Kant*, 118). There is a second line of argumentation, although Heidegger does not bother too much to distinguish it from the first. If pure reason is transformed into transcendental imagination, the *Critique* ruins its own ground. Kant's intuition was not powerful enough to let him invert absolutely the traditional positions. Therefore, "the problematic of a pure reason amplified in this way must push aside the power of imagination, and with that it really first conceals its transcendental essence" (118). For these reasons "the obscurity and 'strangeness' of the transcendental power of imagination, of the ground cleared in the first ground-laying, and the sheer power of pure reason, were worked together in order to veil once more the line of vision into the more general essence of the transcendental power of imagination, a perspective which was broken open, so to speak, only for an instant" (119). Had it been kept open, the consequences would have been considerable. If post-Kantianism had understood that time is the essential structure of subjectivity, then Transcendental Idealism, and Hegel in particular, Marx after him, would have been unable to continue to posit the preeminence of the old ontotheological conception of being as production.

The idea of being as production remained operative during German Idealism, offering a philosophical cover to the first ontotheological militancy we have been discussing, and it turned self-consciousness, in the sense of self-conception, and self-production, into the only true substance. The secret Guha analyzes of the Hegelian hypostasis of the state is rooted in the fact that for Hegel the essential nature of substance is the concept of its own self-identity. It was then only logical that, first, spirit, and later, the state, or perhaps the other way around if you wish, would hegemonize temporality in order to turn the radical historicity of the ego and of the world into the ordered concept of *Weltgeschichte* that is for Guha the condition of suppression of full historicity, hence of subaltern history and of subalternist historiography. But a subalternist recoil in Guha's sense also imposes a shrinking back from the abyss of unthinkability on the basis of a hegemonic understanding of politics. Faced with the impossibility of either an affirmative or indeed a negative reply to the question about the end of subalternity, the thinker who prefers not to dwell on Spivak's "absolute limit of the place where history is narrativized as logic" will recoil into the hegemonic corral. A hegemonic subalternism, that is, an anti-Hegelian subalternism but still a subalternism of the hegemonic turn, is the place of deconstitution of the very radicality of the subaltern idea. Through it subalternism becomes yet another species of progressivism, one more, which also means, if this chapter is half right, inevitably, another instance of reaction.

Through the first form of ontotheological militancy the emphasis of the subject of the political seeks the exhaustive exploitation of being, of the unlimited continuum, in the privilege of the autism of the substantial subject as absolute singular. It literalizes it, understanding the residue of its immanence as the infinitely reducible. It denies the distance between subject and world, and it affirms its own potential apotheosis in the tendential closure of the One-All. We have called this option progressivist subjectivism, emblematized in Hegel. In the second form of ontotheological militancy the emphasis is on distance, in the loss regarding which the subject constitutes itself, subjectivizes into, infinite resistance. It affirms a blind transcendence regarding that which, on offering itself, loses itself. This is reactionary subjectivism, emblematized in Donoso Cortés, in the Marquis of Bradomín, or in the hegemonic subalternism that seeks an impossible total restitution of the historicity of the world, like Ranajit Guha does. Both forms are radically dependent on the notion that, as Parmenides said, "thinking and being are the same."

We have seen the possibility of a third option in Martínez Marzoa's notion of a distance from distance, "only the distance that there is in the very fact of understanding" the play of distance and negation. But that "only" does not minimize anything, because such a double distance is enormous and immeasurable. The becoming relevant of loss, its appearing or happening also at the core of the very possibility of subjective militancy, Martínez Marzoa's "appearing only insofar as subtracting" (*Heidegger*, 46), dwells in the unthought of modern subjectivism and offers therefore the possibility of an alternative understanding of politics, immeasurable as regards the previous ones, and nonmilitant, for the same reason. If thinking and being are not the same, if their relation implies a deeper and more decisive nonrelation, then subject and world do not match up, and progressivism and reaction are not only empty options, but they are also mutually supportive and interdependent. If thinking and being are not the same, the options that conditioned political decisions in modernity—secularizing the sovereign Good, restraining despotic evil—are no longer defining options, because they can no longer exhaust the horizon of politics. They only open it, genealogically. But we are still far from knowing to what. We can only imagine it.

3
Infrapolitical Distance
A Second Note on the Concept of Distance in Felipe Martínez Marzoa

If it is true that the history of thought in the West is a history of the progressive voiding out of being until, with Hegel, which brings to a particular end the inception of philosophy started by the Greeks, being is substance and substance is the subject, and being becomes the most abstract and general of words, substantial exhaustion turns into a final point of abstraction, and abstraction, having reached a point of no exit, an end, having become *aporos*, becomes distraction. Nietzsche, who turns the Hegelian subjective substance into a transubjective will to will, insists on the distraction upon projecting it into a last doctrine of the being of beings under the name of will to power. We live in distracted times, in aporetic times. Why does it have to be so? Why should the history of Western thought resolve itself into a history of distraction, a history of the progressive voiding out of experience? Felipe Martínez Marzoa develops his notion of distance, in the context of a long meditation on historical nihilism, in a close relation to that question. I want now to supplement Martínez Marzoa's notion of distance, which I have used in previous chapters, appealing to the difference between *polis* and politics as described by Martin Heidegger in his 1942 interpretation of Sophocles's *Antigone*. My intent is to place both things, that is, Martínez Marzoa's distance and Heidegger's differentiation between *polis* and politics, in their proper place regarding the genealogy of infrapolitical reflection.

Reiner Schürmann begins his posthumous, monumental text *Broken Hegemonies* with reference to Oedipus's nocturnal knowledge. "The tragic condition" is the specific infrapolitical condition of our aporetic time: "To think is to linger on the conditions in which one is living, to linger on the site where we live. Thus to think is a privilege of that epoch which is ours, provided that the essential fragility of the sovereign referents becomes evident to it" (4, 3). The "singularizing withdrawal" that opened the tragic in pre-metaphysical times through its conflict with "the universalizing impulse" of "political" or historical principles is again with us. Both instances cannot be reconciled through any appeal to higher principles. This "*kenosis*" of the principle opens a new time of tragic anarchy (4). Founding speech gives way to "insurmountable silence" (17). Ours is a "pathetic site" that once again reveals, against all abstraction, "the tragic condition" of being (532).

For Martínez Marzoa, the Greek *polis* was, for the West, the first and also the last possible instantiation of political community, the last because the first, in the sense that, once the *polis* thought of itself as the explicitation, through law, of community, the *polis* could not but implode, destroy itself, as a consequence of such an explicitation: a game that studies itself as a game, he tells us, can and will no longer be played. Community has not been given to the West as a political possibility since then, Martínez Marzoa says. When Heidegger says about the *polis* that it is "the site of history, the Here, in which, out of which and for which history happens" (*Introduction to Metaphysics*, 162), Martínez Marzoa will want to say that, if so, history is over and has been over since the Greeks. But history is not over, which would mean that we have to investigate the very history of the ruin of the *polis*, the very history of the destruction of the possibility of political community, in order to understand what history might still mean, today, for us.

In the pages of *Hölderlin's Hymn "The Ister"* (1942) where Heidegger reframes the interpretation of the first choral ode of *Antigone* he had offered in *Introduction to Metaphysics* (1935), he speaks about the *polis* as the site of a turning/counterturning that organizes the historical existence of the human being: "Perhaps the *polis* is that realm and locale around which everything question-worthy and uncanny turns in an exceptional sense. The *polis* is *polos*, that is, the pole, the swirl [*Wirbel*] in which and around which everything turns. These two words name that essential moment that the verb *pelein* says in the second line of the choral ode: that which is constant, and change" (*Hölderlin*, 81). For Heidegger the *polis*, as "the site of being homely in the midst of beings as a whole" (82), is also the site of a counterturning in the sense that, as it is determined "in terms of its relation to the essence of human beings" (83), and as the choral ode defines the human being as *to deinotaton*, the most uncanny or "unhomely," then the *polos* of the *polis* organizes the turning/counterturning of the homely: "that which is unhomely is not merely the non-homely that seeks yet does not find itself, because it seeks itself by way of a distancing and alienation from itself . . . what properly characterizes the unhomely is a counterturning that belongs intrinsically to its essence"

(84). The *polis*: the homely-unhomely site, the originary site, the founding site of any and all historical appropriation, and by the same token of any and all historical disappropriation. But this means that "the *polis* is and remains what is properly worthy of question in the strict sense of the word, that is, not simply something questionable for any question whatsoever, but that with which meditation proper, the highest and most extensive, is concerned" (85).

It is here that Heidegger pronounces some fateful words we must think through. There is no politics without the *polis*, and yet the essence of the *polis* is not political. There is a difference, uncanny in nature, between the *polis* and the political, and yet that difference is also a logical one. This is the logic: "if 'the political' is that which belongs to the *polis*, and therefore is essentially dependent upon the *polis*, then the essence of the *polis* can never be determined in terms of the political, just as the ground can never be explained or derived from the consequence" (85). What determines the essence of the *polis*? Politics cannot explain the *polis*, even if, or precisely because, the *polis* determines the political. The political may have always already started, but the *polis* finds its beginning, its origin, in a realm that cannot be reduced to the political.

I understand Martínez Marzoa's own meditation on the *polis* in this context—and I will venture that his work is entirely contained in such an effort, in a way that is at the same time systematic and thoroughly idiosyncratic. As a consequence, an isolated citation of it is always insufficient. In *Heidegger y su tiempo* he says, for instance: "We call *polis* [the site] where the game that is already being played aspires to become relevant as such. That is not a doctrine on the *polis* but precisely the *polis* itself. We could refer to the fact that such a relevance means at the same time the loss [of the *polis*] by pointing out that the *polis* dies not through the attack of the barbarians, rather precisely because it stands" (28). Or, in *El concepto de lo civil*, Martínez Marzoa says: "the *polis* is not a State or anything civil, [but] it *is* a community . . . the *polis* pertains to a historical situation where the exchange of things, flourishing as it may be, is in principle limited to determinate types of things, or, said otherwise, alienability is what is relevant, not what is obvious, so that one cannot talk, not even tendentially or structurally, of an absence of binding contents" (105). The *polis* is a space where exchange happens prior to any general principle of equivalence, and it is at the same time a space where exchange is thematized as such. The thematization of exchange, as politics, is the *polis*, so that the *polis* explicitates the political game, it is the site of the explicitation of the political game, which means: it stands at a distance from the political game. This distance will be its downfall, because "the centrality of the exchange means that the community in question [the *polis*] is embarked on the adventure of expressly recognizing its own status as such; hence on the process of recognizing something that would be the same for all and for all cases, hence on assuming a uniform space, consequently an unlimited space; this sets the basis for something that will take long to be taken for granted and even longer to become the very concept of validity" (106). The loss of community, in and through politics, is a direct result of the self-recognition of the community. As a "community" the *polis* binds the homely, but as a community that explicitates its own game it opens itself to the unhomely. This is the first historical inception, a thematization of the game of common life as a game of binding loss that opens, as such, the space of the political and the death of community.

We can bring the history of the *polis* to our own times. "Distance" is for Martínez Marzoa "the distance or reserve that irretrievably remains at the root of the modern project itself, the irretrievable secondariness of the modern, irremediable in the sense that recognizing it is in no way going back to the primary, rather only attempting to understand what is secondary as secondary" (*Concepto*, 111). The political is a thematization of secondariness in respect of the very question-worthiness of the *polis* itself. But the political is also a secondary, always belated reflection on the loss of the turning/counterturning relation to being that first makes the *polis* historical as such. For Martínez Marzoa only distance can bring up, minimally, the very difference between the primary and the secondary that organizes the very possibility of a step back in politics from contemporary politics. Such a distance is infrapolitical distance. Infrapolitical distance, which is the absolute limit of the place where politics narrativizes into its logic, invokes a nearness to something without which life would be unlivable, hence an absolute condition of politics. That something is not politics, it is precisely not politics. It is, rather, the extrapolitical necessity of which Antigone is the historical emblem. The very notion of ontological difference—that is, the distance between beings in the ordinary sense, things, and being, which establishes the horizon of their appearance and presencing (and absencing)—opens infrapolitically as a recourse to that something. This seems consistent with the second Heideggerian interpretation (1942) of *Antigone*, which ends with the notion of becoming homely in the unhomely. To take on a distance is a terrible and empty gesture if the taking on is not always already seeking something other than distance itself. A distance is tolerable only in its relation to an (other) nearness, and the nearness is what matters (the most).

Chapter 4 of *Introduction to Metaphysics* (1935) is entitled "The Restriction of Being." It has four subdivisions, and in the third subdivision, "Being and Thinking," Heidegger's first confrontation with *Antigone*'s choral ode happens. "Being and Thinking" names for Heidegger the space of "the fundamental orientation of the spirit of the West that is the real target of our attack"

(123–24). If there is to be a new history, the West must undo its own fundamental misunderstanding and corruption of the relationship between being and thinking that obtained during the first Greek inception. A destruction — a destruction of a false, merely apparent, only seeming structuration of the relation of being and thinking — must take place. Such a destruction will clear the way for a new determination of the essence of the human being, which is also at the same time a new determination of history, and a new historical dispensation. The ode begins with *"polla ta deina kouden anthropou deinoteron pelei,"* "manifold is the uncanny, yet nothing uncannier than man rises beyond him" (*Introduction*, 156).[1] If nothing is uncannier than the human being, then the human being is the uncanniest. For Heidegger, "the saying 'the human being is the uncanniest' provides the authentic Greek definition of humanity. We first press forward fully to the happening of uncanniness when we experience the power of seeming together with the struggle against seeming in its essential belonging to Dasein" (161–62). Oedipus, we recognize, was uncanniest, as the struggle against seeming undid him, and by undoing him turned him into the man he was. This is the tragic condition of the human in the Greek way.

There are three passages in the ode that receive Heidegger's special attention: verses 360, *pantoporos aporos ep'ouden erchetai*, 370, *hupsipolis apolis*; and 372–73, *met' emoi parestios genoito met' ison phronon*. *Pantoporos aporos* is translated by Heidegger as "everywhere trying out, underway; untried, with no way out he comes to nothing" (the usual translation, as dutifully indicated by editors Gregory Fried and Richard Polt, is quite different, and "where Heidegger sees a paradox in the sentence, most translators would see merely an expansion of the notion 'resourceful in all'" [*Introduction*, 157n52, 157]; the Loeb Library translation says: "all-resourceful; he meets nothing in the future without resource" [Sophocles 37]). It is obvious that Heidegger's translation introduces the possibility of a new reading, as also happens with his translation of verse 370. *Hupsipolis apolis* is translated by Heidegger as "rising high over the site, losing the site is he for whom what is not is always for the sake of daring" (Fried and Polt add: "A more conventional translation would be: 'If he follows the laws of the earth and the gods' sworn justice he is high in the city . . . , but he is cast out from the city if he dwells with dishonor for the sake of daring'" [n53, 157–58]). And verses 372–73 are rendered as "let him not become a companion at my hearth, nor let my knowing share the delusions of the one who works such deeds" (158) (which the Loeb Library translation gives as "May he who does such things never sit by my hearth or share my thoughts" [37]).

Pantoporos aporos and *hupsipolis apolis* are presented by Heidegger as interpretations of the uncanniest in the human (*deinotaton*) (162). As such, they are characterizations of the human in the context of the explicitation of the originary unity and disjunction of being and thinking. If thinking means apprehending (*noein* as *Vernehmen*), apprehension is, Heidegger says, "a happening (*Geschehen*) in which humanity itself happens" (150). How does it happen? Thinking is a relation to being that is channeled, at the time of the inception, as reciprocal violent appropriation. If the human can dispose of the sea and the earth, of animals, of language and passion, it is because it is disposed to them and by them, through the violent prevailing of Being. And so humans ultimately look at their own perdition in various ways: they are *aporos* and *apolis* because "they stand in the no-exit of death" (169) as essential, constant limitation—a limitation that rules over the fact that human *techne* clashes against *dike*. The confrontation *techne/dike*, which he finds clearly expressed in *Antigone*'s choral ode, is also at the same time what, at the end of his book, Heidegger would claim constitutes "the inner truth and greatness of National Socialism," the historical confrontation at the end of metaphysics that could restitute the possibility of a resolutive "encounter between global technology and modern humanity" (note that this latter phrase was added in a 1953 revision of the 1935 text; *Introduction*, 213). This too is being:

> The one who is violence-doing, the creative one, who sets out into the un-said, who breaks into the un-thought, who compels what has never happened and makes appear what is unseen, this violence-doing one stands at all times in daring (*tolma*, verse 371). Insofar as he dares the surmounting of Being, he must risk the assault of un-beings, the *me kalon*, disintegration, un-constancy, un-structure, and unfittingness. The higher the peak of historical Dasein rises, the more gaping is the abyss for the sudden plunge into the unhistorical, which then only flails around in a confusion that has no way out and at the same time has no site. (172)

The sacrificial is hinted at here. Perdition (*Verderb*), then, is the possibility that ensues from the oppositional relation of the two forms of the *deinon*, *techne* and *dike*. Perdition is the uncanniest. It does not come at the end of any failing activity, it "holds sway and lies in wait fundamentally" (173). Oedipus faces disaster because disaster faces Oedipus. If Heidegger pays attention to the conclusion of the choral ode, whose verses exclude the uncanny human from hearth and counsel, it is to say that "one who is in this way [namely, as the uncanniest] should be excluded from hearth and counsel . . . Insofar as the chorus turns against the uncanniest, it says that this manner of Being is not the everyday one . . . In their defensive attitude they are the direct and complete confirmation of the uncanniness of the human essence" (175–76). The determination of Greek humanity would seem to assume its tragic condition in uncanny errancy and the necessary loss of the hearth and of the sharing of collective counsel, of communal thought. For Heidegger, for the time being, that is, in 1935, this is the first inception of the West as history, or of history in the West. I should add that such is also the drift of Felipe Martínez Marzoa's interpretation of the loss of the *polis* and of the *polis* as necessary loss, to which I referred earlier.

The uncanny, which translates into English the Greek *deinon*, is in German the *Unheimliche*, the unhomely. Heidegger says that the reciprocal relation of *dike* and *techne* is the same thing as the reciprocal relation of being (*einai*) and thinking (*noein*) (176). The relation is a violent relation. It makes uncanniness happen, that is, it makes homelessness appear. "The assault of *techne* against *dike* is the happening through which human beings become homeless" (178); "Apprehension is a passage through the crossing of the threefold way. Apprehension can become this passage only if it is fundamentally a de-cision for Being against Nothing, and thus a confrontation with seeming. But such essential deciding, when it is carried out and when it resists the constantly pressing ensnarement in the everyday and customary, has to use violence. This act of violence, this de-cided setting-out upon the way to the Being of beings, moves humanity out of the homeliness of what is most directly nearby and what is usual" (179). Homelessness results, originarily, in the first historical inception, from the mutually appropriating relation of being and thinking. That the chorus will exclude the human from hearth and counsel confirms the unhomely but, at the same time, makes the home first disclose itself as such (178).

Let us now move to 1942. In his seminar on Hölderlin's "The Ister" Heidegger will incorporate some crucial lectures on *Antigone* that fundamentally revise (and it must be noted that such a revision is not explicitated as such, that is, as a revision and a change of heart, in the lectures) his 1935 analysis. The interpretation remains the same in many aspects—it is still an attack on the conflation of *techne* and *dike* that rules over the history of the West—and yet it is totally different as a whole. Where is the difference? It is in the framing. Heidegger no longer directly emphasizes the *techne/dike* difference that presumably was in the 1935 text its central contribution to the analysis—a contribution, to my mind, whereby Heidegger also thought he was saying something essential about National Socialism as a historical movement.[2] But what interests him in 1942 is the relation of the homely and the unhomely, understood no longer in terms of the heroic and the violent but rather in terms of the hearth, the home, and prudent thinking (*phronein*). Again Heidegger centers his commentary on the choral ode, in the elucidation of the very same verses that *Introduction* to Metaphysics had thematized. But now his frame is different, and his interpretation takes its point of departure in what is attributed to Hölderlin: "For Hölderlin, that essence [of history] is concealed in human beings' becoming homely, a becoming homely that is a passage through and encounter with the foreign" (Hölderlin, 54). Accordingly, for Sophocles too "human beings are, in a singular sense, not homely, and . . . their care is to become homely" (71). This is the difference: it is now caring to become homely rather than accepting the destinal character of uncanny violence that describes the essence of the human. An abandonment of politics, in Heidegger's own terms, has taken place through a reconsideration of the essence of the *polis*. I hesitate to include here two additional quotations that could be taken to underline Heidegger's change of position, so I will only do it with a *caveat*: they could be taken to mean just that, which would imply a critique of National Socialism at the time of its decline given the fortunes of war. Heidegger says: "Those who lose the essential site of their history, that is, whatever is fitting in all destiny, in towering high above that site, are in such a way [unhomely] only because nonbeings can be in being for them" (Hölderlin, 87). He is analyzing yet again *Antigone*'s *hupsipolis apolis* verse. The tragic condition resonates: "Where all indulgence is turned towards risk, and every comportment toward beings is as it must be for the sake of risk, the relation of humans to beings is tensioned within the most extreme tension between the supreme heights of mastery of the site of their history and the most profound depths of the forfeiture of this site" (89). The forfeiture of the historical site for Nazi Germany announces a mere possibility at the time of its radical withdrawing, which is the time of its historical death.

In 1942 *pantoporos aporos* and *hupsipolis apolis* are the marks of a counterturning regarding the homely, when in 1935 they were rather the marks of a necessary and heroic perdition (see *Introduction*, 173). The human "everywhere ventur[es] forth (*pantoporos*)" but finds himself or herself "experienceless without any way out (*aporos*)" (73). The human "tower[s] high above the site (*hupsipolis*)" and yet finds himself or herself "forfeiting the site (*apolis*)," site-less (79). Human beings are not accidentally or contingently condemned to those contrary experiences: the *polis* is rather the site where the human being finds its historical essence in the tension or torsion of the turning/counterturning. "Human beings do not 'have' these possibilities in addition and extrinsic to themselves, rather their essence consists in being those who, in ascending within the site of their essence, are at the same time without site" (87). This is the tragic condition, which marks the culmination of the Greek determination of the essence of the human. That the human is the *deinon*, even *to deinotaton*, is asserted by Sophocles for the first and the last time in the

Greek world. Soon, with Plato, perhaps with Socrates (certainly with Socrates in the Nietzschean interpretation), the tragic tension would be concealed for the sake of an affirmation of the priority of one of the sides. "For here alone [in *Antigone*'s choral ode] is there the necessity of remaining within the grounds of that which is counterturning, instead of taking flight into one or the other side. At that historical moment when one side of the counterturning character of being is devalued as the lesser and lower, the Greek world falls out of the orbit of its essence and its downfall has been decided" (77). The latter is obviously the site of Martínez Marzoa's understanding of the ruination of the communal essence of the *polis*, which would set the course of the history of the West, in the Nietzschean and Heideggerian readings, as an ongoing and always failing negotiation of the downfall.

The precise and decisive preparatory moment in Heidegger's reframing of his reading of *Antigone*, which must be understood, in my reading, as a reconsideration of the merely political import of the interpretation of the choral ode, must be found in the discussion of the first dialogue between Antigone and Ismene, which was absent in *Introduction to Metaphysics*. Heidegger focuses on Antigone's words to her sister, announcing to her that she is willing *pathein to deinon touto*, in Heidegger's translation "to take up into my own essence the uncanny that here and now appears" (103). To suffer the terrible, to bear the unhomely: Antigone takes it on, she does not flee from it: "within the most uncanny, Antigone is the supreme uncanny" (104). And then Heidegger asks: "What if that which were most intrinsically unhomely, thus most remote from all that is homely, were that which in itself simultaneously preserved the most intimate belonging to the homely?" (104). Everything will now depend on the interpretation, which is a reinterpretation, within the context of the tragedy, of the last few verses of the choral ode, where the chorus affirms its rejection of the uncanny ones: "*met' emoin parestios genoito met' ison phronon hos tad' erdoi*," which Heidegger renders as "such shall not be entrusted to my hearth, nor share their delusion with my knowing, who put such things to work" (92). Are we to think, as the 1935 interpretation still hinted or left radically ambiguous, that the chorus rejects Antigone, the rebellious, who will not conform to the laws of the city? If so, the choral ode, Heidegger now says, would have become, in these last verses, "a song in praise of mediocrity, and a song of hatred towards the exception" (97). But the tragedy does not support that. Heidegger returns to the thought that a difference is being sustained through those very words between the *polis* and the political, of which he adds "for the Greeks, the *polis* is that which is altogether worthy of question. For modern consciousness, the 'political' is that which is necessarily and unconditionally without question" (94–95). The interpretation according to which the chorus rejects Antigone, expels her from the hearth, can only be the interpretation of modern consciousness, a political (and fallen) interpretation: the interpretation accessible to those for whom politics is the ground itself, and functions without question. But there is an alternative reading even for us—for us moderns, when we embrace a certain distance from the distance.

Antigone's willingness to bear the burden of the heart, to suffer any suffering in her commitment to honor the dead, her dead brother, must be understood otherwise. There is a stupid unhomeliness, sinister and obtuse, which consists in "a forgetting and blindness" (109) of the hearth, but it is not Antigone's—it is, rather, Creon's. Antigone's unhomeliness is of an entirely different kind, since it consists of a radical affirmation of the hearth: "The hearth, the homestead of the homely, is being itself, in whose light and radiance, glow and warmth, all beings have in each case already gathered. *Parestios* is the one who, tarrying in the sphere of the hearth, belongs to those who are entrusted with the hearth, so that everyone who belongs to the hearth is someone entrusted, whether they are 'living' or dead" (114–15). Antigone is able, that is her supreme action, to assume the passage through unhomeliness and death for the sake of taking up unhomeliness into her own essence. Antigone, says Heidegger, "becomes homely within being" (117). She is exempt from the rejection of the chorus because she herself founds the very sense of hearth the chorus enacts. "Becoming homely in being unhomely" (121) is Antigone herself, her essence. Heidegger calls this the "poetic:" "The unhomely being homely of human beings upon the earth is 'poetic'" (120). Deprived of the simple recourse to homeliness among beings, Antigone's decision appeals to the higher homeliness of being, which founds the *polis* as it founds any and every other possibility of historical dwelling for the human. The ontological difference translates here into the difference between politics and infrapolitics.

I prefer to call Heidegger's "poetic" infrapolitical—it seems to me more precise as a term. The wrenching shift from an everyday engagement with things to a radical engagement with the darkness of the originary home, never to be reached, but approachable through nearness, could perhaps be described poetically, but becoming homely through the unhomely remains primarily not a poetic but an infrapolitical task. The infrapolitical task is not to look for a hearth, a home, only to seek a nearness, an approach counterposed to the forgotten distance of the distance. The nearness is infrapolitical distance. It is not a minor task: it has to do with establishing an existential attunement to the fact that everywhere today politics, beyond the dignity of its concept, today everywhere experienced as farce, is nothing more than venturing forth with no way out, a siteless undertaking. From the perspective of the step back, politics, even when it thinks of itself as counterhegemonic, or as resistant, is today everywhere the uncanniest were it not the most ridiculous of tasks. Politics is Creon's doing, the headless and errant assertion of unhomely power lost in nonbeing, lost in the nothingness of administrative and ideological claims. Is that the injustice of the world imagined by Otto Dietrich Zur Linde in Jorge Luis Borges's story "Deutsches Requiem"? Or should we keep awaiting a new historico-political dawn, Hegelian or otherwise? If the latter, there is some work to be done.

I also want to translate the notion that the *polis* is the most question-worthy, in its very difference from the political, into the notion that, for us non-Greeks, it is infrapolitics that is question-worthy when there are no longer any extant questions for politics: politics, considered by so many the site of the identification of being and thinking, is technology today, a technological endeavor, in a context where *dike* is no longer overwhelming, because it has been thoroughly absorbed into political *techne* in the form of social administration under the principle of general equivalence. There is no longer a *polis*—it remains only as a ghost from the tradition. Its spectrality subsists in the form of infrapolitics as a dark memory of the origin, as a reminder of the fact that we too were historically appropriated once. But no more. We have all been unmoored as heartless *marranos*, which is not without its promise. We are all disavowing Antigones. And such is our tragic condition, to which we remain, for the most part, blind, but not blind like Oedipus.

Reflecting on the (spectral) *polis*, Martínez Marzoa notes, "either the community itself does not make itself relevant in any way, remains opaque as such, and then to a certain extent it can be said that there is no community, it does not take place, since it never becomes manifest . . . or else the community is not in a position to rest content with its own opacity, and the links, that is, the countersettings, always already taken for granted, are forced into becoming said, becoming relevant, and then the community certainly takes place, it certainly exists, but then it is to be seen whether what happens is not that the community explodes" ("Estado y *pólis*," 106). Once the distance of the game becomes not just relevant, but obvious, once the distance has been naturalized and has assumed a patency, has become primary, then distance is all there is, but empty distance, distance that rules over a space that is no longer the space of community but an undifferentiated and continuous space, an unlimited space where only arbitrary cuts are not just possible but customary. The consequences reach modernity in the following way: the "political problem" in modernity is that "consensus is limited to one thing only, which is not to seek any consensus; there is to be agreement only in creating and maintaining conditions so that it is possible to live without any agreement at all, not communing with anything" ("Estado y legitimidad," 88). This is for

Martínez Marzoa the "democratic republic" or just "democracy" in modernity ("Estado y *pólis*," 113). But the other side of this coin concerning the dissolution of consensus and communions in modernity is "what happens when those dissolutions and delinkings begin to be (partially) real and the State begins to find itself not even opposed to those things, but alone with itself; it would need to be seen whether there is some reason then for the State to feel panic before itself and to hurry and look for new reconciliations and syntheses with those other things" (89). The emptiness of the political determination, its modern democratic formulation, anchored in the principle of equivalence according to which everything is exchangeable for everything else, and there is nothing outside the system of circulation, means there are no substantial, only formal, links, there is no possibility of a political home or a nearness to any kind of origin. But this also means: "that structure or formation that projects as its concept of legitimacy the absence of links, to the point where it cannot function otherwise, at the same time fails to function without constantly making up some or other supposedly given links, in the name of which, sooner or later, the set of conditions that the concept of legitimacy acknowledges is violated. . . . Nihilism must above all avoid recognizing itself, it must always fabricate something to hold on to, and this is because precisely the recognition of nihilism would be the only non-nihilist thing" (100). This is nihilism with a bite. In the state's reaction to its own empty formalism, oppression ensues. Nihilism recognized is, however, infrapolitical nihilism.

And yet it was Schürmann who said: "Only a wrenching of thinking allows one to pass from the 'time' that is concerned with epochal thinking to originary time, which is *Ereignis*—to agonistic, polemical freeings. So, it is not as an a priori that temporal discordance fissures the referential positings around which epochs have built their hegemonic concordances" (*Broken*, 598). This wrenching of thinking—do we need to refer to it as capable of a new determination of the essence of the human being, a new determination of history, a new historical dispensation? The answer would have to be negative, particularly since those intended "agonistic, polemical freeings" would not coalesce into any new hegemonic concordance. Infrapolitics is the mere possibility of the wrenching of thinking toward the nearest. Infrapolitics is not a politics, yet it sets the conditions and opens the way for a posthegemonic practice of democracy, which is the liberation of infrapolitical time in and for existence.

The originary logos of the West, the logos of the first inception, evolved through Platonic and later times into today's cybernetics and logistics following a process of abstraction that has turned being into the most general, hence empty, of concepts. I have made an effort to give some concreteness to being by associating it to the home of infrapolitics. In a late lecture entitled "On the Question Concerning the Determination of the Matter for Thinking," Heidegger maintained that the change from the dominance of the principles of modern subjectivity into the dominance of cybernetics, which stands for the total orderability of the world, consummates the final avatar of the history of presence, and it is no longer possible to go past it. In that impossibility, which is the confirmation of the hypothesis of metaphysical closure, the question of presencing in a verbal form, still a part of the Greek experience of life but covered over and forgotten, comes up once again as a hint about today's impasse. The total orderability of the world, which the present age and its politics will continue to bring on in an ever-increasing manner, constitutes the final principle of metaphysics. Total orderability is general equivalence. But general equivalence as total orderability is also the end of politics—not its factual end, since there will be politics, but rather the end of politics as historical mediation. What is essential today is orderability as such, which cannot be fought politically. Orderability can only be fought infrapolitically, by developing a relationship to existence that dwells on and questions the other of orderability, which, as mere trace, is the remnant of the free historical being of the first inception. As another, even later Heideggerian essay puts it, it is the attempt to dwell in what "sustains and determines and lets us grow in the core of our existence" (Heidegger, "Messkirch," 51) against every imposition of conformity: an Antigonic trace, and as such the hyperbolic condition of any possible political democracy.

4
Infrapolitics and the Politics of Infrapolitics

Previous chapters show the gradual and tentative development of the notion of infrapolitics, but it is perhaps time to speak of it more directly. The first section of this chapter was written for an academic conference held in March 2015. During the discussion that followed my presentation, a number of interlocutors made the point that they were mystified by the perhaps abstract tone of what was proposed—that they would like to see it contextualized within political struggle proper; that, while they recognized that what I call infrapolitics does not propose itself as a form of politics, but rather as a peculiar withdrawal or retreat from the political field, the retreat is still itself politically significant, and that such significance needs to be made explicit. Such reactions, while legitimate, already spring from a misunderstanding concerning the specific work infrapolitics sets out to do. But merely appealing to the fact that misunderstandings may or do happen, that infrapolitics runs the risk of being misunderstood structurally and consistently, that infrapolitics is precisely the choice to dwell in a particular, murky zone of ambiguous indistinction, is hardly satisfactory, both for the readers, I suppose, and for me.[1]

Addressing the misunderstanding as such, but only in a certain way, is the purpose of the second section in this chapter. There is no amount of precision that might dissolve the constitutive ambiguity of the infrapolitical prospect, of the infrapolitical exercise, and that might undo its refusal of politics in favor of a new form of politicity. The affirmation that infrapolitics is not a politics must be left to stand. The third section in the chapter introduces the notion of posthegemony, for me something like a properly political supplement to infrapolitics.

Infrapolitics—the Project

The thought of infrapolitics started to circulate about ten or twelve years ago in discussions within the field of Latin American studies. Of course it was already a known term, from James C. Scott's theorization, but we were looking for something else, which does not preempt intersections.[2] There was a long period of latency—infrapolitics would be mentioned here and there as a place-marker, or as a hint, but we were not ready to launch into a sustained discussion of its potential. In 2014 after some critical references in publications and social networks, we decided to form a group on the issue which lasted more or less until 2017. It was a fairly complex group, in its larger avatar comprising about forty scholars of all ages and from several countries (Spain, Chile, Mexico, Canada, Italy, the United States), perhaps fifteen of them truly active. Jorge Alvarez Yágüez made a presentation on it at a conference in Madrid in June 2014, and that may have been its first public presentation.[3]

What is infrapolitics? What does one talk about when one says "infrapolitics"? But even so: is "talking about" something or other what one attempts through infrapolitics? No, it is rather a matter of "speaking from" a place or a site we would rather not thematize in order not to turn it into an "object" of research, which would imply the sort of structuration of things, the sort of "image of the world" out of which we are trying to pull ourselves in the first place. If language can hardly speak representationally about language without turning language into a representation, then infrapolitical language refuses to turn infrapolitics into yet another mechanism for representation, another brand of thought in the marketplace of ideas, another "political option" in the university, for instance, another flavor of academic discourse.[4] Our interest is not to thematize infrapolitics, to turn it into another form of computation of the world.

In his 1983 "Letter to a Japanese Friend," Jacques Derrida responds to a demand to offer "a schematic and preliminary reflection on the word 'deconstruction'" (1), and he says: "What deconstruction is not? Everything of course! What is deconstruction? Nothing of course!" (5). We could perhaps *say* the same thing of infrapolitics, a nothing that is also at the same time (not) everything, a (not) all that becomes a form of nothing as a response to the metaphysical question par excellence, which is the *what is?* question. In any case, like deconstruction, infrapolitics may turn out to be "not a good word" (5), simply something that one can only use more or less casually, not systematically, seeking specific effects "in highly determined situations" (5). That being so, there is more in the Derridean text about the bad word deconstruction that we can use, casually and unsystematically, for infrapolitics—without attempting in any way, and at any rate not yet, not for a time, to indicate that deconstruction and infrapolitics may *be* the same thing or come to the same thing. Although why not?

Derrida complains about the sheer difficulty of fighting off the truism that "deconstruction" was negative, mostly negative, negative for the most part. True, there were some ostensible reasons for that, as people simply could not figure out what it was that deconstruction aimed to offer when it became evident it was not seeking any of the habitual things. For instance, Derrida says, deconstruction could not propose itself as an "analysis," since "the dismantling of a structure is not a regression toward a simple element, toward an indissoluble origin" (3). And deconstruction could not propose itself as a "critique," since "the instance of *krinein* or of *krisis* (decision, choice, judgment, discernment) is itself, as is all the apparatus of transcendental critique, one of the essential 'themes' or 'objects' of deconstruction" (3). And, Derrida says, the same thing can be said about "method," which has the pleasant/unpleasant corollary that deconstruction, therefore, is not a methodology for reading and interpretation and can therefore not be "reappropriated and domesticated by academic institutions" (3). Finally, Derrida says that deconstruction is also not "an act or an operation" (3), because there is something more passive about it than the passivity that is customarily opposed to activity, and also because deconstruction does not return "to an individual or collective subject" (3). The most that can be said, therefore, for deconstruction, is that it happens, there is deconstruction, "*ça se déconstruit*," and the "*se*" bears the whole enigma (4).

There is a case to be made that infrapolitics, as we think of it or as we let it think us, is neither an analytic tool nor a form of critique, neither a method nor an act or an operation, that infrapolitics happens, always and everywhere, and that its happening beckons to us and seems to call for a transformation of the gaze, for some kind of passage to some strange and unthematizable otherwise of politics that is also, it must be, an otherwise than politics. In the brief "Letter," there is a hint of this strangeness, which infrapolitics and deconstruction would share, which comes when Derrida, quite unexpectedly, I think, for most readers, says, abruptly and without elaboration, that deconstruction is, therefore, and this seems to be a definition or the beginning of a definition, "a discourse or rather a writing that can make up for the incapacity of the word to be equal to a 'thought'" (4). Infrapolitics is also a region, or a site, as we called it before, where some incapacity of the word to be equal to thought, to a "thought," that is, where an unfillable gap or a fissure between language and thought also happens, but infrapolitics cannot even claim the status of a "discourse or rather a writing" (infrapolitical reflection is of course both, but not infrapolitics as such, if there is or could be an "as such" of infrapolitics).

What is its interest? Can infrapolitics make up for an incapacity, a lack, a gap between language and thought?

If infrapolitics cannot speak of itself without betraying itself, then everything that is said will be an act of destruction, or a prolegomenon to it. But one must start somewhere. Infrapolitics is, minimally, as a thematizable region, a field of reflection open to the exploration of conditions of existence at the time of the accomplishment of the ontotheological structuration of modernity. At such a time, now, we understand that experience, everyone's experience, is crossed by politics, that politics marks and determines and frames it in irreducible and fundamental forms; but we also understand, or think we understand, or would like to understand, that politics cannot exhaust, and does not exhaust, experience. Experience exceeds or subceeds politics, and it can therefore be thematized and studied infrapolitically. At the time of accomplishment of the ontotheological structuration of the known world, politics cannot merely be understood as a taken for granted, natural event, or procedure. Politics is itself subject to historical conditions of manifestation, quite apart from obvious intrahistorical divisions such as, for us, Left/Right, or liberals/conservatives, or populists/technocrats. Politics, in its present range of manifestation, still responds to a particular historical epoch and to a particular structure of civilization. In other words, the nature of politics is not itself political, but rather historical through and through. There is no intemporal politics, rather politics happens once every time, even if it is a matter of a program being implemented, for government or for access to power, but the manner of its happening is not independent from a basic social ideology that frames the range of its occurrence. At the time of accomplishment of ontotheology, politics is ontotheological through and through, even when it finds itself playing a so-called counterhegemonic or resistant role, and the fact that such determination may have been forgotten is no obstacle—it simply furthers its ideological nature.

But infrapolitics does not seek to determine the nature of politics, not even in its contemporary dispensations. Infrapolitics is not primarily a critique of politics. Its interest, and we can call it hermeneutic, phenomenological, or deconstructive, is to be found in the attempt to delimit the political determination in favor of its excess—or its *subcess*; at any rate, its difference. Infrapolitics dwells in the difference from politics. Infrapolitics, as a field of reflection or a site for reflection, reflects on the *subcess* of politics, that is, not on politics as subcessed, but rather on the active *infra-excess* of the political, in whatever underflows politics as we know it. As a subcess, that is, as an excess that precedes, as a site for reflection not circumscribable or determinable by any political determination, to the extent the latter generally remains blind to the former in order to constitute itself, infrapolitics may reach a critical dimension—infrapolitics thinks of politics insofar as it thinks the otherwise-than-politics—but its primary exercise is not politico-critical, rather interpretive (even if its final purpose is not interpretive but experiential: infrapolitics does not aim at sense but at being). Infrapolitics, as a difference from politics, lives and opens up in the withdrawal or the *retrait* of the political field, which means it does carry along an intense politicity, but it is the impolitical politicity that suspends and questions every apparent politicization, every instance of political emergence, every heliopolitical moment, and places them all provisionally under the sign of a destruction.

There is a name for the impolitical politicality of infrapolitics: we call it posthegemony, or even democratic posthegemony. Infrapolitics meets in posthegemonic democracy, or in its praxis, which is posthegemonic democratization, the supplementary interruption of its own *subcessive* praxis. Infrapolitics is not a politics, but posthegemonic democratization is a political praxis, and it would be hard to have one without the other. There can perhaps be infrapolitics without posthegemony, but there is no praxis of posthegemony without infrapolitical reflection. Both infrapolitics and posthegemony attempt to think the gap between epochal politics, as it can be available to us, and its difference from itself—*that* in the human experience, or in existence that, while marked or even covered over by politics, is itself not political, is not itself political, while it subtends every politics. We may have forgotten about it, which makes bringing it back up more and not less urgent.[5]

If the project of Infrapolitical Deconstruction has a common genealogy, and it must have it, although it is lived differently by everyone, we must find it in our provenance—the common link is the university, and the specific field of Latin American studies in it. Of course the older members of the Collective have more scars than the younger ones, but this is all a matter of disciplinary history and can be traced back to texts and specific discussions, and even events. After the late 1990s, in our perception, the general cultural studies paradigm, which had already been used by us as an escape from the constrictions of disciplinary life as we knew it, hit a wall and became unproductive. At the same time, the so-called political turn in cultural studies, which was no more than an intensification of claims of political salvation through academic work, although it included in principle a critique of identity politics (which was for years and even decades the only perceptible if unbreathable claim for "politics" in the North American university) in the name of universalism, became mechanical and dogmatic, and it still is. A critique of the history of the Left, quite neglected by representatives of the so-called political turn, who actually seemed to be much more invested in a mere repetition of the history of the Left in modernity, provoked a general or even terminal dissatisfaction with available or dominant theoretical paradigms both in the larger field of the Humanities and in the smaller field of the Latin Americanist Humanities, including, by the way, subalternism, which, in retrospect, had been the last illusion or delusion of the field.

All of this had effects, and for a very long time effects that were mostly negative and disorienting. It still has them. But finally, as Sergio Villalobos-Ruminott put it in a set of "Seminar Notes" that circulated among the Collective, "there was a need to move forward towards the constitution of a horizon of problems that could articulate a posthegemonic understanding of the political understood as a-principial thought [in Reiner Schürmann's sense] and infrapolitics, understood as a reflection on existence beyond political demand" ("Notas," 2).[6] In the meantime, the university was evolving into its increasingly absolute and seamless neoliberal, corporate avatar, and ceased to be interesting as a usable institution except in the most trivial sense (a relatively secure job, a check at the end of the month, not something to be dismissed). All of these negative or critical predispositions developed in the wake of a certain congenital *marranismo*, which we came to understand as the productive side of the Hispanic intellectual and existential tradition, or at least the side of it we were interested in continuing to preserve and even develop. This last thing is perhaps what makes our project not exportable to everyone, and not even likable by everyone, thank God—it is simply what we do, from a certain understanding of things, and in the wake of many historical failures, which are by no means only ours. Others are welcome to continue to do what they do, and there is nothing further from our interests than any proactive spirit of persuasion. We simply take the right to do what we think is feasible, given time—which is not a right, we know, the professional field will generously provide for us. But so be it. I for one could not care less.

For the fact is that the project of infrapolitics is only derivatively an academic practice—most of us work at the university and we do our work in the context or the ruins of the university apparatus such as they are today. But we understand all too well that the university is subjected to conditions of production and reproduction, themselves derived from the ontotheological self-accomplishment of modernity, that are incompatible with the future of the infrapolitical project. Infrapolitics is postinstitutional to the very extent that it seeks its necessary radicalization. We could see it as a modality of savage thought, or of what Cathérine Malabou calls "the irruption of the fantastic in philosophy," which of course overwhelms us as much as it calls us, and destroys us as much as it informs us.[7] But the fantastic in philosophy is about the time of life against the time of work, about the suspension of monetary equivalence and its equivalential tropes as the general principle of our lives, which is today the very principle of the university (and there is no other). From there, and precisely from there, in rejection and rebellion, infrapolitics does not look for inscription, for celebration, is not looking for community or filiation, it is countercommunitarian and hostile to any capture formation. And its wager is for a long and incalculable time of reflection against every kind of excellentist or salvific productionism.[8]

It must have become clear already that our project places itself in a tradition of thought marked by the work of Martin Heidegger, which it seeks to interpret or reinterpret by learning from a number of thinkers in his wake: from Reiner Schürmann to Cathérine Malabou, from Simone Weil and Luce Irigaray and María Zambrano to Felipe Martínez Marzoa and Arturo Leyte, Jacques Derrida, Jean-Luc Nancy, Massimo Cacciari, Mario Tronti, Miguel Abensour, Oscar del Barco, Agustín García Calvo, Giorgio Agamben, the Invisible Committee, Roberto Esposito, or Davide Tarizzo, from Sigmund Freud to Jacques Lacan, Jorge Alemán and the Lacanian tradition, including of course many others. There is nothing too original here, except that we aim to keep alive a certain simplicity in Heidegger's thought that he himself covered up at times—a problem that has repeated itself in its reception. If infrapolitical reflection is a sustained attempt at working out and releasing the subceeding passage from politics into a region of existence politics occludes, this is not to be taken as a flight from politics, but rather as an attempt to determine, even to thematize, the conditions under which an alternative conception of the political could perhaps become manifest. In "Overcoming Metaphysics," a text written between 1936 and 1946, Heidegger indicates the possibility of a historical opening into explicit infrapolitics when he says:

> The struggle between those in power and those who want to come to power: On every side there is struggle for power. Everywhere power itself is what is determinative. Through this struggle for power, the being of power is posited in the being of its unconditional dominance by both sides. At the same time, however, one thing is still covered up here: the fact that this struggle is in the service of power and is willed by it. Power has overpowered these struggles in advance. The will to will alone empowers these struggles. Power, however, overpowers various kinds of humanity in such a way that it expropriates from man the possibility of ever escaping from the oblivion of Being on such paths. This struggle is of necessity planetary and as such undecidable in its being because it has nothing to decide, since it remains excluded from all differentiation, from the difference (of Being from beings), and thus

from truth. Through its own force is it driven out into what is without destiny: into the abandonment of Being. (100)

One may not like the tropology of being, the ontological difference (but infrapolitics, which thinks ontological difference as the subcess of politics, is also and therefore an attempt at thinking out the conditions for a coming politics of the ontological difference), or other aspects of the Heideggerian jargon, but there remains the fact that an alternative politicity is announced that would not be blindly based on the will to will, of which in another section of Heidegger's essay we are told that it can only bring about what is already with us, namely, "a collapse of the world" and "a desolation of the earth:" "Man wills himself as the volunteer of the will to will, for which all truth becomes that error which it needs in order to be able to guarantee for itself the illusion that the will to will can will nothing other than empty nothingness, in the face of which it asserts itself without being able to know its own completed nullity" (86). We call all of this, in political things, hegemony, and the search for hegemony, and the hegemonic conceptualization of politics, of which one of its greatest interpreters, Ernesto Laclau, has said that it necessarily exhausts politics *tout court*. But we disagree: hegemony cannot exhaust politics, as there is posthegemonic politicity, without which politics is a siteless undertaking.

At the same time, even if infrapolitics aims to continue to let itself be inflected by the Heideggerian schematics concerning the history of being, the completion of metaphysics, the end of epochal history, the ruin of principial thought, it is not our intention to be in favor of any valorization (or, indeed, devalorization) of particular historico-cultural horizons or specific human profiles. The attempt so far to provide genealogical conditions for the project should make it clear. The notion of value, or any form of cultural value, has been denounced by some of us as incompatible with a subalternist approach even at its most superficial. Our *marranismo* has a few teeth, but not to chew on the exaltation or denigration of any form of human life. The publication of Heidegger's *Black Notebooks* makes it clearer than it has already been that our project must also affirm a certain anti-Heideggerianism as well. If we take the Heideggerian scheme on the history of being as a variation on the Hegelian one, hence a hardly renounceable part of the history of thought, the explicit, intentional undertones revealed by the *Black Notebooks* affirming an "ontic" or "existentiell" plunge into both anti-Semitism and an overvaluation of "German" destiny in the preparation of a transformation of thought must be rejected not just in themselves but also as a master tropology for any kind of alternative cultural-historical valorization. In other words, even understanding and endorsing the shame of the anti-Semitic or any other racist legacy, and opting radically for equality and against domination, we do not pretend things would change when we substitute, say, anti-Spanishness or anti-Europeanism for anti-Semitism or if we value subaltern culture over against so-called bourgeois culture. I must refer here to the considerations on un-legacy in Zambrano in Chapter 1 of this book.

The revision and adaptation of what was originally a pro-Nazi tropology—one can qualify this in various ways, but the overwhelming fact unfortunately remains—has been a rather endemic problem in the so-called Heideggerian Left, as can be seen for instance in Massimo Cacciari's 1976 *Krisis*.[9] Infrapolitical reflection must affirm the suspension of any cultural-historical comparative valorization as just another form of principial thought, which, as principial thought, is and would be always already committed to hegemonic power and hegemonic accomplishment. The Heideggerian thematics of the end of epochal history can only be referred by us to the end of the hegemonic/sacrificial structuration of history and historical life. Infrapolitical reflection abandons power as principial force—as the will to will understood as the final principle of metaphysical history—for the sake of an anarchy whose foundations can be traced back to Heidegger as well, mediated by Emmanuel Lévinas, Reiner Schürmann, María Zambrano, and others.

There are two false exits from the Heideggerian schematic structuration of the completion of ontotheology, both of them possibly favored by Heidegger and certainly by, in Heidegger's wake, the Heideggerian Right: one of them is the rupture of the principle of general equivalence, as the dominant structuration of all hegemonic thought in our time, in favor of an alternative hierarchization, that is, in favor of a new hegemony, a new establishment of order and rank. But there is another false exit, and I will merely hint at it. I will do it with another quotation from Heidegger, this time from *Contributions to Philosophy: Of the Event*. There, in the first section, in the *Prospect*, under the heading *Historicality and Being*, Heidegger gives us a notion of what we could call double sovereignty, which, we contend, is the very possibility of a continued hegemonization of the time of life. This is what Heidegger says:

> Sovereignty over the masses who have become free (i.e., groundless and self-serving) must be erected and sustained with the shackles of "organization." In this way can what is thereby "organized" grow back in its original ground, so that what is of the masses is not simply controlled but transformed? . . . Still another sovereignty is needed here, one that is concealed and restrained and that for a long time will be sparse and quiet. Here the future ones must be prepared, those who create in being itself new locations out of which a constancy in

the strife of earth and world will eventuate again. . . . Both forms of sovereignty, though fundamentally different, must be willed and simultaneously affirmed by those who know. (49–50)

The second false exit is the pretense that thinking or poetizing, as a supplement or internal fold within hegemony, could change the nature of hegemony, that is, of sovereignty, that is, of a politics of the will to will finally become conscious of itself. In *Contributions* Heidegger is clearly addressing his remarks to Nazi Germany, but there is a sense in which every structural compromise, such as the one Heidegger is proposing here, of the thinker with the party, the principle of organization, the leading arm of hegemonic power, will always result in the demand for a double structuration of sovereignty. Many leftist thinkers have factually shared this demand, in their appeal to party leadership for instance, which ultimately has to do with the connection of thought and governance, over the last two centuries. We think, however, that there is no non-somnambulistic hero of thought who can or should claim infrapolitical sovereignty. There is no infrapolitical sovereignty, and infrapolitical reflection claims no edge, no advantage over anything else. It is simply a wager for an otherwise of thought. We continue to reflect on this otherwise, which we have sometimes called "transfigured infrapolitics," but it is not yet the proper time to discuss it.

Infrapolitics—the Politics (Allegory and Denarrativization)

In 2004 the Argentinian journal *La Intemperie* published an interview with former revolutionary militant Héctor Jouvé, who had been a member of the Revolutionary Army of the People at the time the guerrilla killed (executed or murdered, take your pick) two of its own members after having determined that they had broken down, or simply broken, as revolutionaries. Shortly after the publication of the interview, Oscar del Barco, a senior figure in the Argentinian intelligentsia, a philosopher, a poet, and a painter, himself a former member of the Argentinian Communist Party and a sympathizer of and collaborator with the guerrilla movement, sent the journal an open letter entitled "*No matarás*" (Thou Shalt Not Kill). This gave rise to a fierce and profound controversy in Argentina.[10]

Let us assume from the outset that the description of the murder of Adolfo Rotblat and Bernardo Groswald in the famous interview could be taken to be, at least in Del Barco's rendering, an allegory or an extended metaphor of the political, itself understood in a certain way. And let me assume that the allegorization is not innocent, but itself a political intervention meant to indict that said "certain" understanding of politics (which in other texts Del Barco has referred to as the politics authorized and enframed by the "System," which is his way of referring to the system of modernity or the system of ontotheological metaphysics)—in other words, my initial contention is that Oscar del Barco, through his open letter, at the same time allegorizes and denarrativizes, or, if you wish, narrativizes and deallegorizes, revolutionary politics as understood by a considerable sector of the Argentinian, and by extension, world leftist intelligentsia after World War II if not also before. Beyond the open letter, the notorious polemic that followed itself allegorizes the fundamental breakdown, hence a terminal denarrativization, of revolutionary politics in modern society, that is, in the society we know, which is perhaps *the only* society we know or believe we know. From Del Barco's letter, and from the responses and counterresponses it gave rise to, well beyond what has been published, we can infer the becoming-true, the entry into full historical consciousness, of a rumor that has long plagued the Left: the disturbing, indeed deranging possibility that the effective triumph of political revolution, far from constituting a new historical time, could only mark what Felipe Martínez Marzoa, in his book *La filosofía de El capital de Marx*, called "the abstract liquidation" of modern society, its (unproductive, were it not so productive for some) fundamental intensification and consummation. This thought can perhaps appear comprehensible if we take the following words at heart. For Martínez Marzoa,

> in Marx, in effect, the difference between the point of view of modern society ("natural consciousness" in Hegelian terms) and the point of view of the revolution resides in the fact that, according to the former, the calculability of being (the physico-mathematical mode of knowledge [that articulates modern society according to the principle of general equivalence, or law of value]) expresses, purely and simply, the "nature of things," and the equality of rights is a requirement of "human nature" (or "pure Reason"), that is: in both cases we have a "truth in itself" that has no dependency on the phenomenon called "modern society," whereas, from the point of view of revolution, things are different: the revolution must be wholly radical in its self-exigency that those postulates [that is, the calculability of being as general equivalence, and the equality of rights] must be fulfilled, precisely because it does not consider them as realities simply "in themselves," comfortably installed in a given "nature," rather as the criteria for a task to be accomplished. (190)

If revolution is the means through which the postulates of universal general equivalence and equality of rights come to be fulfilled, then revolution is indeed internal to the system of modernity, and it can only accomplish modernity. In fact, revolution is to be understood in Martínez Marzoa's perspective, which I share, as the very essence of modern society, and not as a departure from it. From that realization it becomes clear, according to one's preference, either that there would have to be a fundamental change in the very notion of revolution or that revolution is as exhausted as any of the other primary concepts in the architectonics of political modernity. Why, indeed, would we have to assume that "revolution" could survive the entropic catastrophe that has befallen its other systemic terms, from "representation" to "the people," from "the subject" to "the nation," from "legitimacy" to "hegemony"? Unless, of course, the project of a finished or finally accomplished modernity is still good enough to capture democratic hearts and minds. Otherwise, it is time either to abandon the term "revolution" to the dustbin of the history of modernity or to start imagining what revolution could perhaps be once unmoored from its current and at this point rather exhausted systemic haven.[11] The latter is not an easy task—certainly not at the level of imagining it, let alone at the level of making it present. Politically, the challenge is to reach the possibility, in thought first, of an equality, that is, of an end to hierarchies of power, not based on the general equivalence of beings, not based on the leveling down of all substance to its exchange value: a reinvention of the thing, which is always a political invention.

An allegory is an extended metaphor. Denarrativizing metaphors, as metaphors that point to their own end, to their own destruction, are singularly powerful and could convey something of the sense of an ending. But we must not take ending in the mechanical sense of termination—the ending I am referring to might be with us for a very long time, as indeed the responses to Oscar del Barco's letter make clear. My contention is that Del Barco's position ("not an argument," he says somewhere, but not in that letter) splits modern political history in two or begins to split it. That is, in other words, what he offers in specific reference to Argentinian, and Latin American, political history: the beginning of a fundamental refusal of modern politics, and of modern revolutionary politics, which is first expressed as an arrest of political subjectivation. From such a beginning we can begin to unravel the hairball of militant ontotheological politics with a view to its radical destruction, and for the sake of a new figuration. This transfigured politicity includes infrapolitics, and also posthegemony.

Del Barco's letter has to do with the so-called "armed struggle" that developed in the 1960's in many countries partially as a consequence of theoretical developments within Marxism (themselves consequent for the most part with a long history of subjectivity, with a deep ideological production of triumphant subjectivity—it is not Marx we are considering here necessarily, but the history of Marxism). Del Barco merely opposes them, in retrospect, through claiming that "there is no 'ideal' that could justify the killing of a human being, be it General Aramburu, or a militant or a police officer" (115). Armed struggle is not justified, Del Barco claims, and his opposition to it is a consequence of his opposition to the voluntary taking of human life. The letter says little else, really. It does say that its author can understand that the injunction "thou shalt not kill" will not be fulfilled, since, even as a principle, he says, it is an impossible one: "I know that the principle that thou shalt not kill, like that of loving one's neighbor, is an impossible one. I know that history is in great part the history of pain and death. But I also know that upholding this impossible principle is the only possible thing to do. Without it, human society could not exist. To hold the impossible as possible is to uphold what is absolute in every human being, from the first to the last" (116). It is not necessary to belabor it, because it is clear enough, and in fact the simplicity of what is said, the lack of elaboration and argumentation, proves to have been the most anxiety-producing factor of this letter, and what earned Del Barco the most insults.

What counts is the very restraint, the very simplicity of the position that affirms, resolutely, the validity of the statement, impossible in its fulfilment as it may be, "thou shalt not kill." And not only because it establishes, or perhaps reestablishes, for the Argentinian Left, a prohibition its members are then forced to deal with ("Insofar as we do not assume the responsibility of acknowledging the crime, the crime remains active" [116]), but primarily because the prohibition (it is a negative injunction, it concerns, therefore, a prohibition, and the prohibition is the taking of human life, for whatever purpose, in whatever circumstances) has a fundamental consequence: from it, the revolutionary narrative of the Left, the actually existing narrative of the Argentinian Left, for instance, stumbles and falls and cannot be sustained in the daylight. There is something absolute about the human being, Del Barco says, and this absoluteness forbids killing and being killed. If it were said by someone else, a priest, a newspaper columnist, it would be a matter of opinion merely, itself a matter of political combat. But it is said by Oscar del Barco, himself associated with the Argentinian Left, himself an old Communist militant ("Perhaps you forget that I was a Stalinist?" Del Barco would ask some of his critics ["Comments" 162]), and then a supporter of armed struggle. The combat had moved inside, it was an internal debate on a fundamental position, and it was no longer a matter of nuances or mere light position-taking within a general agreement, and this was and is seen as intolerable by many.

The prohibition, the negative injunction, functions as a de-allegorical tool, as a powerful instrument of denarrativization. There is an allegory—every story, every narrative of political effort, of political militancy as militancy, is an allegory, militancy is always allegorical of the promised triumph, of the end of times—and it is the story of the killing, under Jorge Masetti's orders, of the two *"quebrado"* (broken) militants of the Ejército Revolucionario del Pueblo. The retrospective injunction, we should not kill, we should not have killed, destroys the allegorical aura by reducing the narrative to its sordid literalness, by ruining the validity of the figural plane, by indicting the ground of sacrificial militancy on which revolutionary practice has been based: there will be no triumph on killing, and that is that, and it kills the narrative and its figure. The loss of allegorical value is extreme political violence. I do not think we should harbor any illusions that Del Barco's gesture has nothing to do with violence: it is an extreme violence, the violence of a fundamental denarrativization, which is to say, the violence of a fundamental desubjectivation. The heroic subject of sacrificial revolutionary militancy is debunked—through its simple negation.

I insist on Del Barco's own violence because it seems to me important to retain the thought that Del Barco's action is not an abandonment of politics—far from it. It is not a renunciation of politics in favor of some ethics, whether Levinasian or Kantian or properly DelBarquian.[12] The injunction is political because it has political intent. It is aimed at the heart of revolutionary Left practices for most of the twentieth century, and it is aimed at it, with devastating effects, in my opinion, not as one would oppose ethics to politics, but rather as an internal fold of politics, as an alternative politics, as a wholly other politics. Del Barco confirms this when, in his response to articles by Jorge Jinkis, Juan Ritvo, and Eduardo Grüner, he tells them, "the letter is not strung 'on high' but laid out on the 'ground,' in 'politics,' contradicting what you say about my supposed 'abandonment' of politics, which in reality is an abandonment of what you understand by politics" ("Comments," 155). In the same counterresponse Del Barco refers to what he is trying to do as "in-politics, or . . . non-political politics" (158), in order to mark what is announced as a break, a differend that cannot and should not be reconciled. Later on he says:

> You refuse to understand that in fact I am rejecting your idea of politics, which in my judgment (and I must repeat myself) is that politics that respects the limits fixed by the System for thinking "politics" and acting "politically." . . . I must tell you that not only have I not abandoned politics, but I am up to the neck in politics, in what I consider politics: painting, poetry, music, ecstasy, meekness, philosophical thought, mercy, justice, responsibility, joint action, solidarity. (162)

One of the most prominent antagonists to Del Barco's position was León Rozitchner, who, in addition to his punctual polemical intervention, decided to write a full book on it, posthumously published as *Lévinas o la filosofía de la consolación*. His general indictment of Del Barco's position comes down to a disagreement on the prevalence of the prohibition, that he considers patriarchal, and that he would want to substitute with the positing of what he calls a maternal value: "*Primero hay que saber vivir*" (first you must know how to live, 161). For Rozitchner the positive "*vivirás*" (you will live) trumps del Barco's injunction, and changes everything, that is, it restitutes, not necessarily the convenience of killing (Rozitchner is also opposed to political crime), but definitely the casuistry of human actions, that should now be evaluated on the basis of their relative support of the fundamental value of living, and living on. Rozitchner, therefore, not Del Barco, is the one who bases his political reasoning on an ethics of life in avoidance of the absolute injunction not to take life. Life can be taken for the sake of some other life, Rozitchner ultimately says, on properly ethical, value-laden grounds. Rozitchner's "counterviolence" is an ethical counterviolence before it is political, the counterviolence of an oppressed subject, of the slave against the master, ultimately consistent with the division of the world between the powerful and the poor, or the master and the slave in the Hegelian account: "And don't forget that Hegel's philosophy is a (the) system (and not only of 'philosophical' thought)," says Del Barco ("Comments," 172). Rozitchner calls for counterhegemonic violence over against Del Barco's posthegemonic, and properly political, violence — and it is the latter that thus emerges as true countersystemic counterviolence. I believe that one of the consequences of Del Barco's position, not the least hard of them, is a radical abandonment of ethical calculation, that is, of ethics in the conventional, ontotheological sense. "Thou Shalt Not Kill," politically speaking, is the injunction that marks the beginning of a wholly other politics not from an ethical stance, rather from a sort of reckless or savage moralism for which I prefer to use the term infrapolitics (which would be a friendly correction to Del Barco's nonpolitical politics or in-politics — contra Rozitchner, it seems to me the real position of the not-all as maternal injunction, as impossible possibility).[13]

"I am saying that the end does not justify the means. I am saying that every human being is sacred, amongst other things because his meaning cannot be referred on to anything or anyone" ("Comments," 167). Sacredness, as the positive side of the negative injunction, is not a value — it is the very radicality of the absence of valorization in the absence of every sense-producing principle of legitimacy, in the absence of principial thought as such. Sacredness always and in every case demetaphorizes, de-allegorizes, to the extent that sacredness is the uncompromising holding-fast to the literalness of a nonequivalent singularity. From infrapolitical sacredness it is simply not possible to move on to the always figural, always metaphoric calculations (the weighing of the relative in the face of the cause, in the face of the absolute goal, which is Rozitchner's politics, for instance) that have turned modern politics into a game for hegemonic power without reprieve. Del Barco tells his critics:

> For you to desacralize is to laicize, that is, in the last instance . . . to submit man to the growing alienation and reification of the System, making him revolve in metaphysics and its depredations. . . . What I call the sacredness of man or the attempt at passive totality of so-called self-consciousness as excess-of-self is the opposite of consciousness augmented to omni-potence as superman (in reality the superman is the opposite of the beyond-man: he should be seen as man invested onto-theologico-rationally, that is as Being, God or Reason, and, I would add, Will to Power. ("Comments," 177)

In his 2008 essay "Memory Between Politics and Ethics," Patrick Dove unearths the comments Ciro Bustos, a former guerrilla member, made to Jon Lee Anderson about the situation Jouvé himself narrates, which prompts Del Barco's letter. In Bustos's recollection, the decision to kill came in the wake of the following: "[Groswald] had flat feet, was frightened of going down slopes, and he began animalizing. It was truly repellent, and as the days went by he began physically to look more like an animal. To go down a hill he went down on his ass, walked on all fours; a pathetic image for a guerrilla. . . . He was dirty, unclean, and finally he was punished, given the hardest jobs, that kind of thing" (Anderson quoted in Dove, 286). Dove presents this as "an allegory of militant reason and its crisis: the psychological collapse . . . indicates . . . the disgusting . . . possibility of a reversal of developmental history" (286). The decision to kill is a consequence of so-called animalizing: the man who animalizes is no longer a man. Technically, I suppose, the injunction "Thou Shalt Not Kill" still holds. The revolutionaries do not kill a man, they kill less than a man, a degenerate man, a man that does not correspond to the militants' idea of manhood. It is because manhood can only obtain in its equivalence. For the sacrificial revolutionary Left—and there has hardly been any other so far—manhood is nothing but a metaphor of the final goal, which consumes singular sacredness for the sake of the sacredness of a cause turned totality. Which is why Del Barco says:

> If you believe that everything is politics, then any discussion becomes useless. For my part, I repeat, I do not believe in this politics, because

I consider it a closed space that disempowers essentially autonomous practices, which when subsumed into a unity can be dominated-assimilated by the System. I would rather define politics (or in-politics) as a multitude of erratic or perverse actions without a centre, or a polyphony that no theoretical unity or political practice by parties can suppress. I would prefer to be treated as a theologian or a mystic or a man of religion . . . than as just a politician. ("Comments," 158)

The refusal of the politics of the politician is an affirmation, inaugural, I believe, in the Latin American context, in favor of an infrapolitical alternative, perhaps leading to a wholly other politics whose effective possibility we lose nothing for exploring. Oscar del Barco comes close to making the infrapolitical position explicit. Perhaps he was only missing the word.

Unearthing Posthegemony

In the Conclusions to her *Courage Tastes of Blood: The Mapuche Community of Nicolás Ailío and the Chilean State, 1906–2001*, Florencia Mallon indulges in a bit of confession. She says: "At first it was especially difficult for me to recognize, and to put aside, one of my most enduring and lovingly held prejudices: that oppressed or subaltern groups are in reality morally superior, that in some ways their lives have not been touched by the power struggles that mark the rest of society" (233). Her remark has the virtue of making the rest of us question ourselves: is that a belief or a prejudice we share and endure? Do we happen to think that there is a moral or ethical superiority to subalternity, and does our interest in subaltern life perhaps then ensue from such charming self-deception? I call it self-deception following Mallon, who in the course of her research, as she tells us, came to recognize her prejudice as a prejudice, but also because I do not believe that there are any groups untouched by power struggles, somehow beyond society.

The belief that any number of disenfranchised or disadvantaged or oppressed groups are morally superior to the rest of us in virtue of their historically produced misery can be called self-deception, which immediately raises a number of issues. Is self-deception, that is, lying to oneself, first of all possible, and under what conditions? What regulates it? Can one lie unintentionally? Or is self-deception always hypocritical? Or does it come, the self-deception, that particular one, perhaps others as well, as part and parcel of some larger ideology that we embrace in the course of our work, and that would founder the moment we sober up and see a particular thread of the real for what it is, and pull from it? Was the realization that the people of the

Mapuche community of Nicolás Ailío were not after all morally superior good or bad? Was it something of a traumatic awakening for Mallon? She does not say, and it does not matter. But we might benefit from the sort of traumatic awakening Mallon hints at, while she may or may not have undergone it.

My interest in the question has to do with the possibility of construction of posthegemonic democracy, and not just in Latin America but anywhere. Of course, the word "democracy" already has something to do with superiority, through that *kratos* that makes the notion of democratic force different from "monarchies" and "oligarchies" and comparable only to "aristocracy." According to Nicole Loraux, in a fascinating essay entitled "Notes on the One, the Two, and the Multiple," which is a commentary on Pierre Clastres's work and an attempt to measure the difference at the level of political ontology between, say, the Guaraní and the Greeks, the difference between *arkhe* and *kratos* has to do with the fact that "*kratos* says less about power than about superiority" (162). "Democracy" is to be understood, in the Greek way, beyond any moral judgment or comparative valuation, as the clear affirmation of the superiority of the *demos* over everyone else, in the same way that an aristocracy would contend that the upper classes of society are better endowed for rule; but this, in ancient Greece, not because the *demos* was conceived as somehow immune to the power struggles of the social, uncontaminated by them. The superiority of the *demos* was, for Greek democrats, always already a political fact, hence, conceivably, it had nothing to do with morality in Mallon's sense. But the general *kratos* of the people was, in Loraux's understanding, in every case tempered by *arkhe*, the rotatory function of command that made democracy what it was—a place of indistinction between the governed and the governors, which was the specifically egalitarian, demotic function of Greek politics.

Pierre Clastres, in his classic 1974 book *Society against the State*, refers to the frequent accusation launched by all manner of European preachers and imperial servants, who were under no illusions concerning the superiority of the indigenous, against many groups of Indians, particularly in sixteenth-century Brazil. The Indians were deemed to be "faithless, lawless, kingless" (205). The Europeans looked at them from the perspective of what they were lacking, and what they were lacking was invariably a state. It was the lack of a state that deprived them of faith, law, and king, in other words, of a logic of filiation and submission to despotic authority meant to produce or to sanction inequality. Indian groups, essentially egalitarian in Clastres's ethnology, were characterized by the fundamental prohibition of inequality (199), which was a prohibition of the state, that is, a prohibition and an interdiction regarding the state. Clastres's question then becomes:

Primitive societies are societies without a State because for them the State is impossible. And yet all civilized peoples were first primitives: what made it so that the State ceased to be impossible? Why did some people cease to be primitives? What tremendous event, what revolution, allowed the figure of the Despot, of he who gives orders to those who obey, to emerge? Where does political power come from? Such is the mystery . . . of the origin. (205)

The question of posthegemonic democracy must come to terms with the question of the origin of power. The question of liberation, which, in order to be such, cannot be conceptualized as merely a liberation from empire, but should be liberation from hegemonic power, cannot be answered without recourse to the question of the nature and origin of political power, which postcolonial studies has been singularly remiss to ask, if it has ever asked it, by essentially taking it for granted that the postcolonial task was the construction of a postcolonial state, today understood as a multinational state in countries such as Bolivia or Ecuador. It is in the very last pages of his book that Clastres intimates a hypothetical response to his own question. For him, the history of the Tupí-Guaraní, who in the few decades before the Conquest were agents of a massive messianic movement that led many of them "to forsake everything and launch out in search of the Land Without Evil, the earthly paradise" (215), provides the possibility of an answer.

The hypothesis is: the Tupí-Guaraní, in virtue of demographic growth, were coming close to the creation of a system of chieftainship that devolved political power on the chief, which until then had been kept away from him. It is at that point that the shamans, the *karaí*, began to engage in "a prophetic speech, a virulent speech, highly subversive in its appeal to the Indians to undertake what must be acknowledged as the destruction of society. The prophets' call to abandon the evil land (that is, society as it existed) in order to inherit the Land Without Evil, the society of divine happiness, implied the death of society's structure and system of norms" (215). For Clastres, what obtained then was tragic: "the insurrectional act of the prophets against the chiefs conferred on the former, through a strange reversal of things, infinitely more power than was held by the latter. . . . Prophetic speech, the power of that speech: might this be the place where power *tout court* originated, the beginning of the State in the Word?" (218). The state came to the pre-Conquest Tupí-Guarani through the very attempt to ward off the state.

We are now stuck with the state. Mallon says that much. For her, regarding the Mapuches, "the Chilean state seems to set the rules of the game, in the sense that it establishes the structures, institutions, and political discourses within which people must struggle and exist" (237). It is, for the time being, either too late or too early to return to Tupí-Guaraní originary ground. But, learning from the past, in order to establish posthegemonic democracy, or, more modestly, to pursue the path of posthegemonic, egalitarian democratization, the path must then be radically nonprophetic. Whatever equivalence could be traced between the Tupí-Guaraní move toward the destruction of society and contemporary resistance to capitalist coloniality, it is prophetic speech that, then or now, manages to gather the people under the power and the spell of the One, and constructs hegemony. But what if the originary ground were not to be conceptualized as a ground of filiation but as a ground of alliances? What if we could learn from contemporary anthropology that the structure of filiation that regulates all our mostly Western notions about the ground and about the originary is precisely a notion always already rejected by the so-called nonhistorical peoples that still populate the Amazon basin? What if we could set our political expectations not on a return to a pristine Tawantinsuyo, which was already a state society, based on tribute and forced labor, but on the possibility of a savage democracy, based on the potential virtue of a posthegemonic theoretical practice? What if the demotic principle of noninterference were to be replaced on the basis of the ontology of war—war between equals—that Eduardo Viveiros de Castro has explicitated as proper to the Tupí-Guaraní, that is, on an ontology of exchange not identity, never subsumable into identity, on an ontology that always already looks for interference, beyond the One, with no reversion to the One, as the only possibility for a manifestation of being open to difference?[14]

We can explore a transversal line of flight against violence and empire and beyond postcolonial parameters that I will indifferently call geophilosophy, following Gilles Deleuze and Felix Guattari, or cosmopolitical thought, following Jacques Derrida.[15] In many parts of Latin America such line of flight must be thoroughly invested in the anthropology of indigenous life that Tim Ingold used to call "philosophy with people in it."[16] Cosmopolitical thought has a demotic agenda, but it is a minoritarian agenda that wants to look both beyond the ruses of colonization and the rhetoric of liberationist decoloniality for the sake of a return to a ground of thought that should think of itself against every configuration of filiational thought. Cosmopolitical thought might make Deleuze and Guattari's words about Captain Ahab its motto: "I have no personal history with Moby Dick, no revenge to take, any more than I have a myth to play out; but I do have a becoming" (*What Is Philosophy?* 245). Becoming, which as they say is "always of a different order than filiation, it concerns alliances" (238), is something for which "only a minority is capable of serving as the active medium" (291). And becoming is the very possibility of history, or at least of a new history. It would involve both Indians and non-Indians, that is, everyone, and precisely everyone.

Clastres refers to Heraclitus in his explanation of the politico-intellectual becoming of the Tupí-Guaraní *karaí*. He says: "the mind of the savage prophets and that of the ancient Greeks conceive of the same thing, Oneness; but the Guarani Indian says that the One is Evil, whereas Heraclitus says that it is the Good. What conditions must obtain in order to conceive of the One as the Good?" (217). Heraclitus, also a believer, like most Amazon Indians, on war as foundation of the universe, was, for Clastres, a shaman who had already fallen into his own prophecy, who had already invented political power through the very desire to oppose it. Western metaphysics would eventually lead into the theorization of the state as ethical substance (in Hegelian metaphysics, which only explicitated a state of affairs), but the exemplarity of the Tupí-Guaraní consists of the refusal to countenance the goodness of the One. This is posthegemony ground zero—the first *karaí* prohibition of the state can be traced to the interdiction of hegemonic domination, but there is no hegemonic interdiction without consequences. The *karaí* are always in the position of remembering an immemorial prophetic language, which is repeatable like every prophetism.

Clastres tells us that the Tupí-Guaraní did not oppose the One to the Multiple, but rather to duality or complementarity. From the *karaí*'s statement that "things in their totality are One; and for us who did not desire it to be so, they are evil" (170) he glosses: "to name the oneness in things, to name things according to their oneness, is tantamount to assigning them limits, finitude, incompleteness" (173). The extent to which this sentence is both a philosophical and a political sentence, or rather an antipolitical sentence if politics is precisely originated with the rise of the despotic principle, the extent to which a refusal of the One within a universe of general war is an opening to the mystery of complementarity, would guarantee the need for a practice of alliance on grounds of radical equality as cosmopolitical, and even infrapolitical, geophilosophy.

Florencia Mallon's book concludes with a series of questions concerning the historical understandings of community among the Mapuche from which I would like to retain the one silent question that is precisely not there but which emerges between the lines. She says:

> Is the community a kinship network built around the family of the original cacique (definition created by the resettlement and the land-grant titles)? Is the community constructed through struggle

and solidarity among all the poor and oppressed (definition of the left
and the agrarian reform)? Is it simply a place of residence like any
other (definition of the military dictatorship)? Or is it a trade-union or
syndicalist organization under legally defined statutes and bylaws (the
Indigenous Law of 1993 and the postauthoritarian governments of the
1990s)? (241)

For Mallon all of those versions of the community are active today in Mapuche self-understanding, all of them a result of the impact of their own history on Mapuche life. The key issue is, there are no other versions. We are far here from, for instance, Alvaro García Linera's notion, in *Forma valor y forma comunidad*, that the overcoming of capitalism as labor form, and therefore the substance of all systemic, that is, antisystemic struggle, must appear as the restoration of archaic community and a return to the originary unity of nature.[17] The contemporary emphasis on substantial community, the need to return to originary ground in radical, prophetic decoloniality: well, perhaps it runs the risk that, through it, the State of the One will come, and return, and keep returning, through its very attempt to ward it off. It is, after all, old history. And what one says of prophetic decoloniality can also be said of so many other pronouncements in the contemporary Left that keep telling us, in spite of themselves, since they disavow it, that any refusal of the One is always at the same time an embrace of insidious, many-faced capitalism.

5
The Absolute Difference between Life and Politics

They harass me with the demand for definition—What is infrapolitics? What is not? Is this infrapolitics? Is that infrapolitics?—as if it were important to fix a meaning, to cipher an essence, as if it were not only important but a *sine qua non* condition for moving forward, for using the word, to see how it may move or stumble, to find its limits, to witness its deployment. Inevitably I suspect they want to entangle me—they want me to get lost in contradictions, ambivalences, inconsistencies, they want me to be swamped and to have mud and dirt in my mouth, because the worst thing that can happen, absolutely, in such a petty and narrow-minded field of reflection as the one determined by our tongue, is for a new idea to show up, a different way of looking at things. And infrapolitics is, or was until recently, a new idea and a different way of looking at things. It still is, insofar as its generative force is active, no matter how that may offend some. If it were really necessary to offer a definition, let me suggest the following, one of many, one in a legion: infrapolitics is the absolute difference between life and politics, therefore also between being and thinking. Of which no expert can speak. Of which you can speak only while not speaking. With a great deal of patience. Absolute difference? The same way we do not know how much glory inhabits a body, we do not know what an absolute difference is, and we cannot talk about it. At any rate a difference can only bind the two terms that differ, and if it is absolute so is the binding between them. Between thinking and being there is a cut that liberates both terms, each one to its own realm, and the liberation does not hinge on mutual restraints. It is the same between life and politics. A caesura has no lock, it is perfect in its opening, but, since it is a caesura, a rift, between two terms, it absolutely and perfectly links them. It is a matter of emphasis, or how to look, how to see. It is not just that politics and life are not the same: there is an absolute difference between them that, as absolute, cannot be relativized in discourse. It can only be unconcealed, glimpsed, felt, touched upon, sniffed at, also through words, not just with one's body. But I will try to elaborate a bit on the contours of infrapolitics as an ever-inconspicuous presence in the field of thought in order to satisfy the monster of the question. So that it will not be my fault if they fail to understand or if they claim they do.

One of the most interesting, and at the same time most widely disregarded, aspects of the legacy of May 1968 is the perhaps silent and nevertheless effective sundering of any possible identification between life and politics. This might be counterintuitive at first sight. The notorious slogan "the personal is political" implied the obvious acknowledgment that a politicization of life was needed, because it was lacking, but the intent of the explicit politicization of life, compensatory in nature, was not the turning of life into the instrument or even the consequence of politics. On the contrary, the intent was that of a liberation of life, whatever that may have meant in concrete terms for the different constituencies that claimed and have not stopped using the slogan. So many years later, the capture of life by politics is undeniable—biopolitics, in ways perhaps unimaginable in 1968, has indeed made the personal political, perhaps even terminally, and not always in precisely liberating ways. My contention is that a reversal of the slogan—not "the personal is political" but "let infrapolitics be"—remains within the legacy of May 1968, even if it means taking a step back from the political sphere that claims us exhaustively.

General Equivalence

I think Alain Badiou is right when, in his short essay on May 1968, *On a raison de se révolter* (There Is a Reason to Revolt, 2018), he says, "what is primarily decisive is to maintain the historical hypothesis of a world delivered from the law of profit and of private interest" (*Raison*, 51). But can we have a world beyond profit, private interest, calculation, general equivalence? And is the destruction of the structure of general equivalence preliminary to any possible "liberation of life" from capture by the law of profit today? In *After Fukushima: The Equivalence of Catastrophes* (2015), Jean-Luc Nancy discusses how the Marxian notion of "general equivalence," applied of course to money as the general equivalent, has come to absorb "all the spheres of existence of humans, and along with them all things that exist" (5).[1] This is a fundamental phenomenon of our age, of course tendentially present since the beginnings of modernity but now endowed with a new intensity. If general equivalence is today the totalizing principle for the administration of life, the very region of politics, then a subtraction from it destroys the totality; no totality will subsist if exceptions multiply that undo its all-encompassing character. Hence the importance of its thematization, that is, the thematization of the possibility of a radical existential subtraction from general equivalence, even if it is just, or primarily, a conceptual and not a practical thematization. But all conceptuality is practical too. To think of infrapolitics is always in every case to think of exceptions to the general equivalent.

Nancy wants to situate equivalence today within a catastrophic horizon. Or rather, as he says, "it is . . . equivalence that is catastrophic" (6). Not all catastrophes are the same, and we cannot compare Auschwitz to Fukushima, or global climate change to the 2008 financial crisis. There is, however, a comparison to be made, since equivalence itself is our catastrophe. General equivalence, in fact, preempts the possibility of noncomparison; and this is, in a marked sense, because general equivalence ciphers the general ontological horizon of our time. It is the last doctrine of being, the last metaphysical ontology. Nancy's thoughts on general equivalence are powerfully premised on the later Martin Heidegger's critique of the technological gigantic.[2] The gigantic, which takes globality as inception, is total interconnectedness. But it is the interconnectedness of that which has crossed a limit and has reached the unlimited. I think it is important to understand properly what Nancy is proposing here. He says:

> What is common to both these names, Auschwitz and Hiroshima, is a crossing of limits—not the limits of morality, or of politics, or of humanity in the sense of a feeling for human dignity, but the limits of existence and of a world where humanity exists, that is, where it can risk sketching out, giving shape to meaning. The significance of these enterprises that overflow from war and crime is in fact every time a significance wholly included within a sphere independent of the existence of the world: the sphere of a projection of possibilities at once fantastical and technological that have their own ends, or more precisely whose ends are openly for their own proliferation, in the exponential growth of figures and powers that have value for and by themselves, indifferent to the existence of the world and of all its beings. (*After Fukushima*, 12)

What holds for Auschwitz and Hiroshima holds also for many other events of technological gigantism, including the development of surveillance society, of expository society, down to the not-so-banal everyday extreme, in the workplace for instance, of any technical system regulating compensation, or travel expenses, or labor time, or performance, always looking for its own relentless completion, for the execution of consistency, no matter how lunatic and alienating, and regardless of collateral damage. Whether it is 50 million Facebook users, or 87 million, or even 200 million instrumentalized by Cambridge Analytica in the 2016 US elections, with a lot of subsidiary complicities, to undermine or destroy the ostensible essence of the liberal-democratic system of rule, the indifference across the limit marks a threshold. The indifference across the limit unleashes the unlimited, and first organizes an absolute illimitation that is radically metaphysical in nature, gigantic indeed, and from which equivalence ensues as a paradoxical and deceiving way of warding off madness, of indexing the continuum, of mapping the grid. Within the catastrophic gigantic names do not pass beyond but rather "fall below all signification. They signify an annihilation of meaning" (13) that equivalence must both signal and make up for. Not all catastrophes are the same, but the inevitability of catastrophic comparison based on equivalence turns the principle of equivalence into the principle of the annihilation of meaning. Within the principle of general equivalence all words and all bodies fall below signification. Calculability fights the incommensurable, which alone grants meaning. Nancy establishes the very narrative of why an unlimited principle of equivalence is the very interruption of relational rapport between nonequivalents; but this means that, in the gigantic unleashing of productive forces, something inconspicuous takes place, which is the loss of every possibility of relation. From now on, there is only measurement in a continuum—the personal, indeed, has become political. A certain modern apocalypse has already taken place. This is Nancy:

> Forces fight each other and compensate for each other, substitute for each other. Once we have replaced the given, non-produced forces (the ones we used to call "natural," like wind and muscle) with produced forces (steam, electricity, the atom), we have entered into a general configuration where the forces of production of other forces and the other forces of production or action share a close symbiosis, a generalized interconnection that seems to make inevitable an unlimited development of all forces and all their interactions, retroactions, excitations, attractions, and repulsions that, finally, act as incessant recursions of the same to the same. From action to reaction, there is no rapport or relation: There is connection, concord and discord, going and coming, but no relation if what we call "relation" always involves the incommensurable, that which makes one in the relationship absolutely not equivalent to the other. (26)

Not just Auschwitz and Hiroshima calculate, not just Fukushima and the 2008 financial crisis are the results of catastrophic calculation. We live our entire lives, increasingly, and with diminishing margins, within a horizon of exhaustive calculability. In political terms, even hegemony theory, which is the last political doctrine of the Left, based as it is on the formation of chains of equivalence, is little more than a methodology for political calculability at the service of an effective alternative administration of the body politic.[3] Research today, at the university, is nothing but accumulation and quantification. Our Facebook posts are produced, or not, according to the number of projected "likes." Soon our life expectancy will hinge upon our ability to pay deductibles for "extraordinary" (that is, more expensive) medical treatment.[4]

For Marx the pure technology of calculation is money. In Nancy's words, "by designating money as general equivalence, Marx uttered more than the principle of mercantile exchange: He uttered the principle of a general reabsorption of all possible values into this value that defines equivalence, exchangeability, or convertibility of all products and all forces of production" (31). We calculate the incalculable even when we refer to the incalculable as incalculable, or precisely by doing so. If my post has fewer likes than yours, we calculate respective values on the basis of the principle of equivalence. If your book sells better than mine, I calculate as well, and my resentment—even when, or precisely because, I know that my book is better than yours, which is another calculation—is based on a calculus that throws a deficit that happens to be mine, not my book's but mine. "The incalculable is calculated as general equivalence. This also means that the incalculable is the calculation itself, that of money and at the same time, by a profound solidarity, that of ends and means, that of ends without end, that of producers and products, that of technologies and profits, that of profits and creations, and so on" (32). The extension of general equivalence as the incalculable itself posits general equivalence as the latest, if not the last, name of being, and as the ultimate metaphoric background and purveyor of metaphors that equivalence itself reduces to nothing: all metaphors under the principle of equivalence are, after all, dead metaphors.

But—and this marks Nancy's difference from Marx and any Marxism—breaking away from general equivalence means abandoning the calculations of production. Against Marx, there was no production at the beginning, and there can be no production at the end. There can be no demystification of production for the sake of a proper communist production (at least if we understand that phrase in its historical, conventional meaning)—production is always necessarily its own mystification. The real movement of things may be a movement of production, yet that is the movement that infrapolitics at the same time identifies and then brackets and rejects. About communism as production Nancy says: "The possibility of representing a 'total' human, free from alienation, emancipated from all natural, economic, and ideological subjection, has faded away in the very progress of general equivalence becoming the equivalence and interconnection of all goals and possibilities" (33). This amounts to nothing other than the collapse, not of politics, but of any possibility of a new (human) subject of the political, perhaps even the end of the possibility of any political or philosophical anthropology. Still, adds Nancy: "This condition imposed on our thinking surpasses greatly what we sometimes call 'a crisis of civilization.' This is not a crisis we can cure by means of this same civilization. This condition also goes beyond what is sometimes called a 'change of civilization': We do not decide on such a change; we cannot aim for it since we cannot outline the goal to be reached" (35). The end of political anthropology is also the end of any possible philosophical anthropology—something else is called for.

What is to be done? Short of giving ourselves over to thoroughly accomplished general equivalence, since there does not seem to be any other thing to do? What is there to do in order to suspend the sway of general equivalence, in order to subtract from the totalizing principle of civilizational life? Nancy says, "no option will make us emerge from the endless equivalence of ends and means if we do not emerge from finality itself—from aiming, from planning, and projecting a future in general" (37). But, with this, the difference between general equivalence and its critique emerges as the very difference between politics and infrapolitics. Infrapolitics would then be—Nancy does not say it; I am extrapolating—"the care for the approach of singular presence" (40). Nancy refers to persons and moments, places, gestures, times, words, clouds, plants. When they come, they come incommensurably. Nancy's "communism of nonequivalence" is my infrapolitics, where "democracy should be thought of starting only from the equality of incommensurables: absolute and irreducible singulars that are not individuals or social groups but sudden appearances, arrivals and departures, voices, tones—here and now, every instant" (41). The proposal here is for the recognition of an equality not premised on equivalence but rather on radical singularity—there can be no value calculation, no comparison, hence no hierarchy between incommensurable singularities. As we say in Spanish, *nadie es más que nadie*. We could add, a bit gnomically, *nada es más que nada*.

Capitalist Discourse

As we saw, for Badiou the refusal of general equivalence in the abandonment of the law of profit is essential. He states that a "fidelity" to May 1968 hinges on that very issue. He calls his "historical hypothesis" the "communist hypothesis" (*Raison*, 51), which is the hypothesis of a social world delivered from the law of profit, but we should recognize that the "communist hypothesis," in that determination, remains a merely negative one: yes, we may want to exit capture by the commodity and by the common equivalent, money. How communist is that? For Badiou an "idea" is necessary today for the reformulation of the communist hypothesis and to escape "corruption" (55). For Badiou—and he does claim in his little pamphlet that May 1968, "*c'est moi*"; he claims to be, "with some others," the embodiment of its survival (35)—the communist idea is the embrace of what he terms a "true politics" and a "true life" (56). True politics leads to a true life in the same way a false life is possible through bad politics. Communism can fix both, it is said.

In spite of Badiou, I believe the notion of a "true politics" and the notion of a "true life" do not necessarily imply each other. Politics and life are not coextensive. To think that politics and life are in fact coextensive—a common conceit today in our academic world, perhaps everywhere—implies life's sacrifice, and it is a reactive position itself thoroughly dependent upon capitalist discourse and its principle of general equivalence. There will be no sundering from the law of profit and of private interest, no exit from capitalist discourse, if we persist in the deluded presumption—even if everything seems to point at it—that politics and life are coextensive. The true legacy of May 1968 might in fact be the dissolution—the cutting—of the link between the notion of politics and the notion of life in favor of a reformulation of the notion of existence. We know this much: May 1968 was the declarative end of the old politics in favor of a new existential experience, itself not deemed antipolitical. But this became forgotten, the Left has forgotten it.

Martin Heidegger mentions in his seminar on Heraclitus, in 1943–44, an old word of the Ephesian thinker. In R. D. Hicks's translation, Diogenes Laertius's paragraph reads: "But he [Heraclitus] would retire to the temple of Artemis and play at knuckle-bones with the boys; and when the Ephesians stood around him and looked on, 'Why, you rascals,' he said, 'are you astonished?' Is it not better to do this than to take part in your civil life?" (Diogenes, 9.3). *Touto poiein*, to play at knucklebones with the kids, to do just that is better than *politeuesthai*, to take care of the *polis*. *Politeuma*, the substantive, refers to the business of government, to administrative issues, and *politeuo*, the verb, goes from meaning "to live like a citizen, *polités*" to "getting involved in politics" or to "concerning oneself with the business of city management." Heraclitus says, according to Diogenes Laertius, that playing with the kids in the temple of Artemis is better, *kreitton*, that is, "stronger" and "more powerful," than devoting oneself to politics, than assuming the condition of the citizen. There is a nontrivial context for this, which according to Diogenes has to do with the banishment from the city of Heraclitus's old friend Hermodorus. Heraclitus thought his city, Ephesus, was badly run, there was no proper *politeuma* there. He had no respect for the politicians, for those near him who filled their mouths with political talk. "The Ephesians," Heraclitus said, "would do well to end their lives, every grown man of them, and leave the city to beardless boys" (9.2). So he preferred to play with the kids.

We will never know, and can only imagine, what old Heraclitus thought of the *kakoi*, the rascals and scoundrels that stand around him and pretend to be surprised that such a great and lofty man, a philosopher, would waste his time that way rather than join them to do administrative business and cunning maneuvering. But something translates. I am not interested—I could not do it—in recreating the Heraclitean moment, but only in what, perhaps banally, translates into our own time—when the shrinking of experience has reached such proportions that many among us would think that nobody should or ultimately could talk of anything but politics, nobody should do anything but politics, because everything, alas, is political. Politicize, always politicize! And yet is it still possible to hear Heraclitus say that sometimes it is better to play at knucklebones than politicize? Even for the sake of a better politics? Can we take it seriously? Perhaps against Badiou, although things are not so simple for him either, but certainly not against the spirit of May 1968.[5]

Lacanian theory always had reasons to posit a difference between life and politics as point of departure. Jacques Lacan gave a lecture at the University of Milan in May 1972, in which he claimed that he was rescuing notes from three years earlier ("Du discours," 1), putting therefore his lecture's materials chronologically very close to 1968. It is a rather enigmatic lecture, but some things in it are clearly comprehensible. Lacan says at one point: "The crisis, not of the master's discourse, but of capitalist discourse, which is its substitute, is open" (10). In the previous page, and talking to students at Milan, Lacan recasts or repeats well-known 1968 lines of his. He says: "To make revolution . . . you should have understood that that means . . . to return to the point of departure" (9); and "there is no master's discourse as severe as the one that obtains where revolution is made" (9). But what is more seriously striking in this lecture, titled "On Psychoanalytic Discourse," is perhaps the assertion that "it is now too late" (10). Too late for what?

There is a capitalist discourse that has left the master's discourse behind, that has substituted for it, that promises to "march on like a roulette, could not march any better, but precisely it marches too fast, it consummates itself, it consummates itself to such an extent that it consumes itself" (10). This does not mean, as I understand, that capitalist discourse will come to an end. Rather it means that it consumes itself as discourse because it has left all limits behind. What may be paired to it now is perhaps no longer an oppositional analytic discourse, as the case may have been a few years earlier, when it would have been possible to oppose a master's discourse to it, but rather some other "pestiferous" discourse, Lacan says, "at the service of capitalist discourse" (10). This is what makes it already too late politically speaking. There is no doubt that Lacan is certainly talking about politics in that speech. It is up to us to determine what kind of discourses can be classified as politically "pestiferous" — and what the range of them may be. Let me limit the reach of the adjective a bit: a "pestiferous" discourse is a discourse that serves capitalist discourse in the sense that it will not move toward an exit from it. Another way of putting it could be to say that capitalist discourse implies the capture and cancelation of the absolute difference between life and politics (and then "too late" begins there, in that capture), which (pestiferously) undermines the position of every other discourse. Discourses are now only possible in reference to capitalist discourse. We can be certain that some discourses are pestiferous precisely in that regard, but we may not be able to be so certain about others. What about, for instance, Etienne Balibar's recent insistence on the renovation of a philosophical anthropology? Is philosophical anthropology a discourse at the service of an exit from capitalist discourse? Or does it serve capitalist discourse, no matter how equivocally or counterintentionally? Balibar's position — from the old hermeneutical rule that we must critique every position at its strongest not weakest point — will stand here for a host of other positions that are quite common in US university discourse. Is philosophical anthropology not still an attempt to suture life to politics, an attempt not to permit an outside to politics that could not be discursively controlled? Are there discourses, on the other hand, that could be said to subtract themselves from this Lacanian pest?

Balibar's mantra is: "the becoming-citizen of the subject and the becoming-subject of the citizen" (*Citizen*, 17). There is a silent articulation here of a total historical project based on a philosophy of history, even if it is more tenuous as philosophy of history than Hegelian phenomenology. Balibar invokes an "anthropological difference" that becomes foundational for the question of philosophical anthropology, and is thus, from the Balibarian perspective, itself the very motor of a new politics. Balibar is not seeking to establish philosophical anthropology as a regional ontology, his attempt seems to have little to do with responding to the old Kantian question "What is man?" through a series of precise theoretical determinations that would allow for the establishment of a disciplinary object among others. The attempt is, however, still perhaps essentially Kantian in a specific, transcendental way: to place the anthropological question at the very center of philosophical reflection in the present, that is, to turn the question into the object itself of philosophical reflection. This is not trivial. It calls for a suture of life and politics, of the real and of reflection on the real, of being and thinking—and it is a suture that, lamentably enough, is not recognized as a choking ideologeme, but rather saluted as a somehow liberating truth.

Balibar goes even further, in a way that is perhaps no longer so Kantian. He posits a necessary supplementation and torsion of philosophy that dislocate the latter and make it synonymous with thought in general. Balibar's "philosophical anthropology" emerges in that way as a theoretically totalizing attempt concerning philosophy—it does not much matter that the totalization may refer to an unfinishable task, a totalization of the *plus d'un* (more than one) or of the *pas tout* (not all). This is the sentence that gives Balibar away by revealing more than it says: "the adjective 'anthropological,' more than a given field or a regulative idea, designates a critical question apropos of the necessary but ambivalent relation that exists between philosophical or sociological concepts and modern politics" (17). As the context makes clear, Balibar is saying that the task of philosophical anthropology is the suturing of practico-theoretical reflection, that is, of modern theoretical practice, to politics. It announces that there is no thought outside politics and that there is no politics outside thought. And, to my mind, he is wrong on both counts (but the first count matters more). Is it a harmless mistake, or is it an error that makes Balibar complicit with a reading of history that will end up strengthening the claim of capitalist discourse in its Lacanian characterization?

"Modernity is the age or rather the 'moment' defined by the overlapping and contradictory processes of the becoming-citizen of the subject and the becoming-subject of the citizen" (17), says Balibar. He is moving toward a final formulation that will make things tight and clear and leave the tautology behind: "modernity is the 'moment' at which the human can only become coextensive with the political (which no society has ever known)" (17). This is the dead center of Balibar's project—to establish the nonsimple "coextensiveness" of humanity and politics, itself "overlapping and contradictory," never lineal, never merely progressive or merely reactionary, but at the end of the day normative for the Balibarian tenuous or dissembled version of a philosophy of history: Balibar is offering us in his book a phenomenology of the forms of consciousness (I would even say: a phenomenological teleology of forms of consciousness, a kind of phantasmatic summary of Hegel's *Phenomenology of*

Spirit, no less) that may regulate the precise interpretation of the posited coextensiveness at every stretch of the way. Perhaps humanity and politics were not always coextensive, perhaps life and politics have never been the same thing; no previous society has ever known their identity, even if its latency was always there, but now, in modernity, in our times, well, now what was always necessary but remained concealed has finally become explicit. From there it is no longer possible, and it will no longer be possible, to affirm any *Kehre*, any turn, any radical exit from the historical continuum. Modernity continues through the present its old itinerary, and there is no room in it to speak of any alternative beginning for thought.[6] The idea is here, then (Is this consistent with Badiou's communist hypothesis or yet something else? Would Badiou's hypothesis also be at the service of the reproduction and advancement of capitalist discourse?), to continue the old, to let the old continue itself, in a renewed and sufficiently complex way, and thus to revitalize a form of thinking whose ambition is to dissolve the frontier between political praxis and theory, making the two not just the same and more of the same, but subordinating both to an ontologico-historical sameness, an identification of humanity and politics, that no society has known until now, but that ours may indeed be starting to know. The identity between humanity and politics is of course the corollary to the deceitful alternative "becoming-citizen of the subject/becoming-subject of the citizen." This is a grand, ambitious plan to restore and restitute metaphysical thought, without compunctions, in the modern tradition. It takes its point of departure in the identification of (human) life and politics, whose absolute difference modernity would have come to relativize, hence cancel out. But I think it is preferable to imagine an alternative.

The Lacanian discourse of the master is sometimes assimilated to absolute knowledge, that is, to philosophy in a Hegelian vein. The identification of life and politics has Hegelian and Hegelo-Marxian roots (even if Marxism could have followed a different route).[7] Balibar's discourse, by making philosophy coextensive with politics, indeed by making humanity, the subject of philosophy, coextensive with politics, removes a final barrier and makes philosophy circular—the citizen-subject is the subject-citizen, who is the citizen-subject, for ever more. There is no longer a limit. A revolution has been accomplished that may mean, however, that we are back where we started, at the point of departure, that is, no longer in the discourse of the master, but now in its substitute and successor, capitalist discourse. There is no exit, only a meek acceptance of a dialectic that triumphantly moves forward into total assimilation, which is also total transparency—assimilation into transparency, radical consummation of an accumulation without remainder, full blown equivalence, total disposability, an unlimited continuum: life is politics, which is life, which is politics, and thinking and being are now finally the same. And what has been excluded is the possibility of taking a step back, looking for a sheltered place, to breathe freely, and to play at knucklebones in open dismissal of the makers of politics, the business administrators, the Heraclitean rascals, and the academic scoundrels. Is there no longer a function for thought that may vindicate its own extreme politicity otherwise, namely, in its rejection of the pretension of a unity in the field of the real now granted by a (quasi-)totalizing philosophical anthropology? The identification of life and politics is not just an offense against life; it is also an offense against politics, since it devalues it and reduces it, brings it down to size. Our freedom does not depend on any "anthropological difference" but rather on an absolute difference that subtracts itself from the anthropological closure of the world and rejects the discourse of transparency in favor of a phenomenology of the inapparent, to which infrapolitics is committed.[8]

I use "absolute difference," an ultimately Freudian expression, in the sense invoked by Jorge Alemán in a booklet entitled *Lacan y el capitalismo* (56).[9] I confess I am not able to interpret the Lacanian algorithm for capitalist discourse, which of course depends on its difference from the algorithms for the other four discourses, namely, the discourse of the master, university discourse, the analyst's discourse, and the discourse of the hysteric (see on this Lacan's Seminar XVII, also known as *The Other Side of Psychoanalysis*). So I trust Alemán to interpret it for me. He notes that capitalist discourse thrives on the logic or the law of the superego—that is, it forces us to give up on our pleasure in order to feed the instance that takes pleasure in the renunciation itself. Or, in other words, it forces us to forfeit pleasure in order "to accumulate a satisfaction that nurtures itself from the satisfaction on which the subject gives up" (*Lacan*, 22). Is that not precisely the type of enjoyment affirmed by the partisans of the seamless identification of life and politics, the great revolutionists and/or the great bureaucrats that end up meeting there, in the *jouissance* of cumulative renunciation, in the death drive? Alemán's "absolute difference"—ultimately the expression of an existential *jouissance* not controlled by the superego or the death drive—is the counterpart to the "absolute rationality" of capitalist discourse, which he assimilates to the Heideggerian notion of technology. Both capitalist discourse and the discourse of technology, which wish to bring to absolute fulfilment the illimitation of the continuum of humanity and politics—a politics now turned, amidst all the noise, mere administration—are discourses of the unlimited, and themselves discourses without a limit. But the absolute rationality of capitalist discourse—and its supplement: a philosophical anthropology that feeds the subject into politics with no way out, that feeds politics into the subject as its apotheosis and final consummation—is also the absolute rationality of an unhinged death drive that will "make the world uninhabitable" (*Lacan*, 28). Philosophical anthropology, in Balibarian terms, as the index of an exhaustive coextensiveness of humanity and politics, is also the emptying out and the nihilist leveling of existence. Should we not be looking away from philosophical anthropology into a possibility of thought, namely infrapolitics, that would allow us to look for an exit to the illimitation that links both life and politics to the death drive?

Absolute difference refers to whatever obtains in the constitution of a mortal, sexuated, and speaking existence that cannot be "absorbed by the circular and unlimited movement of capital" (Alemán, *En la frontera*, 124–25). It is what remains, if it remains. Alemán calls this "the Common," and defines it brilliantly as "that of which no expert can talk" (*Lacan*, 60). Nor can any nonexpert, to be precise. Alemán is referring to a facticity of existence that will not be reached by any totalizing anthropology, and that remains enigmatic.[10] It does not have a name, in the sense that it cannot be reduced to a concept or essence—it is not a "thing," but the remainder of the thing, something that subceeds or exceeds, noncapturable insofar as one can only deal with it suppressing it or letting it be, but never taming it, never appropriating it. I call it the infrapolitical region, as a way of naming without naming it—in that failure of nomination existential facticity perhaps emerges as a site for thought. The infrapolitical region is an exception to political existence—for instance, but it is only an instance, it is the region of the Ephesian temple to which Heraclitus could withdraw with the kids, under the protection of no lesser a goddess than Artemis—that nevertheless holds the secret of a radical politicity (or ultrapoliticity, or perhaps impoliticity—since it is a form of nonpoliticity that becomes a condition of every politics and of every enjoyment of being).[11] In that secret of which no one, no other, may speak—the secret that opens a caesura in every politicization of existence and that offers itself to it as its most intimate exception and its ultimate radical impossibility—what is common for another beginning of thought that will not end in absolute knowledge plays itself out. True, infrapolitics does not have Hegelian roots, and subtracts itself from any Hegelianism, from the moment when it departs from an absolute caesura between being and thinking (which means the denial of the old Parmenidean word on the identity of the two).[12]

Egalitarian Symbolization

In a book published a couple of years before *On a raison de se révolter*, that is, *La vraie vie* (True Life, 2016), Badiou sets forth his notion of a true life, which he thinks must arise in the context of a universal "egalitarian symbolization"

(54). This egalitarian symbolization would be to my mind the region of difference, of the rupture of the principle of equivalence, of the exit from the commodity and from private interest: in other words, the (common) place of communism. It is interesting that also in Badiou there is a recourse to the kids, as in Heraclitus. The philosopher feels old and wants to talk to the young ones. Badiou speaks of two errancies. The first errancy is the errancy of those who have a confused destiny ahead, crossed by the death drive, inhabited only by a proliferation of empty *jouissance*, consumerist, senseless, "suspended in the immediacy of time" (16)—this is the possible but dominant errancy of the young. There is an alternative to this, of course, for a certain percentage of the population: "to find a good place within the existing social order" (17). But there is a second errancy, the errancy without errancy, the immobile errancy of the old ones without authority, condemned to await their second death (since their first death, the death of old age, has already happened) in medicalized living spaces (residences, hospices, sanatoriums). Badiou states that a conjunction of both errancies can produce "a militant idea" (34), that is, an alliance, "against today's adults" (34), in favor of the true life. This would be a properly philosophical alliance, since "true life is philosophy, its theme" (14). The alliance would seek to secure a true life in the militant conjunction of the two errancies in favor of the communist idea, that is, in favor of a new and universal egalitarian symbolization.

Young and old understand that today's crisis is not primarily a crisis of financial capitalism. It is rather the great symbolic crisis, a crisis in the symbolic, in preparation since the Renaissance, which is now understood as the final accomplishment of modernity, and that consummates itself, through the power of money as *Grundwesen*, Marx's "common substance," in the principle of general equivalence. For Badiou we are in the midst of "a gigantic crisis in the symbolic organization of humanity" (43) for which there is no precedent—("it has no precedent" [43]) even if it is very precisely announced by Marx and Engels in *The Communist Manifesto*. Our world is factically the world of the icy waters of selfish calculation mentioned there, in the face of which there are three possible reactions: one is of course the "unlimited apology of capitalism" (45); the second one is the "reactive desire for a return to hierarchical, traditional symbolization" (46)—which is starting to wreak political havoc all across Europe and the United States and beyond, and it has only just started. Those two are no good, according to Badiou, but there is a third one: "communist desire," which posits the invention of a new "egalitarian symbolization" (48).

These three options present any number of false confrontations among them, from the secondary contradictions between capitalist enthusiasts and

Arcadian reactionaries to the mere competition between political options within a liberal democracy itself overwhelmed by the death of symbolization. But the real conflict, according to Badiou, is the conflict between "communist desire," which is the new egalitarian symbolization (no further precisions or determinations are given in this text, but we know from other texts it is not old Stalinism Badiou has in mind), and the forcefully "a-symbolic vision of Western capitalism" that today cannot but create "monstrous inequality and pathogenic errancies" (47). For the old philosopher, there, in the invention of what one can or could do under the communist invocation, which is always necessarily the construction of "a new idea of collective life" (51), there arises "true life, situated beyond mercantile neutrality and beyond old hierarchical moons" (52). But also, we should add, beyond the line of encounter of those who have nothing to lose, because they have already lost their time, and those who have everything to lose, since they still have time. Communism, in Badiou's terms, is egalitarian symbolization—of universal humanity. He claims that only egalitarian symbolization can offer a positive exit from the planetary nihilism that results from money and its extrapolation into the principle of general equivalence as the new name of being and the only universal referent. But this is a *desideratum* more than a *demonstratio*. As a *desideratum*, however, is it not necessarily conditioned by an overwhelming finality? We must remember here Nancy's abjuration of finality.

How do we go about egalitarian symbolization? From where can we even start to think about a situation that, from our present, cannot find more than a hypothetical and all-too-willful trace of itself, not even a concept, not even the beginnings of an articulation, only the rescuing of a dubious (from twentieth-century politics) historical term? Surprisingly, Badiou says, without quite saying it, by just omitting the political dimension of it, like Heraclitus at Ephesus, hence bracketing for a moment the question of finality, that it is not primarily a question of politics. His assignation of "true life" is more a question of gender. It is necessary, first, to conceive of a "true life," which cannot be done in any old way. In fact, it requires at least two constructions, two positions, "according to whatever a girl or a boy are" (117). Boys will get the short shift. Boys, destined in traditional society to be men through the fulfilment of a number of initiation rituals that would culminate (or not) in the incorporation of the Name of the Father, that is, on the structure explicitated by Freud in *Totem and Taboo* and *Moses and Monotheism*, are ill-starred today. They have been badly affected by the fact that the death of traditional symbolization, that is, the death of the order of the Law, means "a thought of truth despoiled of transcendence. God is really dead. And since God is dead, the absolute One of masculine closure can no longer rule over the total organization of symbolic and philosophical thought" (114). At best we are left with a sort of "Christianity without God: Christianity, since it is the son that is promoted as a new hero of an adventure that, in mercantile modernity, is nothing but fashion, consumption, and representation, all of them attributes of youth; but without God, which means without an access to a true symbolic order, because, if the sons rule, it is only over appearances" (64). The Freudian myth is now liquidated in a scansion without foundation, "doomed to repetition, hence governed by the death drive" (66). In other words, according to Badiou, there is no longer the rise of the son, only the fall of the father, which dooms the masculine position to ruin.

Within that context, the initiation of the boy is only an initiation into the market, "into the circulation of objects and the vain communications of signs and images" (68). It is an initiation without initiation, an empty initiation that will not carry the boy into manhood but that will reduce him to perpetual adolescence. Within this perpetual adolescence that defines masculine possibilities today, Badiou finds three distinct options that are in fact, come to think of it, a sort of philosophical anthropology, except that they do bring it to an end in philosophical terms: they are what Badiou calls the "perverted body," which is a body without a subject, a body sustained in inert repetition, a body without an idea (69–70); the "sacrificed body," which is the body that desperately seeks a return to tradition, that seeks to get rid of the perverted body through the lethal embrace of the Law and that finds its impossible subjectivation in martyrdom (70); and the "deserving body," the average body of he who has some merit or makes merits, the body that embraces general equivalence as the only possible law, selling himself in the market at the proper, that is, properly equivalent price (71). Unless you are too old or too young you will have to recognize yourself, impossibly, in one of those figures that mark what Badiou calls the destiny and the mystery of the "de-initiated son" (73). Are you not an uninitiated son, if you are male, given over to general equivalence as a meritorious idiot, gainfully employed, or a pervert, with drunkenness and other addictions defining your everydayness, or a sorry-ass sacrificial victim working in heroic soldiering? If not, what are you? Is there a fourth position? Do you claim it?

Badiou's philosophy is generally speaking optimistic, so he does point out that there is a way for the terminally deinitiated boy to come close to a new practice of truth: the perverted body could find rescue and redemption in love; the deserving body could transcend himself in intellectual invention, be it science or art; and the sacrificed body could opt for a politics of nonpower, a communist politics maybe. But we just do not know how, through what mediations. Or do we? We want to believe it, or we believe it to be possible to exactly the extent that philosophy has as its only function to aid life, which means "to help so that the question of the son, now subtracted from the typology of the three bodies, can be given back to the order of truths" (80–81). In other words, philosophy can help rescue the otherwise doomed body. It does not seem to me a particularly promising state of affairs, to have to trust the finality of philosophy, which now substitutes ambiguously for political finality—and the alternative is of course a resignation to the fact that the boys can in the future do nothing but occupy themselves with the "servicing of the goods," to use the Lacanian expression, unable to access any possible subjectivation (since subjectivation for Badiou amounts to subjectivation to truth). But there will be no truth for the deinitiated boy.

Women, however, seem to have a better shot at things, a potential destiny not as ominous as that of men, but not without a price to pay. If for the boys the end of initiation implied the fixity of infinite adolescence, for the girls "the absence of separation—a separation that was in the past structurally provided by masculine mediation through marriage—between daughter and mother, between the young daughter and the adult woman as mother, implies the immanent construction of a femininity I will call premature," Badiou says (90). A girl is today always already a woman, prematurely. The end of symbolization doomed life to be a life without an idea, so that the categorical imperative of contemporary capitalism is "Live without an idea!" (90). The young males are given over to stupid life, which could be ciphered in an "eternally competitive and consumerist adolescence" (94). For women—for girls, that is—adolescence arrives otherwise, "through the impossibility of being girls, of living in the glory of being girls, through the premature woman-becoming that orients the cynicism of becoming social" (94–95). Under those circumstances we need to forgive Badiou a tendency to exaggerate a little and present the world as composed of a "troop of stupid adolescents led by skilled careerist women" (96). But things of course do not end there in his analysis. There is extraordinary pressure on contemporary women: "Contemporary capitalism demands, and it will end up requiring, that women take upon themselves the new form of the One that capitalism itself seeks to replace the One of symbolic power, to replace the religious and legitimate power of the Name of the Father" (107). That new One is the one of consumerist and competitive capitalism, to which the men-boys, that is, the boys-men, can only offer a playful but precarious longing. The demand to women is that they offer, that they take it upon themselves to offer, "a hard, mature, serious, legal, and punitive version" of such a new One. Badiou says: "this is why a bourgeois and dominating feminism exists" whose project is not to build a new world but rather "to release the world such as it is to the power of women" (107). Badiou is serious and provocative both, when he says that, in that precise sense, women are today "the reserve army of triumphant capitalism" (108). Under those circumstances, with women whose One is increasingly more solid than the One of the men, why should we not start foreseeing the disappearance of the masculine genre? What would be the latter's function, other than perhaps rather uninspiring entertainment, in a world where technology can compensate a hundredfold for the absence of the reproductive drone?

Badiou also thinks, however, as it was the case for men, and with equal optimism, that, for women, we can also postulate the destruction of their traditional role and function without having to endorse their dubious function as the new reserve army of capital (112), even if a certain number of them demand it. We can also here, in the case of women, imagine a new interruption of the death drive that would necessarily consist in linking woman to a philosophical gesture, since it could be "neither a biological, nor a social or a juridical one" (113). Women, Badiou trusts (he says he "gives them his trust, absolutely" [115]), will "become the new woman" (115) able to give herself over, in her embrace of the four types of truth (namely, amorous, political, scientific, artistic), to a new symbolic production, a "new universal symbolization" that would have to be communist—women are, therefore, privileged, from the point of view of the true life, and dubiously, I think, as the new subject of history and the only possible future of communism. Except that this would seem to break the very axis of egalitarian symbolization.[13]

In the first essay of the book, Badiou proposes a militant commitment to the idea of a new symbolization that receives no specification; in the second essay, he proposes a destruction of traditional sexual difference that continues in the third, where it resolves into a question of optimistic faith in the capacity of every youngster, whatever their sex, to embrace a new dispensation of truth. We can only imagine that such a dispensation, regulated as it would be by a nontraditional or even antitraditional perspective, could only be radically egalitarian. But it has not been decided, or at least it has not been demonstrated—I think it has perhaps been hinted at, insinuated, suggested, but never stated—that such universal symbolization would be something other than the mere inversion of the general principle of equivalence as money into a general principle of equivalence as truth or militant faith. Badiou's communism, based on the production of an idea led by women, may still be or still sounds very much like a communism of equivalence, based on the reduction of absolute difference in favor of political finality, in favor of a commitment, led by gender, to militant fidelity. Its egalitarian symbolization, pending new theoretical developments, dooms difference, starting with sexual difference, to its dissolution into a certain idea of the common that may not go far enough, may not be useful enough. The common, Badiou seems to offer, is a potency: it is the common subjectivation to truth. We can talk about that, and every expert will in fact never cease chattering about it—Badiou's common subjectivation to truth, standard in the Left, standard for every affirmation of hegemony as an instrument of politics, may after all be not very far from the unlimitedness of the superegoic law of capitalist discourse. It might be a bad exit, a distraction, like the one we found in Balibarian philosophical anthropology.

For Badiou philosophy is, or it seeks, true life. I cannot avoid thinking of the definition a young Heidegger would have proposed of philosophy in his 1922 essay on Aristotle. There Heidegger states that philosophy is "fundamentally atheistic" ("Phenomenological Interpretations," 367) to the precise extent that it occupies itself with factical life, seeking its destruction in favor of a concept of existence, that is, of proper existence (367). Factical life against *Existenz*, this is Heidegger, and he does not seem so far from Badiou's claim regarding the possibility of a true life that can be acquired in a commitment to a type of truth that would follow or posit as precondition the destruction of patriarchal and capitalist symbolization. Philosophy is, Heidegger says, "simply the explicit interpretation of factical life" (369), but it is of course an oriented interpretation, and it is an oriented interpretation that goes through destruction: "Existence becomes understandable in itself only through the making questionable of facticity, that is, in the concrete destruction of facticity with respect to its motives for movement, with respect to its directions, and with respect to its deliberate availabilities" (366). In reaching for existence Heidegger is looking at philosophy as "true life," as an initiation into true life. The concrete destruction of facticity in the relentless attempt to analyze, in every case, the concrete conditions of everyone's time, of the historical time of everyone, can only be done from the singular existent, since factical life is in every case the factical life of the individual. Heidegger's philosophical hermeneutics, like Badiou's, in fact, takes its distance from God and abandons the Name of the Father as archontic or principial being, as guarantor of the symbolic edifice. And, like Badiou, he also fundamentally sends us back to history and to the history of the present as the only possible path for entry into another history. Heidegger says: "The very idea of facticity implies that only authentic [*eigentlich*] facticity—understood in the literal sense of the word: one's own [*eigen*] facticity—that is, the facticity of one's own time and generation, is the genuine object of research" (369). Heidegger goes on to say that "the hermeneutic carries out its task only on the path of destruction" (371). This destruction—how does it compare to the Badiouan one, and to Badiou's own path?

Heidegger's facticity is always in every case one's own. This seems to imply—we already saw it in Nancy—that a radical nonequivalential egalitarianism obtains: the symbolization of the world that starts in facticity, in fact, in the destruction of facticity, is an egalitarian symbolization (it behooves everyone, in every case) that does not rely on equivalence. Badiou supplements it with the possibility of access to types of truth. From there, is it really possible to name this new egalitarian symbolization communism prior to having submitted communism to its necessary phenomenological destruction? If one cannot have true life—or *Existenz*—without an infrapolitical destruction of factical life (which would have to distinguish, in every case, what pertains to life and what pertains to politics), would it not be necessary to add that no infrapolitical destruction is possible from the overwhelming postulation of a communism of equivalence? And isn't Badiou's communism of the idea always a communism of equivalence? Although if we call communism the mere new egalitarian symbolization, against the exhaustion of the traditional world in the exit from modernity, against the technical closure of the world, then perhaps communism, infrapolitics, and existential hermeneutics come to the same thing. This can in fact only be worked out in concrete historical experience. But we might be able to use Badiou's two errancies not in order to request from them the construction of an idea, which would be just more errancy, and errancy of errancy, but rather to move toward an explicitation of their truths in a common infrapolitical destruction. Is this not a condition—the very condition—of a clearing in which all politics must test itself? The recuperation of the instance of existence—and we all have it, insofar as you are not reading this beyond your grave—as the knucklebone game, as the enigmatic region of thought, against both politics and life, against their coextensiveness, is no refuge from politics—it is rather an act of extreme politicity without which all politics will end up where they started. That is, badly, as Lacan suggested. There is too much to lose.

The Inconspicuous Incident

What could dwelling in the absolute difference between life and politics of which no expert can speak (and of which nonexperts would seemingly rather not speak) mean for young and old, men or women? Infrapolitics refers to the need for a thematization of existence, for an explicitation of the facticity of existence, as a condition of political thought, of any thought about politics, but also in order to think about the clearing to be found in the difference from politics. Politics is not the master referent of infrapolitics. Existence is. Another way of putting it is to say that existence is the horizon of infrapolitical practice, even if we limit the idea of practice to that of the use or exercise of thought. By "existence" it is not just "life" that is meant, and this is so not because infrapolitics has no interest in life in general, but rather because it comes to life from an interrogation of existence, where existence is provisionally understood as the human way of relating to life. Not long ago, in an informal discussion, a Heideggerian scholar whose conservativism is well known reacted in what for me was a surprising way by immediately linking every possible thought on existence to the Sartrean notion of commitment, and to Sartre's calls to "social, economic, and political action," as he said. We must undo this misunderstanding and insist upon the fact that infrapolitics wants to think of existence not beyond its use (infrapolitics is after all and before everything else a use of thought) but certainly besides its directly political (or economic, or social) instrumentalization, which is perhaps what Jean-Paul Sartre might have recommended. In that sense infrapolitics is a step back from politics, but not through any desire for depoliticization, not through any antipolitical passion. Rather, infrapolitics refuses to accept the notion that politics could conceivably constitute the first or last horizon of thought, since it posits that any thought about politics is derivative and secondary to modes of existential exercise. Thinking and being are not "the same," and it is existence (thinking) that refers to politics, and not politics (being) that refers to existence. The statement, although it may be said to run counter to the general drift of contemporary thought, should be sufficiently comprehensible in itself.

At any rate, in the 2014 Preface to the English edition of his book *The Origin of Politics* (1996 in the original Italian version), Roberto Esposito proposes something that might help. Esposito remarks that, had he written his book at the time of the new preface, he would have spent more time reflecting on what both Simone Weil and Hannah Arendt attribute to the nonsubjective "dimension of thought" (*Origin*, xi). What Esposito says is relevant to make clear, and to uproot any possible suspicion to the contrary, that infrapolitics has nothing to do with contributing to the thinking of inner experience, of the subjectivity of the subject, of private and nontransferable intimacy. The infrapolitical dimension of thought, on the contrary, enters the impersonal, which is where the absolute caesura between life and politics plays itself out. Esposito says: "Without doubt thinking is in itself an impolitical and an unproductive activity. Like the sound of the flute, it is a part of those forms of life that do not leave any material residue on earth" (*Origin*, xii). For Arendt, Esposito explains, the relationship of thought and judgment—thinking is a condition of judgment, and judgment is "the most political faculty" (xii)—links thought to the plane of the impersonal. Thought, "the only non-political activity par excellence" (xiii), gains direct political relevance upon its conversion into judgment, but thought is not identical to judgment, and it may in fact affirm its absolute separation from it. But Weil rather than Arendt takes the link between thought and the impersonal to the center of her position. For Weil freedom must be understood in its Spinozian form, as the capacity to adjust conduct to the necessity of the real. Since thought has no sense or object other than the world and its necessity, its absolute difference from being can be affirmed. There is thought and there is world, and the contact between them happens through a "decreative" ascesis that passes through a radical subjective destruction. "The impersonal, that is, the rupture of the subjective enclosure of the person, is not at all equivalent to the 'collective' or the 'social,' which for Weil is the placeholder of extreme idolatry. In contrast, the impersonal is a relation to singularity as the result of an antinomic binding of the singular to the common. In this way, thought is precisely that which binds these two opposite poles in the form of the nonsubjective, the nonanterior, and the nonpersonal" (xiv). Thought is here understood, infrapolitically, as the explicitation of a material facticity, as the ceaseless binding to a real that includes and overflows politics. Infrapolitics is not on the side of the real or on the side of thought, it is rather between them, in the elusive caesura that is constitutive of their relation, and which marks both of them as a reciprocal form of use.

A consequence of understanding thought as the use of existence—which depends on a certain overdetermination: thought that uses existence and that is the use of existence insists on thinking the relationship between thought and existence—is the immediate emergence of its imperative dimension. One thinks because one must think, thinking is existing and inhabiting, thinking is inhabiting existence, and it is not an option among others, but a human need, even if frequently unthematized. But, if the relation of thought to existence is imperative, then it can be said that so is the relation of existence to thought: that is, thinking inhabits existence, but existence imposes its necessity on thought.[14] If we can distinguish between two modes of infrapolitics, one of which would be factical infrapolitics, unavoidable as such, because it is infrapolitics as always already there, as a constitutive dimension of existence, of every existence, as the simple precipitate of the caesura between life and politics that subtracts from the language of the expert, there is also a reflective infrapolitics that accepts its imperative dimension and takes it on. Of the latter it can be said that it is at the same time cause and consequence of a certain existential rupture—Reiner Schürmann, in his meditation on Meister Eckhart, called it *Durchbruch*, breakthrough.[15] Infrapolitical rupture, which is for most part inconspicuous, an incident rather than an event, is still acquiescence to a certain necessity, but the necessity is of a special kind, Spinozian or quasi-Spinozian: it commands the acknowledgment that the existent does not only use existence but is also used by it, that she or he is trapped in her or his conditions of existence, which are conditions of thinking and being, and that only those conditions may tolerate relative practices of freedom; the acknowledgment that only in the acquiescence to the imperative dimension of existence can we find something other than command and domination: a freedom that can be understood not just as political freedom but also and crucially as a freedom regarding politics, that is, a freedom from politics.

Esposito finds that option for freedom in Arendt and Weil, but perhaps it was also the great Heideggerian intuition—perhaps this was the intuition that sustained Heidegger's work beyond any "turn" or internal division in his work during periods that were defined by changing emphases. Infrapolitics is neither a Heideggerianism nor a Derrideanism, except in the conventional sense in which one could claim that Heidegger himself was a Nietzschean, or a Husserlian, or an Aristotelian. But infrapolitics, for essential reasons, does not admit of an exegetic relationship in submission to any textual corpus—its decisive vector is somewhere else, on the other side, not beyond the text, but rather in the site of every textual trace, in its anonymous and unsigned wake. It seems fair, however, to recognize previous steps in the movement of thought that have been and will continue to be instrumental for the very formulation of the infrapolitical endeavor. I want to look briefly at three of those texts: Jacques Derrida's "*Ousia* and *Grammé*," Jean-Luc Nancy's "The Decision of Existence," and Thomas Sheehan's "But What Comes before the After?" (the last an essay on the continuation of *Being and Time*'s existential analytic in the later Heidegger). I think all three of those texts configure approaches to a thematization of existence, explicitly in Nancy and Sheehan, only implicitly in Derrida, that infrapolitical reflection must take on board. I will also add a coda on a certain aspect of a 1957 text by Heidegger. I must insist that these four brief probes are to a certain extent arbitrary—they are convenient for me, handy, and they will do a work that could be done also with texts by Nietzsche, Lacan, Blanchot, with the work of Luce Irigaray, Sophocles or Gracián, Teresa of Avila, Simone Weil or Paul Celan or Fernando Pessoa. But I wanted to be explicit regarding the Heideggerian legacy, which those texts share, at this point in the book.

"Ousia and Grammé"

In the last and decisive section of "*Ousia* and *Grammé*: Note on a Note from *Being and Time*," entitled "The Closure of the *Grammé* and the Trace of Difference" (63–67), Derrida comments on Heidegger's 1946 text "The Anaximander Fragment." Derrida detects in it a deep vacillation. On the one hand, Heidegger thinks or makes an attempt to think of modalities of presence; on the other hand, he seeks to call all modalities of presence in general *"the*

Greco-Western-philosophical closure" (65). Derrida states that all the arduous fundamental meditations by Heidegger on presence, including the text on Anaximander, are *intra*-metaphysical meditations, but he also says that Heidegger is aware of it and that in such an awareness he prepares another gesture, "the more difficult, more unheard-of, more questioning gesture, the one for which we are least prepared" (65). This would be a gesture that "only permits itself to be sketched, announcing itself in certain calculated fissures of the metaphysical text" (65). Derrida will try to recreate that gesture in the figure of the trace, of which he thinks it cannot give itself to be read under any modality of presential thought, neither through the copula nor through its negation, which of course would only refer to negative modalities of presence. Trace is therefore the Derridean name for the site of Heidegger's "difficult gesture"—it is neither present nor absent, neither perceptible nor imperceptible. The trace is not a Heideggerian or a Derridean gesture; it rather belongs to the metaphysical tradition, but it belongs to it as erased, as forgotten. The very ontico-ontological difference gets lost as trace, gets forgotten as trace. If the ontological difference is only detectable as a forgetting, then the forgetting of the forgetting of the difference is a trace of the trace, a second-order trace. The unheard-of (but constantly rehearsed) possibility of the Heideggerian gesture—unheard-of also for Heidegger—opens up here: if the ontological difference is the trace of a forgetting, it is not possible to make the trace appear "*as such*" (66). The trace *as such*—*Ereignis*, perhaps, for instance, *Das Viertel*, perhaps, or *Be-reich*, or even the absolute difference I have been calling infrapolitics, but Derrida produces no such examples—is always in each case, and to the extent one insists on naming it, on applying to it expert discourse, the name of the being of beings, an intra-metaphysical name. The trace *as such* establishes in each case the new plane of principial figurality, and it restitutes thought to hegemony or to the enterprise of hegemonization. But there is no trace *as such*. The trace is only the remission to the facticity of the thing. What opens up in that step back that places a something into the not-all, not in order to relativize it, but rather in order to expose it to absolute difference?

If the forgetting of the ontological difference is a second-order trace, there is still a trace of forgetting that would be in the third order: "there may be a difference still more unthought than the difference between Being and beings . . . Beyond Being and beings, this difference, ceaselessly differing from and deferring (itself), would trace (itself) (by itself)—this *différance* would be the first or last if one could still speak, here, of origin or end" (67). *Différance* points at or names in Derrida the difficult gesture that allows for an abandonment of the presential horizon, and in that sense solves what Derrida identifies as Heidegger's residual hesitation in the Anaximander essay: *différance* would be "older than Being itself" (67) to the extent being itself is conceived as originary *arche*. The play—it is not a game, nor its contrary—is to bind trace and *différance*, which reject by definition the naming of any *arche* and refer only to a ceaseless and dispersed facticity, to the movement of existence. Derrida does not do it explicitly, but perhaps Nancy and Sheehan might indicate the way.

"The Decision of Existence"

For Nancy a decision of thought takes place when the existent attends to what I called the imperative character of her or his relation to thought. "Philosophizing decides to think . . . when it grasps the fact that existence unfolds in the midst of an understanding of Being, and the fact that, while understanding Being in a 'vague, average' manner, existence finds itself, in a wholly exceptional and precise way, in an essential (that is, *existentiell*) relation to its own understanding. . . . Thought in its decision is not the thought that undertakes to found Being (or to found itself in Being). This thought is only the decision that risks and affirms existence on its own absence of ground" ("Decision," 84). The "decision"—itself the "only" content of thought—has no positive content: it is merely "the disclosive projection and determination of what is factually possible at the time" (85). The relation of decision to the "event" is indicated here: "Decision, in this sense (in a sense that no meaning of the word 'decision' will suffice to open, or to decide), is what most escapes existence, or it is that to which and in which existence is most properly thrown— and what offers existence its most proximate, its ownmost or most intimate, advent: *Ereignis*. . . . *Ereignis* is, or makes, decision, and decision is, or makes, *Ereignis*" (87). Thinking is therefore the exercise, appropriative, of decision. Everything moves in the ontic, *existentiell* terrain. There is no transcendent here. Thinking is a relation to facticity, never the discovery of something other than facticity. Note that, in this understanding, a decision is always "passive," in the precise sense that the notion of holding back on it, of leaving it "undecided," is meaningless.

In the same way that it is possible to distinguish two modes of infrapolitics, the factical and the reflective, Nancy speaks about two modes of facticity: if the existent is for the most part suspended in her or his everyday existence, first facticity, it is a matter of suspending the suspension—without, on the other hand, going anywhere else. It is a matter of factically suspending facticity itself. It is a matter of thinking the facticity of facticity, so that a modified relation to it emerges, second facticity. It is inconspicuous always in every case. It does not discover anything, it does not transcend toward anything, it does not cut anything, and it does not found anything. If there is *Durchbruch*, breakthrough, in the suspension of factical suspension, what is accomplished is merely a modification in the existential relation to existence. It is nothing, but it is more than nothing. It is the entry into reflective infrapolitics.

Nancy speaks, therefore, about two decisions. One of those decisions of thought is the average one, the metaphysical one, the subjective or identitarian one, the egoic one—the decision of the hero who cuts through some Gordian knot in order to reach, or to fail to reach, a new level of existence. We can call this decision, or this modality of decision, the "heroic machination," and it is the properly political decision, the political subjectivation that would be in any case not renounceable in any average process of political decision or partisanship. Most contemporary discourses privileging politics as the last horizon of our lives are there, and they are subsidiary to their heroic vocation. But there is then the other decision, from a modified existential grasp. In it, the existent, quite aside from her or his constitution as subject, sutures or binds her or his own relation to existence, and that is all. Nancy does not call this decision infrapolitical, but I do. He speaks of a "joy" that comes from the modified grasp of the one who decides "to exist, to render oneself passible to non-essence" (106). It is a joy that happens "in an existence that exists only in its existing—that is, in the free 'nullity' of its foundation of Being" (107). It is the primary infrapolitical affect, the joy that inhabits the rejection of the foundation of presence in favor of an affirmation of facticity and of an affirmation in facticity. It is infrapolitical because "thought has no decision of practical, ethical, or political action to dictate. If it claims to do so, it forgets the very essence of the decision, and it forgets the essence of its own thinking decision . . . the essential, active decision of existence. Its necessity is also called freedom . . . but freedom is not what disposes of given possibilities. It is the disclosedness by which the groundless Being of existence exposes itself, in the anxiety and the joy of being without ground, or being in the world" (109).

Nancy adds: "It is necessary to understand that decision, its anxiety, and its joy take place 'outside' the 'text'—in existence" (107). Existence seems to subtract itself thus even from the trace, from any *différance*, but it is a subtraction that makes them visible, suspending their suspension. Nancy uses "exscription" for this: "The exscription of a text is the existence of its inscription, its existence in the world and in the community: and it is in existence, and only therein, that the text decides/reaches its decision—which also means in the *existentiellity* of the text itself, in the anxiety and joy of its work of thought, its play of writing, its offer of reading" (107). In the notion of exscription a parergonal possibility of infrapolitics emerges. Because the infrapolitical breakthrough moves nowhere, it is always and everywhere only parergonal rupture, exscription.

"But What Comes before the After?"

Thomas Sheehan also takes his departure from the imperative or protreptic dimension of thought in the Heideggerian text. He says that following it "is the final goal of all Heidegger's work" (3), and it was never abandoned. In a way that is consistent with what we have seen of the Heideggerian hesitation between forms of presence and its other (not absence, but the other of presence/absence), with the Derridean demarcation of the trace against the *arche*, and with the presentation in Nancy of the forms of existential decision, all of it received by the modalities of infrapolitics already mentioned, Sheehan insists on a dual structure of existence in Heidegger. To "existence" Sheehan prefers "Ex-istence," in order to underline the ecstatic standing of Da-sein, its fundamental "ejectivity" (against every subjectivity and every objectivity). Ex-sistence has a dual structure, as it refers to the structure of Da-sein (*existential*) and to the "persons and activities (*existentiel*) that this structure makes possible" ("But What Comes," 44). The existential structure opens the field of signification, while the *existentiel* is always in a multiple relation to it. One of the forms in which the *existentiel* may project itself is by tracing its relation to the existential, for instance in the thematization of the ontological difference or of the trace-structure in Derridean terms.

The task of Da-sein is to make her or his own facticity explicit—this is also Heidegger's own definition of philosophy (from his 1922 essay on Aristotle). This matches Nancy's second decision. It is the parergonal or ex-scripted form of relation to the relation itself, the step back which consists of making the relation explicit and of living it protreptically as explicit. At some point, certainly in *Being and Time*, Heidegger called that protreptic parergon the "authentic" form of existing, but he soon abandoned that terminology. Sheehan reflects on what may have substituted for it and finds it in the Heraclitean *hapax legomenon* that Heidegger uses in *Conversations on a Country Path*: *ankhibasie*, the "ever-approaching" that determines an asymptotic condition that cannot be calculated or planned beforehand (50). If the relation of infrapolitics to politics is a version of that relation, it is so not because infrapolitics wants to "approach" politics. On the contrary, infrapolitics seeks an asymptotic approach to an outside that cannot be tamed by the anguished pretention that everything is political. To think that outside, the parergonal outside of exscription that is not an exterior but only another way of existing in the experience of the trace, is the infrapolitical relation itself. One lives there, or ek-sists, not knowing whether the nearness that *ankhibasie* refers to will make itself accessible. But such ignorance is also a form of joy, to be conjugated in the future perfect.

The liberation of facticity into itself—that is, making it explicit—is the *exercitium* of post-epochal thinking in Sheehan's terms: "One can get free of being restricted to metaphysics as an 'epoch,' by embracing one's appropriation and living out of it" (12). Epochs—always subjected to principles, *archai* in the Schürmannian sense: every epoch is ruled by a principle, a hegemony, that organizes it and determines it as an epoch—are sequesterings of history, "the bracketing out of the Open" (12) in every case.[16] Infrapolitics is post-epochal thinking, or its asymptotic attempt, always an exercise in epoch-destruction, an exercise in anarchy for the sake of an existential/*existentiel* breakthrough. This is why infrapolitics should be thought of as a countergaze into politics and history, as it is also an exodus and a rejection of hegemonic principles for the sake of another inhabitation. It is neither ultrapolitical nor metapolitical, as we will soon see. It actually looks for a fully political adjustment with politics but claims that it could not take place without the previous acknowledgment of the difference between life and politics that no expert can discuss.

Coda

In his 1957 Freiburg Conferences, Heidegger talks about the silent and quiet incidents that motivate changes in the "principles of thinking" that have defined the history of metaphysics—all of them arriving on doves' feet. I have referred to the inconspicuous in a different sense, in order to name a step back from the epochal modalities that infrapolitics aims to leave behind. My gesture wishes to acknowledge and repeat the Heideggerian one, or at any rate it is not alien to it. In the first of his lectures Heidegger, after having narrated how what is inconspicuous in the historical emergence of the basic principles of thought "remains veiled in the dark for us" (88), says that such darkness is at play in all historical times. But, he insists, "the dark remains distinct from the pitch-black as the mere and utter absence of light. The dark however is the secret of the light. The dark keeps the light to itself. The latter belongs to the former. Thus the dark has its own limpidity" (*Basic Principles*, 88). From the limpidity of what is dark in those regions, one does not attempt merely to enter into an alternative light. It is rather a matter of securing an alternative gaze for which there may not yet be sufficient or good-enough eyes. A few pages later, in the second lecture, Heidegger adds: "We still lack the eyes to see the essential countenance of the *logos*, to endure its sighting, and to bring to this the fitting countergaze" (100). Infrapolitics is an attempt, tentative and modest, to approach the countergaze from the dark. In that sense it could perhaps be read as the gesture opposite to that of the butterfly that cannot avoid being burned by the burning light of the solar principle, which is the secret end of every and all politics as we know them and have known them so far.

6
A Politics of Separation
An Alternative Politicity

Chapter 2 of Bruno Bosteels's *The Actuality of Communism* (2011) has an organic function in the book. I have analyzed his general perspective elsewhere, so I will not repeat myself here.[1] Bosteels is interested in showing how a certain contemporary emphasis on political ontology, that is to say, on the destruction of political ontology, runs the risk of constituting an obstacle to his brand of communist or neocommunist politics, based on old and perhaps renewed subjectivist and militant postulates, and certainly also on heroic decisions. His excursion through Roberto Esposito's notion of the impolitical and through what I had started to call infrapolitics in my 2007 book *Línea de sombra: El no sujeto de lo politico* (A Line of Shadow: The Nonsubject of the Political), although generous and well done, has a disqualifying intention at its core, no doubt thoughtfully nuanced. Ultimately Bosteels wanted to present antagonists he could dismiss as "beautiful souls" (127), mere "archipolitical" thinkers (125) whose play would be in the best of cases the attempt to revolutionize humanity in a more spiritually felt sense than the one afforded by the calculative presumption of politics and its dirty hands. He could then isolate statements that could be easily conjured as extreme, all-too-extreme, so as to relegate them to the other side of the moon.

He concludes his chapter by saying that what Esposito and Moreiras propose "is a strange case of passive decision, or a decision in favor of passivity and inaction, this being the only remedy against the deafening calls for political effectiveness and activism" (*Actuality*, 128). The deafening demands, I take it, are the ones the people address to Bosteels, or at any rate those Bosteels chooses to hear with strong and resistant ears, and that is certainly his privilege. But nothing is less certain than the accusation against Esposito, or even against infrapolitics, of being in favor of "passivity and inaction." It is more a matter of the fact that both theoretical practices would prefer a form of action and of political activity different from Bosteels's predication. Thus, the political practice I choose, not particularly open to the deafening demands of the people, true, but only because it does not come into my mind that the people would specifically talk to me, has little to do, outside a generic connection to post-Marxism or to the social-democratic Left, with the one Esposito prefers—and neither of them, mine or Esposito's, is measurable from the perspective of the passivity and inaction that Bosteels insists on adjudicating to us. And not just to us, but also, more recently, to the Argentinian thinker Oscar del Barco, and generally speaking to all manner of deconstructors, Heideggerians, Lacanians, post-Marxists, and poststructuralists of every ilk—that is, against anybody who fails to commune with his dearly vetero-Marxist or heroic-Hegelian militancy.[2]

It will be more productive to abandon the analysis of the ultimate intention of Bosteels's text in order to take advantage of his analytic talent in chapter 2 of *Actuality*. When Bosteels writes his text (its first version is from 2008 and was presented at a conference on Italian political philosophy I organized at the University of Buffalo), he only has *Línea de sombra* as a referent. In that book, however, infrapolitics is just insinuated as the text is more fully concerned with the presentation of the figure of the nonsubject in the attempt to undermine multiple academic theorizations regarding the politics of subjectivity. That may explain that infrapolitics is presented by Bosteels for the most part as an explicitation of impolitical presuppositions in Roberto Esposito's work. It is true that there are many common elements to infrapolitics and the impolitical, but there are also considerable differences that Bosteels never touches upon and that I will now try to indicate. It is not primarily a matter of differentiation—it would be an honor for me if infrapolitics were to be considered a discursive artifact in the philosophical register of the Italian impolitical—but rather more modestly a matter of clarification. Let us begin with the common elements, which Bosteels finely captures:

> There are, without a doubt, plenty of echoes and resonances between infrapolitics and the impolitical, beginning with the negative references to political theology or, more generally speaking, to any political philosophy or philosophy of history based on the militant subject of the sovereign decision, whether this subject is called a "person," as the sacred bearer of inalienable rights, or a "victim" of the infraction

of these same rights, all the way to the images or figures of "retreat," "passive decision," the "neutral," and the "impersonal," not as values that are the opposite of politics but as "delimitations," that is, as limit-concepts, or as "determinations," in the nondialectical sense of a taking-to-their-final-terms the premises of politics in its theological and metaphysical essence. (108)

Another similarity is that both in infrapolitics and in the thought of the impolitical, what is sought is not the setting up of a countervalue to the theologico-political tradition, or even to politics itself, but rather to avoid the very disjunction, the value war, since the latter would fall into every trap of moralist determination. It is to be noted that the double rejection of political theology and the reification of the subject of politics (that "militant subject of the sovereign decision" that Bosteels loves is for me a rather terrifying character) do not just go together but are consubstantial to post-Heideggerian thought and possibly to a great deal of twentieth-century philosophy as a whole—if "retreat" refers to Jean-Luc Nancy and Philippe Lacoue-Labarthe, "passive decision" to Derrida and Lévinas (and Lacan), the "neutral" to Maurice Blanchot, and the "impersonal" to Simone Weil. But this also means that those concrete coincidences between infrapolitics and the impolitical are not as remarkable and interesting as they could otherwise be—that is, if they were autonomous developments. Nor is it so interesting if we expand the wave of similarities and we add that infrapolitics and the impolitical, as Bosteels duly notes, also share the notion, taken from Heidegger's 1942 seminar on Hölderlin already studied in Chapter 3, that the essence of politics is not itself political, and if we also add the notion that it is not just a matter of rejecting political theology, which in Esposito's version includes every philosophy of history, including the Marxist philosophy of history, but also every linking of power and the idea, and every recourse to the pretension that politics is in every case the *repraesentatio* of a higher truth. In fact, the extreme secularization of neoliberal globalism, the corollary of which is the handing over of the planet to the technical imperative, which is biopolitics for Esposito, is also to be politically rejected (although not so clearly in Esposito, who proposes a "biopolitics from below" or "affirmative biopolitics," as we will see).[3]

Where then can we find connections between the postulates of the impolitical and those of infrapolitics that cannot be explained through a superficial reference to the general epochality of thought? From Bosteels's coordinates, the point of radical community between those two instances must be located in the following quotation, which Bosteels uses to talk about the impolitical, but that infrapolitics fully accepts:

Esposito defines "political theology" as the articulation of power and value, or of representation and idea. It is that which permits the transit from an idea to its enactment, and conversely, it is that which structures power in the name of a normative value or transcendent idea, which is precisely the representation of the good to be realized in politics. "This is in essence the meaning of the expression political theology, to which from now on I will refer," explains Esposito, namely, "the conception according to which the good would be politically representable and politics would be interpretable in terms of value." All political theology thus presupposes a suturing of politics and ethics, while the impolitical, by postulating the impresentability of the value of the good, at the same time recognizes the radical incompatibility of political power and ethical ideas. (101–2)

Infrapolitics, from the intuition of the absolute difference between life and politics, understands that there is no possibility of real *representation* either of life in politics or of politics in life, of thinking in being or of being in thinking. The approach between those elements is not gradual but proleptic and cannot be bound to any figure of continuity or analogy. A caesura separates them, and thought gives itself over to politics in a leap, from necessity, when it cannot not do it, not in the name of a whim or an ethical conviction that may mediate in the dark field of nothingness, but in the precise name of a naked will to power on the side of life or survival, beyond any value. From that perspective, of course, both infrapolitics and the impolitical would fully accept Jacques Ranciére's postulate regarding politics as the rare irruption on the scene of the part of those who have no part, with a simple modification: every time there is a claim for social power there is politics, and it is not so rare, since by definition the claim to power is made by those who have no share or not a sufficient share of that specific power in every case. There is politics, politics is ceaseless, there is no full outside vis-à-vis politics, there is a constant leap into politics, but at the same time politics can always be exposed to its own finitude, can always be confronted with its limit and its death. The impolitical and infrapolitics have as a common center the intuition that the exposure of politics to its death cannot be done from politics itself, that it requires a step back from politics. Both forms of thought stage the necessity of a step back through which, as we will see soon, the very possibility of a reinvention of democracy at the end of political theology plays itself out. Bosteels is therefore perfectly right when he says that "both Esposito and Moreiras . . . claim that the meaning of politics is not itself political and cannot be thought except when refracted through their respective categories of the impolitical and infrapolitics" (80). The impolitical and infrapolitics are two forms for thinking politics. Except that infrapolitics is not only that: it is also more than that. The impolitical makes of Esposito more than ever a thinker of politics. Infrapolitics is not only a thinking of politics. That is the first fundamental distinction between the two.

Infrapolitics Includes the Impolitical

In a forthcoming book whose provisional title is "Political Grammars. The Unconscious Foundations of Modern Democracy," Davide Tarizzo mentions the Lacanian idea according to which any private grammar is a fundamental fantasy and cannot refer to any substantive truth: it only refers to a type of work, to a structuration. The same is true for any collective grammar regulating our notions of community, from the community around a soccer team to that of the children in primary school or even to the human community as such. For Lacan there is no collective grammar that may function without leaning on a private grammar (the latter organizes, for every one of us, the *cogito* as "true fiction"), nor is there a private grammar that functions without the support of a common language. The gap between private and collective grammar is nevertheless irreducible: a form of absolute difference that I invoke as the relation without relation between life and politics. The attempt to fill in that gap is catastrophic and leads to disaster—both in life and politics. To the extent that politics thinks of itself (but can politics think of itself?) as the attempt to respect the impossibility of filling the caesura between the public and the private, to the extent, therefore, that politics can be enacted as a form of respect for any private grammar, politics is democratic or is oriented toward democracy. To the extent that politics thinks of itself as an attempt to transgress the impossibility of filling the gap between the private and the public and seeks therefore the unification or maximum reduction of private grammars, politics approaches fascism or at the very least distances itself from a democratic perspective.

Why should we not add that infrapolitics inhabits the gap between private and collective grammars? It is a *chora*. It is installed between fundamental fantasies; it is the space between fundamental fantasies—but this means that it itself is not a fundamental fantasy. Reflective or affirmative infrapolitics, the second infrapolitics, the one attentive to its own facticity, is a belligerent position on the impossibility of filling the gap, of closing the absolute difference. Certain critics are therefore right: infrapolitics talks about nothing, refers to nothing. Neither private nor public, impersonal, infrapolitics is the nothing of politics, that nothing of which it is said: "there is nothing before politics (or after politics)." On the impossible ground of that nothing, the infrapolitical site, politics consummates its permanent catastrophe.

What is then the impolitical and what is its real relation to infrapolitics? Massimo Cacciari's important 1978 article "Nietzsche and the Unpolitical" presents it, in its Nietzschean version, as:

> the critique of the political as affirmation of value. The unpolitical is not the nostalgic refusal of the political, but the radical critique of the political. It goes beyond the mask of the political (its disenchantment, its necessity, its being destiny) to discover the foundation of values, the discourse of value that still founds it. Its power analyses, and dissolves, that which even in Weber tends to present itself as the totalizing method of Western spiritualization. The unpolitical does not represent the value that frees itself from the nonvalue of the political, but the radical critique of the political as invested with value. The unpolitical is the reversal of value. (95)

We can for a moment take "the unpolitical," in Alessandro Carrera and Massimo Verdicchio's translation of Cacciari's text, as another name for the impolitical. This is an important definition that must be taken on board in order to dissipate misunderstandings and vulgar perceptions. If politics, as the residue of a disenchanted world where illusion has no future, is a totality, it is a totality immersed in nothingness—it picks up the nothing, as a void of value, and projects it as the foundation for action. But it is not politics that says this; only the impolitical says it about politics. The impolitical is the reversal of the value of politics. In other words, "the unpolitical brings the political back to the acknowledgment of its intrinsic nihilism" (96) and deconstructs the false pretensions of politics to valorization. The unpolitical is the internal force of the radical critique of politics in the epoch of the world-image (in the epoch of the crisis of political theology). It is also the antitheological force that shows how any "absolutization of the political belongs to the theological dimension of Western thought" (97). As "it is, in the political, the critique of its ideology and of its determination" (97), its democratic force stands on "the desacralization of the political" (98), and its ultimate deabsolutization, which is something the current Left, with its desperate notion that any destiny is a political destiny, is unable to hear. Cacciari will be able to say that "the state is one of those powers whose process of absolutization coincides with that of its devaluation. The unpolitical is the recognition of the occurred perfection of the political" (99). But it is perfection no longer. The unpolitical—that is, the impolitical—is therefore the critical instance that, within politics understood as the disavowed general devaluation of all values, prepares an alternative possibility, a possibility other than the silent fall into nihilist entropy (I am preparing this translation during the days of the Trump-provoked crisis of the US Postal Service, which is as good an example as any of the nihilist entropy of political maneuvering, no matter how many pious Christians support it). If it were possible for there to be politics again, Cacciari will say glossing Nietzsche, and it is to be understood that both of them are talking about a politics not deluded about itself ("disgraceful is not the priest, but the priest who states that his kingdom is of this world," 102), it is a remote possibility that goes through "the unpolitical acknowledgment of the nontotality of the political" (102). Impolitical politics is therefore an exception to nihilism—a politics of the not-all that preserves on its reverse side infrapolitics as the not-all of politics, that is, what subceeds or exceeds politics, what is noncapturable by the absolutizing apparatus of politics in the epoch of secularization and at the time of the overwhelming triumph of capitalist discourse. Cacciari's definition opens the space of infrapolitics as the very reverse of impolitical critique. This is the relation of infrapolitics to the impolitical, and also its difference.

Esposito will say in *Categories of the Impolitical*, in the preface to the 1999 Italian edition, that "only the impolitical defines the totality of the real in political terms" (*Categories*, xvi), which in the context of Cacciari's analysis is a paradox that needs to be accounted for. The impolitical, as the instance that destroys the political pretension to absolutization, is also the instance that picks up and destroys the absolutization of the real into politics. There is a logic of the supplement in place here: the impolitical destruction of politics as totality takes on board politics as totality, but also its destruction, and by so doing it takes up more of the real than it destroys. From that position, the banal critique that attempts to reduce the impolitical perspective to a form of passive quietism or of blissful inaction is badly out of joint and shows it has not understood well at all. The impolitical runs through the entire space of politics, but it does more than that, as it reaches an outside where it enacts an ultrapoliticization that turns back on itself. The ultrapolitical is here the political rejection of the absolutization of politics, the maintenance of the open gap between private and collective grammars, the necessary radical democratization of a space where no axiological prevalence gives some more legitimacy than it gives others. The impolitical is an antiauthoritarian and prodemocratic hyperbole, hence posthegemonic, and eminently open to ceaseless praxis. To the extent it includes the labor of private grammar in its confrontation with collective grammars, it understands and affirms that there is no apolitical or antipolitical site for the speaking, mortal, and sexuated being. At the same time, it affirms that not everything is political. Both positions are not only compatible but mutually presupposed. Both of them are shared by infrapolitics. This is why infrapolitics is infra*politics* at the same time it is *infra*politics.

What is then the possible infrapolitical supplement to the impolitical? It has been mentioned already, perhaps lightly and transversally, but after all it is difficult to speak about that which experts cannot discuss. If there is a subcess to politics, something that precedes it and exceeds it, something that occupies the site of the nothing of politics, would it not be on the side of the mortal, speaking, and sexuated existent? It could and would not be prescribed by either capitalist discourse or by the nihilism of a devalued politics. That which remains, the site of what Jorge Alemán calls "common solitude," is something that cannot be measured either by politics or by the impolitical. It is beyond both of them.[4]

Beatitude against Subjection

Within the time that marks the reconstruction of the ideology of the person after World War II there emerged three fundamental zones for research with varying degrees of hegemonic success: existence first, then language, then culture. There was existentialism, and then the linguistic turn, and later the cultural turn, and they inflected or constituted a history or a trajectory of reflection that, in retrospect, and in spite of some years during the 1990s where it looked as if that reflection were having noticeable impact on the social sciences and other spaces of knowledge production, seems to have remained more or less, or for the most part, confined to the academic humanities. We seem to have drifted away from the cultural turn, but it is harder to discern whether a new technopolitical interest, with its radical impact on the notion of the person, is first of all an event in the history of thought or whether it should be more properly considered a turn in the history of humanity—since there is a difference between the history of thought and the history of humanity. The contemporary dominance of technoscientific protocols, even at the level of economic development, challenges and undermines—or consummates, depending on one's perspective—many conceptions inherited from modernity at the most practical and experiential levels. The technosciences will make leaps within the span of one or two generations, and the political implications of promised developments in, for instance, neurophysiology, pharmacology, or genetics, not to mention informational sciences, certainly also in the environmental sciences, will change even more drastically than they have so far many of the conditions of social interaction. Indeed, it is because we are already at the threshold of potentially revolutionary change in at least some societies that there is an urgency to the formation of critical and constructive thought on the various consequences of the technopolitical turn that seem to exceed the conditions under which a fixation on existence in the 1950s, or on language in the 1960s and 1970s, or on culture in the 1980s and 1990s, was or could be considered directly political. For me, infrapolitics is the site of those possibilities for new thought. Esposito, however, has been arguing for years that they will take place in the space of what he calls an "affirmative" biopolitics. I will therefore explore the difference between infrapolics and affirmative biopolitics.

Giorgio Agamben's 1996 essay "Absolute Immanence" was programmatic. Its importance does not reside in its focus on the technopolitical. Rather, Agamben turns to that which the technopolitical seems to threaten, which would constitute the substance of his thought from *The Coming Community* down to his latest work: what he calls "life," in the sense of "bare life," which is a notion found in the work of Walter Benjamin, and which Agamben modulates through his notion of form-of-life understood as the site of a potentiality of thought to be opposed to the general closure of existential experience under the technical imperative.[5] The confrontation between bare life and technopolitical deployment, or rather the fundamental attack on life as we have known it at the hands of technoscientific protocols and their political ramifications—biopower, in short—is to be submitted to a genealogical analysis on the basis of a new conceptuality. This is Agamben's 1996 program:

> The concept of "life," as the legacy of the thought of both [Michel] Foucault and [Gilles] Deleuze, must constitute the subject of the coming philosophy. First of all, it will be necessary to read Foucault's last thoughts on biopower, which seem so obscure, together with Deleuze's final reflections, which seem so serene, on "a life . . ." as absolute immanence and beatitude . . . for Foucault, the "different way of approaching the notion of life," and for Deleuze, a life that does not once again produce transcendence. We will thus have to discern the matrix of desubjectification itself in every principle that allows for the attribution of a subjectivity; we will have to see the element that marks subjection to biopower in the very paradigm of possible beatitude. (238)

Unpacking this program, Agamben says, is a task to be pursued along two main poles: the play between subjectivity and desubjectification and the play between beatitude and submission. In terms of goals, since a program for a coming philosophy must incorporate a teleology, it is perhaps easier to understand the importance of beatitude, given its conventional association with happiness, than it is to move toward a practice of desubjectification. If things are mired in obscurity, well then, the task of the coming philosophy is no doubt to contribute to their clarification. Agamben offers a number of thoughts on the way. I will sum up some of them, since they will be relevant for an adequate evaluation of the stakes in Roberto Esposito's *Terza persona* (Third Person). I think the latter is the text where Esposito makes his best case for an affirmative biopolitics. After its analysis I will move on to briefer considerations on a later text, *Da fuori: Una filosofia per l'Europa* (From the Outside: A Philosophy for Europe).

Most of Agamben's essay is taken up with a celebratory analysis of Deleuze's last essay, "Immanence: A Life . . ." The notion of *homo tantum*, understood or expressed in Deleuze on the basis of a passage in Charles Dickens's *Our Mutual Friend*, seems crucial.[6] It refers, in Deleuze's formulation, to *a life*, that is, to a point when "the life of the individual has given way to an impersonal and yet singular life, which foregrounds a pure event that has been liberated from the accidents of internal and external life, that is, from the subjectivity and objectivity of what comes to pass . . . beatitude; or an *ecceity*, which is no longer an individuation, but a singularization, a life of pure immanence, neutral, beyond good and evil, since only the subject that incarnated it in the midst of things made it good or bad" (387). *Homo tantum* is *a life*, in the sense that it is that in life which remains free from the aporias of subjectification, and even from consciousness. The *homo tantum* is the locus of a "transcendental field" defined as a "pure plane of immanence" (385). For Agamben, with the notion of the pure plane of immanence Deleuze has taken an "irrevocable step beyond the tradition of consciousness in modern philosophy" whose radicality goes or would go beyond anything accomplished by Edmund Husserl, Martin Heidegger, Maurice Merleau-Ponty, Emmanuel Lévinas, or Jacques Derrida (Agamben, "Absolute," 225). In fact, the latter thinkers, Agamben says, to the extent that they are thinkers of immanence, will still want "to think transcendence within the immanent," so that "immanence itself [be] made to disgorge the transcendent everywhere" (Deleuze and Guattari quoted by Agamben, "Absolute," 227). But Deleuze's notion goes beyond his colleagues' "necessary illusions" toward the "most extreme thought" of "a principle of virtual indetermination, in which the vegetative and the animal, the inside and the outside, and even the organic and the inorganic, in passing through one another, cannot be told apart."[7] This is Deleuze's triumph: to the extent that "today, blessed life lies on the same terrain as the biological body of the West" (239), as Agamben offers rather enigmatically, *homo tantum* will have given us something like an analytical lever to initiate a practical countermove to technopolitical subjectification. "A life" is "a matrix of infinite desubjectification," and it is therefore radical resistance to biopower (233). In the notion of "a life," Agamben salutes Deleuze's identification "without residue" of desire and being, and thus the principle of a new and totalizing vitalism commensurate to the present epoch (236). It is fair to say that Esposito would consider the identification of desire and being the condition of any affirmative biopolitics. If politics today is biopolitics, as Esposito contends, hence a form of technopolitics caught up in capitalist discourse and certainly not in resistance to it, we could begin to suggest the thought that infrapolitics is the other side of any biopolitics, and a fortiori of any technopolitical configuration of life.

Deleuze's transcendental empiricism has discovered the plane of immanence on the basis of an *il y'a*, a *there is*, which is less than a whisper in the background: it is the irreducible, what obtains before both being and nothing, pure virtuality attributable to nothing.[8] Imagine a wound. The wound preexists you. A wound is later incarnated in a state of things, in lived experience, it is narrated, it is felt; it can even become a source of transcendence. But the wound, before action, is always already a singularity in the virtual field of immanence. For Deleuze "events or singularities impart to the plane their full virtuality, just as the plane of immanence gives virtual events their full reality. The event considered as non-actualized (indefinite) lacks nothing at all. It suffices to put the event in relation to its concomitants: a transcendental field, a plane of immanence, a life, a few singularities" ("Immanence," 388–89).

We are now in a position to understand Agamben's program for a philosophy of the future a little better: on the basis of the fact that it is the modern notion of subjectivity that has led us to where we are, we must watch over the possibility of a reintroduction of transcendental subjectivity, which is the ground of the possibility of the "necessary" illusions according to Agamben.[9] If *a* life is the matrix of infinite desubjectification, we must uphold the priority of *a* life over against any concrete life. There is a danger that beatitude, power, desire, even when theorized from a postsubjective position, become once again transcendental illusions. Beatitude and subjection lie on the same plane of immanence. The political battle is a matter of making the active side of power overcome the reactive side of power—the virtual against the actual.[10] We must play off beatitude, which is a good thing, against subjection, which is bad. But is that enough? Or rather: is it not too much already? How does beatitude, *that* beatitude—how could it—take us beyond the aporias of a technopolitical administration of life? Can we begin to think of an infrapolitical beatitude? Or is infrapolitical beatitude an intolerable evil for any affirmative biopolitics?

The Zone of Indistinction

"The person, one could say, is that which, in the body, is more than the body" (Esposito, *Terza*, 15), which also means that the body is always less and other than the person. Is *homo tantum* commensurate to the task of a new destruction of the concept of the person? If it is, is destruction what we need? Esposito argues that, whatever goes today under the concept of the person, the latter has enjoyed "an absolute ontotheological primacy" (5) since Roman law, and that even today's jurisprudence makes of the person the very condition of possibility of the subject of rights, and vice versa (5).[11] The category of the person unifies man/woman and citizen, soul and body, law and life. And yet, today more than ever, and despite the category's ideological primacy, we witness a growing disparity between form and existence, subjectivity and the body, life and the law. This is Esposito's fundamental thesis: the ongoing disjunction between life and contemporary conditions, that is, our basic biopolitical fracture, is not occurring *in spite* of the ongoing reaffirmation of the allegedly democratic— because universal—ideology of the person, but rather *because of* it.

We are dealing with a theoretical circle that has a long history. Even if this history antecedes it, Roman law organized a powerful systematic separation between the person as an artificial entity and man/woman as natural beings to whom the status of person could be more or less accorded or from whom it could be withheld. This meant the presence of a zone of indistinction that made of many human beings something less than persons, that is, beings that, while human, were still somewhere between person and thing: the slave is only an extreme point of a social gradation, and perhaps not the most extreme. A partial reification of the human, even when it was a question of distinguishing the properly human from its internal fallenness into thingness or animality, has remained a constant in the long history of ontotheology.[12] Through Western time, and through different historical epochs down to our present, the human was differentially defined, to its glory or its doom, through its rapport with the thing that was inside it, and that always already made it susceptible to appropriation and domination even at the same time that it set the conditions of possibility for its freedom and autonomy.

Even if a person is precisely not a thing, there has never been a definition of the person outside the consideration of the essential and irreducible presence of the not-personal thing within the person, which always therefore contaminates the person. "At the bottom of this convergence we find the Aristotelian definition of man as rational animal . . . the biopolitical corporization of the person or the spiritual personalization of the body are inscribed in the same theoretical circle" (16). In terms of our recent past, there is a difference in the systematic treatment of the differential nexus between the person and the body: for instance, the liberal conception, which assigns the property of the body to the person that occupies it, and the Nazi conception, which assigns it to state sovereignty. But, Esposito says, even this heterogeneity rests on a common trait: a productionist conception of life that makes the body into a property, a piece of property. Contemporary bioethics still reproduces the Roman separation between *persona* and *homo* when theorizing the differences between the full person, the semiperson, the nonperson, and the antiperson (17), which is ultimately the theorization of the technopolitical conditions for the power of decision over life and death, and for everything in between. In the face of technoscientific development we need alternative understandings of the human, and even alternative understandings of the very notion of life.

And yet, Esposito says, "the logic of the person does not occupy the entire contemporary horizon" (18). There is a thought of the impersonal that is beyond philosophy and can also be traced in literature and painting, in music and film, even in science. "The impersonal . . . is the mobile border or the critical margin that separates the semantics of the person from its natural effect of separation" (19). The thought of the impersonal is not a philosophy of the antiperson—it only dwells elsewhere. The notion of a "third person" was suggested by Emile Benveniste's work on personal pronouns.[13] For Benveniste, the "third person," precisely, does not have personal connotations, but refers to another register that is able to bypass dialogical subjectivity and reach the region of singularity, even of plural singularity. To explore this region, to interrogate the possibility that the third person, or the impersonal, can undo the ontotheological primacy of the person (in ways other than thanatopolitical) and can thus provide for the possibility of a thought outside the theoretical circle of productivist life, is the final object of *Terza persona*. I will focus on some aspects of it that seem particularly relevant, and which I will link to Giorgio Agamben's *The Open*.[14] The differences between infrapolitics and an affirmative biopolitics cross the differences with Esposito and Agamben.

The Shadow of the Impersonal

How does one make a third-person politics? The third person is not just another person, but rather it opens a different regime of sense. For Esposito, also for Agamben, Foucault and Deleuze are key figures in the philosophical tradition that has moved against dialogical models in favor of a new theorization of the neuter—the neuter is not "some other that adds itself to the first two, but rather that which is neither the one nor the other, that which escapes every dichotomy founded, or presupposed, by the language of the person" (*Terza*, 21).

A POLITICS OF SEPARATION

For Esposito, Foucault and Deleuze will have succeeded in turning the impersonal not just into a force able to destroy (or "deconstruct") the *dispositif* of the person but, even more important, into "the form, or rather the content, of a practice that modifies existence" (22). And Esposito calls "life" the figure of the third person in Foucault and Deleuze: "Life . . . is for Foucault that biological side that never coincides with subjectivity because it is always caught up in a process of subjection and subjectivation—the space that power invests without ever totally occupying it, thus generating always new forms of resistance" (23). If Foucault's notion of resistance—of life's resistance to subjection/subjectivation in the relentless push toward an outside—can become the "uncertain" basis of an "affirmative biopolitics" against contemporary power/knowledge (but not, by the way, against science as such), then Esposito thinks of the third person as the site for a new political practice against threatening technopolitics, that is, for an affirmative and postsubjective technopolitics. And Deleuze's notion of "animal becoming" "opens the thought of the impersonal" not just to the "liberation from the fundamental prohibition of our time" but also to "the always promised but never truly experienced reunification of form and force, mode and substance, *bios* and *zoe*" (24), that is, to a new univocity of being where, like in Agamben, desire and being, or being and thinking, would coincide without residue. The coextensiveness of life and politics, which infrapolitics denies, is the condition of an affirmative biopolitics. Esposito therefore situates himself in the legacy of Deleuze and Foucault in terms of a coming philosophy now explicitly defined as a modification of existence, a practical politics of the third person (or a practical politics of "neutralization") that is also an affirmative politics of the impersonal. What is at stake is the rupture of the theoretical circle of the person and its originary separation or split of the human between rational and animal, person and thing, subject and object, spirit and body, substance and mode, even thinking and being. Foucault and Deleuze are not Esposito's only companions in this endeavor of beatitude.

But whatever may remain uncertain in the search for a positive biopolitics must be read in the context of the genealogical analysis. *Terza persona*'s first chapter posits a first beginning for it in the "paradigmatic turn" that came to affect or infect nineteenth century political theology at the hands of biology, and in particular through the work of Xavier Bichat. Bichat's two main contributions for our purposes can be summed up in the polemological understanding of life as the set of functions resisting death ("the measure of life is . . . in general the difference that exists between the effort of the external powers and internal resistance. The excess of the former is life's weakness; the predominance of the latter is the index of its strength" [Bichat quoted by

Esposito, 26]), and the notion of two lives or a double life, split into organic life (vegetative functions) and animal life (which regulates relations with the outside). Death is the enemy, and its last triumph is taking over organic life. As Esposito shows, Bichat's work will have had tremendous impact on the understanding of the relations between the living subject and the conditions for political practice over the last two centuries, contributing to the rise of bio- and technopolitics against the founding notions of modern political theology, including modern democracy. In fact, the very presuppositions of the latter, such as the social pact between subjects endowed with rational will, and able to determine their own actions, will have suffered at least temporary collapse at the ideological level precisely through the consequent reduction in the notion of the person. "Divided into an 'inside life' and an 'outside life,' into vegetative and organic life, life is traversed by an alien power that determines instincts, emotions, desires in ways not reconducible to a unique element. It is as if a non-man—something different and prior to animal nature itself—came to be inserted into man . . . From that moment the function of politics—now inevitably biopolitics—will not be to define relationships between men but rather to individuate the precise point of the border between that which is human and that which, inside the human itself, is other than human" (30).

Biopolitics in its modern formulation is thus, to begin with, the decline of the person, and of the ontotheological primacy of the person. Arthur Schopenhauer and Auguste Comte are among the first thinkers who take Bichat's position seriously in terms of its implications for an understanding of the political. There can be no passage from the state of nature to the civil state when men are governed and controlled by their organic life. The function of the state is no longer to produce freedom, but rather to transfer the empire of death from the inside to the outside. Comte's "biocracy," by substituting *bios* for *demos*, places at the center of politics the life of an organism, whether individual or collective, that must no longer abide by representation. Self-preservation is now all. This is far from Kantian republicanism.

Anthropology will be the scientific practice charged with drawing the consequences, and also linguistics, and then racial discourse. The power of life must be strengthened following laws of organic evolution that no longer respond to the Kantian categorical imperative and follow instead an entirely other logic. The human sciences have transferred their object from history to nature (45), which will partially lead biopolitics in the direction of a thanato-politics defined by the absolute superiority of the racial datum. The humanization of the superior animal is only the other side of the animalization of the inferior man (65). The relative opposition between *bios* and *zoe* finds its maximum stretch in the particular humanism of Nazi anthropozoology: "Never like in this case . . . *bios* and *zoe*, form of life and life without a form, are separated into a distance that is irremediable because it is constituted by the direct or inverted relationship with death: on the one hand a life so alive that it can propose itself as immortal, on the other hand a life no longer such—'existence without life,' *Dasein ohne Leben* . . . because from the beginning contaminated and perverted by death" (71). With it, the human, reduced to its position in a legacy of blood, race, species, became only that which remained from the destruction of the person that the French Revolution had made tendentially coextensive with the citizen. The mask had been taken out (73).

The 1948 Declaration of the Rights of Men, from which, arguably, our contemporary understanding of liberal democracy emanates, attempted to reconstruct it. If the emphasis of the 1789 Declaration had been on the notion of citizenship, now, in the wake of the radical depersonalization Nazi thanatopolitics had imposed, the dignity and value of the human person as such are vindicated and put at the center of the juridical and philosophical reconstruction of liberal-democratic culture after World War II. But with it, unavoidably or irremediably, the old dualisms—mask and face, image and substance, fiction and reality (92)—came back to life, and to the notion of life. One consequence of making the person the subject of rights—of human rights—is to restitute the separation that keeps rights away from the nonperson. But the nonperson is always the other side of the person, and its fundamental condition. There is, in other words, no person without the nonperson, as no mask can be recognized as such that does not imply the counterpresence of a face, as no appearance can exist without a founding presence, and as no fiction exists without the counterpositing of a reality, albeit merely imaginary, in the background. Already Hannah Arendt, in her book on totalitarianism, had recognized one key aspect of the aporetic structure that threatens the normative validity of the human rights of the person with the abyss: "the law admits only those who enter it from a given category—citizens, subjects, even slaves, to the extent that they are part of the political community" (87). But those who are excluded from the categorial structure—from the structure of belonging, at any level—can only enter into law negatively, by breaking the law. The separation between the merely human and the person as a subject of rights still radically obtains today. Those two elements, Esposito says, only meet "in the form of their separation" (91), as the contemporary refugee crisis in Europe, not to mention the appalling conditions now obtaining in the US-Mexico border, make once again all too painfully clear.

Esposito's brief analysis of the Hobbesian inversion of objective rights into a subjectivistic notion of law is determinant. In principle, once the individual, beyond any difference in social status, is considered the bearer of a rational will and the total master of itself and its property, the Roman differentiation between man/woman and person seems to lose its very foundation. The French Revolution, and its principle of equality, would have buried the Roman superordination of the subject to the law. But it is precisely at that moment that a new internal differentiation makes an appearance that reproduces at another level the gap between the individual as political subject and its undifferentiated humanity. Hobbes's notion of "artificial person," understood as the person of the representative, or the sovereign, already marks the dimensions of this irreducible gap in the political structure of modernity. The sovereign is "the only agent of personalization to the extent that before its institution no one can in the proper sense define himself as a person, either natural or artificial, because in the state of nature everybody coincides with their own living, and hence dying, being—that is, the transcendence that constituted the necessary condition of personality does not yet exist" (104–5). But from the very moment that the sovereign emerges as an agent of personalization his role in universal depersonalization also emerges. The social pact, which constitutes the agent of the pact as a person, is simultaneously its depersonalization. Sovereignty marks the body of the "natural" person by "turning the person into that which no longer has a body and the body into that which can no longer be a person" (107).

Adapting Sigmund Freud's definition of melancholy, one could say that, from the first modernity on, the shadow of the nonperson has always already fallen upon the person. The *dispositif* of the person traces indeed a melancholy paradigm, as the person can never fully emerge from its underside, the nonperson, which constitutes its permanent state of exception. The infinite effects this phenomenon has upon the contemporary administration of life remain to be worked out in critical analysis. Nazism is no longer our direct enemy, in the sense that it does not directly threaten our political structures so far. Rather, liberal death spreads its wings today, still in the wake of Roman law but immeasurably enabled by contemporary technoscience, through its claim to organic life and its increasing encroachment upon human relationality, which includes the human's relation to animals and to its own body understood now, through a not-so-progressive turn of the screw, as what one is rather than what one has (present being now erases history, and, given the contrived emphasis on performance, a life's career cannot compete with present decline for any number of baby boomers or indeed subsequent generations when it comes to labor relations, for instance: not one's history, only present performance matters). Esposito refers to issues of biotechnology, intangible property, and patents concerning vegetal and animal life as contemporary sites of deployment of the radical structure of separation at the core of the living from the perspective of the *dispositif* of the person, which has proven incapable of arresting the "progressive reification of life" (117). Contemporary bioethics (Peter Singer and Hugo Engelhardt in particular come in for harsh criticism) does not hesitate to insist upon the animalization of liminar zones of the human under the dual thesis that "not every human being can aspire to the qualification of person, and not all persons are human beings" (119). But of course these are only punctual examples of a political macroprocess of disenfranchisement that the contemporary ideology of the person not only does not prevent but even fosters.[15] In yet another paradoxical turn, it is precisely the pretension that the person is master of itself and its property, but only insofar as the person *is* what it has always been, that is, not if the person has deteriorated beyond a certain line, that leaves not just so many of our fellow humans outside their own categorial enfranchisement (the nonpersons, the quasi-persons, the semipersons, the no-longer-persons, and the antipersons Singer theorizes, for instance), but that constantly threatens to destroy even those of us who are otherwise secure or, in our best moments, believe ourselves to be secure in our present condition as persons (think of the current and developing emphasis on post-tenure review in contemporary US universities, for instance). Esposito's main (critical) thesis, namely, that the contemporary predicament has not developed in spite of the overwhelming ideological dominance of the *dispositif* of the person but rather because of it, has a crucial consequence: the need for the elaboration of an alternative understanding, without which no ideological struggle can be effective. The theoretical circle must be broken in order to give infrapolitical way to Esposito's positive thesis. But the emphasis on the impersonal is still compatible with an infrapolitical perspective.

Against Subjectivation

The thinker Esposito invokes as the first radical proponent of a philosophy of the impersonal is Simone Weil, whose work in the 1930s already rose against the personalist ideology that many segments of the European liberal (and Catholic) intelligentsia were proposing as an alternative to fascism. For Weil the person depends on the collective and right depends on might. From this perspective, for Weil both the category of the person and the notion of rights are complementary factors in what Esposito calls an "immunitary drift" whose end is the protection of privilege against the excluded.[16] Weil looks at the notion of person from the perspective of what it excludes, as she also looks at rights from the perspective of what they steal. In other words, right is designed to protect the person against the nonperson, which is always the nonperson that has been defined as such from the very perspective of the right: this is the immunitarian drift. There can be no "universal right" of the person, since right is the mark of a communitarian privilege, which is always had against the community's outside. The category of the person is for Weil, accordingly, a category of subordination and separation that must be fought through a radical appeal to the impersonal. "What is sacred, far from being the person, is that which, in a human being, is impersonal. All that is impersonal in the human is sacred, and only that" (Weil quoted by Esposito, *Terza*, 124).

The passage to the impersonal: this is Weil's political demand. It is a passage beyond the I and the we, and therefore a passage into the third person, into the nameless or anonymous. The radically republican question is indeed of a pronominal nature. Is political justice, and political freedom, to be accomplished through the constitution of a *we*, or through the passage to the impersonal *they*? If my freedom is the freedom of all, is *all* to be encompassed by a first-person plural or by a third-person plural? Is political freedom a question of community or is political freedom a question of the multitude? Esposito will conflate the two parts of that question into one at the end of *Le persone e le cose*, and then again in *Da fuori*, as we will see later.

Right around the time that Weil was dealing with these ideas she spent a few months in civil-war Aragon, close to the front. Had she been able to look beyond the trenches, into the other or anti-Republican side, she might have seen a few women with the letter "Y" patched onto their blue shirts. They would have been members of the Sección Femenina, the Spanish Falangist organization for women, created and developed by Pilar Primo de Rivera, a sister of the founder of the Falange Española. In Paul Preston's words:

> The symbol of the *Sección Femenina* was the letter Y, and its principal decoration was a medal forged in the form of a Y, in gold, silver, or red enamel according to the degree of heroism or sacrifice being rewarded. The Y was the first letter of the name of Isabel of Castille, as written in the fifteenth century, and also the first letter of the word *yugo* (yoke) which was part of the Falangist emblem of the yoke and arrows. With specific connotations of a glorious imperial past and more generalized ones of servitude, as well as of unity, it was a significant choice of symbol. (Preston, 129)

You are a woman, but you have subjectivized yourself as a person in an affirmation of love to the Falange. Your choice of the Falange is your personal freedom, but that freedom is, first of all, imperial freedom, as it commits you to a path of domination of others, the non-Falangists; secondarily, it is also imperial freedom to the extent that you sign up for your own domination, for your own assumed servitude. You choose a collectivity that will not take its eyes away from you. As a member of the Sección Femenina, it is your duty to serve the man, the men of the Fatherland, those fascists that you love. Is Pilar Primo de Rivera and, with her, all the colleagues who thought up the Y symbol to sum up the free presence of Spanish women in the National Movement, giving us the conditions of possibility of all political subjectivation? How does one become a person, politically speaking?

The community of the *we* is always the Y on your shoulder. The passage to the impersonal is the refusal of the Y. The uncanny choice for the freedom of all, not for *our* freedom, but for the freedom of the third-person plural, is a choice to be made outside and even against political subjectivation. It is adrift, since it refuses every orientation beyond itself, beyond its own gesture. It embodies no calculation, no teleology, no program. It is rare—more exceptional than the emergence of the subject itself, which happens every time there is a free choice for community. It stands outside every moralism (as it never seeks personal advantage). It is time to return the impersonal to the heart of the political. Everywhere we hear definitions of politics that presuppose political subjectivation as the goal and can barely think beyond it. There is no doubt that political subjectivation is ongoing in every political process. But political subjectivation is in every case a function of the history of domination. The passage to the impersonal is the attempt to produce politics as the countercommunitarian history of the neuter. But there are different ways of appealing to the impersonal. In the last chapter of his book Esposito draws on a number of thinkers who have attempted the task of the neuter. I will comment on the analyses for Emmanuel Lévinas and Maurice Blanchot and will leave out of consideration Esposito's notes on Vladimir Jankélevitch and Alexandre Kojève, as well as his extensive, although partial, revision of Foucault and Deleuze's thoughts on the issue.

Countercommunity

The significance of Benveniste's essay on the third person is high, to the extent that Benveniste, in Esposito's interpretation, has given us the *grammatical* conditions of possibility for the development of a sustained thought of the nonsubject as the (logically) only possible thought of alterity: "Notwithstanding all the rhetoric about the other's excess, in the confrontation between two terms, [alterity] can be conceivable only and always in relationship to the I—its other side and its shadow" (*Terza*, 129).[17] If the I, confronting it, depersonalizes the you, it only does so to the extent that it awaits its own depersonalization in the reversal of the positions: the you always responds. The third person breaks away from the relationship between a "subjective person" and a "non-subjective person" by creating the possibility of a nonperson: "The 'third person' is not a person; it is rather the verbal form that has the function of expressing the non-person" (Benveniste quoted by Esposito, *Terza*, 131). The third person, beyond the I and the you, always refers to the absence of the subject, even if it can simultaneously refer to potential subjects. It is constitutively impersonal, and it is because of it that it can have a plural: "Only the 'third person,' as non-person, admits a true plural" (Benveniste quoted by Esposito, *Terza*, 132).

It is from this position that a reading of Lévinas opens up for Esposito, not as a thinker of the third person, but rather as the thinker who could not bring himself to the exposition of his own radicality from a political perspective. We are used to thinking of the Levinasian face-to-face as the epitome of Lévinas's philosophical or antiphilosophical position. What Esposito's reading brings out, accurately, is the fundamental impossibility of the second-person suture in Levinasian thought—something that Lévinas himself recognized, of course, and at the same time left undeveloped. At the limit, it would be something from which Lévinas would have recoiled. Esposito says that the question of the third person is for Lévinas both "the theoretical vortex and the point of internal crisis" of his thought (146). But, far from neutralizing it into the I-you encounter, Lévinas recognizes the very originality of the face as the trace of a field of signification that breaks every binary relationship: "the beyond from which the face comes is the third person" (Lévinas quoted by Esposito, *Terza*, 146). The beyond, which for Lévinas means "beyond being," also therefore means "beyond transcendence," or "beside transcendence." But this is the key problem. In the recognition of the third person as the beyond of the face Lévinas's thought opens itself to an unthinkability whose key position at the limit of twentieth-century reflection makes it all the more urgent for us.

It is the problem, not of the impersonal, but of the impersonal's political import: the point or limit at which politics should no longer be thought of as contained in a dialogical structure is also the point at which politics abandons its all-too-human face in favor of a dimension able to affect, beyond and beside the third person and its infinite plurality, what Blanchot came to call the neuter for lack of a better term. Just as language "is spoken where a community between the terms of the relationship is missing" (Lévinas quoted by Esposito, *Terza*, 147), a countercommunitarian politics is a politics no longer structured in terms of friendship or enmity, no longer structured in terms of the interhuman relation. This is where my divergences with Esposito's final position begin to develop.

Biotechnopolitics finds its limit in the fallen dialogics of the subject/object relationship: it is the tendential application of technique to life, for the purposes of an administration of life where life occupies the place of the object. Biopolitical practice, always modeled on the person's *dispositif*, is a practice of the master subject over against an object that constitutes it, and that by constituting it occupies the position of internal interlocutor. If the purpose of biopolitics is to make life, both organic and animal, sing to the tune of the subject, then it should be clear that no positive or affirmative biopolitics—all biopolitics is affirmative, even the Nazi kind: thanatopolitics is never but the dark side of an essential affirmation, lunatic as it may be—will suffice (and this is something that Esposito has not been willing to concede). A radical politics of the third person, hence beyond or beside the person, hence antibiopolitical, finds its point of departure in Lévinas's problem, his theoretical vortex and his point of crisis, which we can here only gloss following Esposito's indications, but with a twist.

If the other is to command radical priority, there can be no common ground between the I and the you—the face comes up from a region of radical separation, or the you would become just another aspect of the I. The other is not just a fold in a communitarian continuum but the signal mark of an essential lack of community, and therefore the opening of and to a radical disymmetry. If the subject suffers expropriation in Levinasian thought, it is because the demand of the other presses upon it from a region incommensurate to community. The experience of the you, when the you is not to be handled according to everyday linguistic convention but comes to us in the form of the face, radically, is then precisely at the same time the experience of that which can never be reduced to a you: an experience of the third person, or of what Lévinas calls *illeity*. Sensing the beyond of the face of the other, that is to say, sensing the face of the other as the beyond, is at the same time encountering the third person.

But the third person recedes, seeming only to come in the form of its absence, as an absence. It marks, in the first Lévinas, a negative experience that might be referred to God as the Unreachable. Lévinas will later say: "Proximity is troubled and becomes a problem with the entry of the third" (Lévinas quoted by Esposito, *Terza*, 149). The third is a problem: its recession breaks proximity, and proximity can no longer suffice. What is often ignored by Lévinas's critics is that troubled proximity, the perturbation of elemental proximity, and not in any way the ethical relation, is the site of politics, which means that politics is the region that opens up in and through the very impossibility of community, in the uncontainable rupture of the immediate ethical relation. It is through the very tension between proximity and its rupture (which is also at the very same time the rapture of proximity), or through the resistance to that tension (as the subject remains hostage to the other), that justice appears as the horizon of the political in the wake of the radical and ongoing failure of the ethical relation to constitute itself as closed or unique horizon. This is what organizes the political as an insurmountable contradiction between the infinite ethical responsibility for the unique other, which introduces a radical limitation in the universality of law, and the equally infinite demand for justice, which is necessarily a limitation of ethical responsibility. Politics is for Lévinas, to start with, this unstable field of relations created in virtue of the theoretical vortex that makes justice, as a demand that originates in the troubles of proximity, and ethics, as a demand imposed by the face of the other, equally unconditional. Esposito calls it a conflict between "partiality and equality," which, he says, reverses "the language of the person . . . into the form of the impersonal" (152). The entry of the impersonal remains a problem because, with it, the subject is liquidated: not even as a hostage can it remain the source of agency. And this is something about which Lévinas left but few, and at best ambiguous, indications. The question, however, arises as to what the best way of supplementing Lévinas's ambiguity would be. What if Lévinas had been right in affirming the impossibility of a communitarian politics?

Esposito claims that it was Blanchot who made it his business to develop the Levinasian point of crisis into the insight of the neuter, "against the hostility, or at least the incomprehension, of the entire philosophical tradition" (156–57). Blanchot mentions a "relationship of the third kind," a relationship that interrupts reciprocity and that opens itself to the nonrelationship, and which is precisely the disaster of every dialectics, and of every dialogics. The neuter is a nonpersonal alterity for which Blanchot rejects the name of "impersonal" as still insufficient (since "impersonal" is grammatically still dependent on a notion of person). Blanchot is looking for a break of the semantic field that will not allow it to reconfigure itself around the usual categories: being and nothing, presence and absence, internal and external. The third kind is the kind that enters no kind: and the neuter a word too much, which Esposito will link to the Levinasian notion of the *il y a* as it was developed, rather unforgettably, in *De l'evasion* and *De l'existence a l'existant*. But for Blanchot the neuter is not primarily a site of existential horror; as the inevitable and destined site of existence, it is rather the "extreme possibility" of thought (159). How is this to be understood?

What would be its political manifestation? A politics of the neuter is a politics of the third person in the sense already specified: an impersonal politics of the singular plural, a countercommunitarian politics of the *they*. Esposito's contention is that only Foucault and Deleuze were able to advance Blanchot's project. This is something that Agamben has also sustained in his essay on the coming philosophy. As explained earlier, for Agamben the active category in the program for a philosophy of the future is the category of "life." Esposito connects the development of the category of life in the later thought of Foucault and Deleuze to a basic Nietzscheanism in both thinkers—to their emphasis on the notion of "force," which will be linked to an irreducible and untamable outside that is, however, and in virtue of its radical univocity, also our most intimate inside. "What is it that we are—beyond or before our persons—without ever taking possession of? What crosses and works us to the point of turning itself inside out if not life itself?" (*Terza*, 168). Power, also constituted by life, and to the extent that it turns itself against the human, never has enough with the person as subject of rights, but must go beyond the person and its end, beyond death therefore, toward the capture of life itself. Life captures itself as power, but at the same time life exceeds itself as force beyond power. This is for Esposito the very possibility of an "affirmative biopolitics" (170) that he identifies with a new possibility of community, beyond the person, "singular and impersonal" (171). "Life itself . . . constitutes the term on which the totality of the theory of the impersonal seems to be summed up and projected towards a still undetermined configuration, but because of that loaded with unexpressed potentiality" (179). The critique of the theoretical circle of the person enables Esposito to announce a politics of the impersonal community ruled over by life as principle, which is a condition of affirmative biopolitics. But this affirmed vitalism, in open reference to Nietzsche, is it not regressive vis-à-vis the true potentiality of Esposito's analysis? To my mind the path toward a republican politics of the impersonal is not the path of affirmative biopolitics. Esposito moves toward a strong binding of affirmative biopolitics and a new communitarianism that I would dare call anti-republican, as I will try to show.

A politics of the neuter is expressed in Esposito through his notion of a politics of impersonal life, even a biopolitics of impersonal life, that must lead, through the tapping of its unexpressed potentiality, not just beyond "the entire conceptual apparatus of modern political philosophy" (179), but toward a new community, impersonal and singular: a community of beatitude that is, finally, the beatitude of the animal, the goal of the Deleuzian "animal becoming" that receives full recognition in the last pages of Esposito's book. Esposito's affirmative biopolitics would finally render the metaphysical separation between *homo* and *persona*, which also means, between person and animal, null. Agamben's *The Open* unquestioningly shares many of Esposito's insights and advances the argument toward a perhaps more nuanced, if to my mind still insufficient, understanding of the political task at least at the theoretical level.

The Critical Threshold

On the face of it, Agamben's *The Open* seeks a reconciliation of "man with his animal nature" (3). Its departure point was also treated by Esposito: it is Kojève's intriguing reflections about "the figure that man and nature would assume in a posthistorical world, when the patient process of work and negation by means of which the animal of the species *Homo sapiens* had become human reached completion" (6). If the destruction of the animality of man could be taken to sum up the humanist project down to the Hegelian system, for Agamben, glossing or critiquing Kojève, "perhaps the body of the anthropophorous animal (the body of the slave) is the unresolved remnant that idealism leaves as an inheritance to thought, and the aporias of the philosophy of our time coincide with the aporias of this body that is irreducibly drawn and divided between animality and humanity" (12). The body of the slave—*homo tantum*. We could define *The Open*'s project as the problem of reconciling *homo tantum* with the "physiology of blessed life" that a risen body—the posthistorical body—would want to enact. It is therefore a problem of beatitude, which remains, explicitly in Agamben, the eschatological horizon, and thus the orientation for an impersonal politics of the *whatever*.[18] We are back into a "critical threshold," and it is not unrelated to the Levinasian one. If for Lévinas the threshold was defined by the incompatible unconditionality of the third person's demand for justice or equality and the particular other's demand for radical priority, for partiality, the threshold in Agamben is also a political threshold, that is, a threshold that determines a politics. It is the troubled separation between animal and human: also a trouble in proximity, seemingly irreducible for Western metaphysics, but which the technopolitical turn may be about to handle—if it hasn't already done it—dismissively and with few compunctions.[19]

Agamben defines humanism's "anthropological machine," on the basis of Pico, Linnaeus, and others, as an "ironic apparatus" that must treat human nature as precisely an absence (29).[20] The human, caught in an endless play of specular misrecognition and projection, ends up establishing a "zone of indifference," a "space of exception" that is "in truth, perfectly empty, and the truly human being who should occur there is only the place of a ceaselessly updated decision in which the caesurae and their rearticulations are always dislocated and displaced anew. What would thus be obtained, however, is neither an animal life nor a human life, but only a life that is separated and excluded from itself—only a *bare life*" (37, 38). The object of a political practice commensurate to the present, which on its positive side would be to promote beatitude, is, on its negative or critical side, to destroy the space of exception, that is, to dismantle the apparatus for the production of bare life. This is still a Foucauldian or Deleuzian politics of life, hence ultimately Nietzschean, which requires the division of force into active and reactive elements for the sake of the former. The active force of beatitude confronts the reactive force of error, not as truth confronts falsity, since truth could only emerge as the other side of error and hence still on the side of the reactive force, but rather as something deeper or higher: as an eschatology, Benjaminean, in any case un-Nietzschean, no longer Nietzschean. Early on in the book Agamben says: "perhaps even the most luminous sphere of our relations with the divine depends, in some way, on that darker one which separates us from the animal" (16).

The second half of *The Open* is almost entirely devoted to a partial analysis of Martin Heidegger's 1929–30 seminar *The Fundamental Concepts of Metaphysics: World, Finitude, Solitude*. In the 1996 essay discussed earlier, Agamben had placed Heidegger at the center of a genealogy of thought that included Immanuel Kant and Husserl on the one hand (the side of transcendence) and Baruch Spinoza and Friedrich Nietzsche on the other hand (for immanence), and that would result in Lévinas and Derrida over against Deleuze and Foucault in the post-Heideggerian constellation: Heidegger's concepts are "the first figures of the new postconscious and postsubjective, impersonal and non-individual transcendental field that Deleuze's thought leaves as a legacy to his century" ("Absolute," 239, 225). Deleuze, counterintuitively, would have completed Heidegger's thought. The return to Heidegger now retraces the emergence of a political philosophy of the impersonal. But is it certain that the path marked by Foucault and Deleuze on the side of immanence must leave aside Lévinas and Derrida as epigones of ontotheological thought that are therefore complicitous with the establishment or continuation of the apparatus of bare life? If Agamben's genealogy is to work, and obviously Esposito gives it credence, we would have to consider Lévinas and Derrida as thinkers of life's power against life, as reactive thinkers unable to reach the sphere of the neuter. But nothing is less certain, as I have already tried to show (as Esposito himself shows) regarding Lévinas.[21] Something nontrivial is missing in Agamben's rather hurried delineation of "sides."

The crucial importance of Agamben's reading of Heidegger's 1929–30 seminar is the linkage he establishes between Heidegger's notion of life and his own notion of the political, and the step forward taken on the association of Deleuzian beatitude (which, toward the end of *The Open*, is conflated with the Benjaminian image of a nature reconciled, a "saved night" [81]) with Heidegger's boredom as fundamental attuning of the human. Agamben succeeds, through Heidegger, in projecting Esposito's critique of the ideology of the person and his proposal for a politics of the impersonal onto productive practical terrain, at least up to a certain point. He directly links the understanding of life in *Being and Time*, which it is the function of the *World, Finitude, Solitude* seminar to explicitate, to the biological and zoological work of the time (Hans Driesch, Karl von Baer, Johannes Mueller, and Jakob von Uexkuell are mentioned [51]). Heidegger's fundamental insight, already from *Being and Time*, is that "the ontology of life is achieved only by way of a privative interpretation" (Heidegger quoted by Agamben, *Open*, 50); "privative" in the sense of a subtraction and a reduction to mere present-at-handness. The concept of life inherited from the tradition is therefore thoroughly anthropocentric, thoroughly premised on the conception of the human as *animal rationale*, and to that extent useless for us. The 1929–30 seminar will reconduct the investigation of both the abyss and the peculiar proximity between Dasein and animals toward a sphere where "*animalitas* become[s] utterly unfamiliar and appear[s] as 'that which is most difficult to think,'" and "*humanitas* also appears as something ungraspable and absent, suspended as it is between a 'not-being-able-to-remain' and a 'not-being-able-to-leave-its-place'" (50–51).

If it is true that "the animal behaves within an environment but never within a world" (Heidegger quoted by Agamben, *Open*, 52), this is so because, according to Heidegger, animals and humans have a different relationship to the open. Animals are "open in a nondisconcealment," that is, they are captivated, captured, by what calls them. If the openness of humans to the world is primarily an openness to the conflict of truth, which is the conflict between concealment and unconcealment, then it follows that "the openness of the human world . . . can be achieved only by means of an operation enacted upon the not-open of the animal world" (62). Boredom is the "place of this operation," which immediately places boredom, as abandonment in emptiness, as the essential phenomenal hinge tracing the human/animal separation. In other words, boredom is the key to the overcoming and dismantling of the bare-life *dispositif* to the precise extent that it leads to an understanding of the difference between environment and world. "In becoming bored, Dasein is delivered over to something that refuses itself, exactly as the animal, in its captivation, is exposed in something unrevealed" (Heidegger quoted by Agamben, *The Open*, 65); hence, both animals and humans "are, in their most proper gesture, open to a closedness; they are totally delivered over to something that obstinately refuses itself" (Heidegger quoted in *The Open*, 65). The *lethe* (concealment) is primary in the unconcealment of *aletheia* as truth. The passage from environment to world is the disruption of animal captivation, but this immediately means: "the open and the free-of-being do not name something radically other with respect to the neither-open-nor-closed of the animal environment: they are the appearing of an undisconcealed as such, the suspension and capture of the lark-not-seeing-the open" (68). This sets the caesura between animals and humans into a structure of mutual belonging: the conflict of truth, the originary and ceaseless struggle between concealment and unconcealment, now emerges as the originary and ceaseless struggle between environment and world, between animals and humans. And "Dasein is simply an animal that has learned to become bored; it has awakened *from* its own captivation *to* its own captivation" (70). This awakening (awakening to a closedness) is the rise of the human, which sets the human as not just the result but the infinite production of the awakening, which is also at the same time, as in boredom, or as in the struggle for truth, the infinite suspension of the awakening. This is, in Heidegger's determination, the difference between the humans and animality in general.

And this is indeed, and therefore, the beginning of politics, even or perhaps particularly of politics for a technopolitical age: politics as awakening, politics as the pursuit of a path of disclosedness against the fundamental occlusion of the possible. According to Agamben, "the ontological paradigm of truth as the conflict between concealedness and unconcealedness is, in Heidegger, immediately and originarily a political paradigm. It is because man essentially occurs in the openness to a closedness that something like a *polis* and a politics are possible because man essentially arrives as opening to a closedness" (73). But the very possibility of a politics does not mean its goodness.[22] Heidegger himself pursued what he thought of as a good politics in terms of a reconstitution of community alongside the production of a *we*. For a number of years he thought that a personalization of the political possibilities of truth was not just possible but in effect historically destined in terms of the authentic possibilities of the German people. At the same time, in a form no more enigmatic than decisive, and even while remaining blind or captivated by his own political investment, he warned against another move of the sinister, which he associated with the destiny of the entire West under metaphysics: the return of disawakening under the sway of technology.

If in Heidegger's position Agamben can recognize a reconceptualization of the political that makes it thoroughly dependent on the struggle of the human against animality; or in other words, if from a Heideggerian perspective we can see that politics is always already biopolitics, then two paths seem to open up for us. One of them is the recaptivation of the human by its own pretenses: the human that has left the animal behind, the human that has thoroughly personalized and reified its own awakening into an ideology of endless production of world, of the ceaseless management of life, increasingly as technical world, and as technically administered life (this is the path that was, according to Heidegger, inexorably followed by the West), is also the human that, in

Agamben's words, "seeks to open and secure the not-open in every domain, and thus closes itself off to its own openness, forgets its *humanitas*, and makes being its specific disinhibitor. The total humanization of the animal coincides with a total animalization of man" (77). This is the biopolitical project, relentlessly pursued today by liberal humanity and its absolute reliance on technology: it is also, inevitably, an impersonal politics of world production as world domination. The night of the world threatens in that path, and it is not the saved night. It is a night because it is the return of the undisclosedness of world under the sign of a radical (technopolitical) disawakening. If a conciliation of humans and animals is to be found there, it will be at the price of a thorough extension of the apparatus of depersonalization in the direction of subjection. There will be no way of inverting the sign of the dominating force into an active force of redemption. No attempt at inverting the sign of biopolitics into an affirmation of the *lethe* at the heart of the living can go beyond humanitarian ideology, which is, as Esposito has shown in his deconstruction of the person, not the obstacle but rather one of the reasons for the present sway of biopolitics and the consolidation of the bare life apparatus, beyond ostensibly political life, into the technocapitalist constitution of postgenomic life and the thorough control of the organic (and this is the other side of nanotechnology's promises).[23] This is a politics to be understood as the setting into practice of a general administration of life, hence a politics that is anything but politics. It moves toward the terminal constitution of technocapitalist life. And it takes its point of departure in the total assimilation of life to politics and of politics to life. In this reciprocal assimilation, which should remind us of the Balibarian mantra studied earlier in this book, the awakening to a closedness vanishes, and politics loses its most precious component. Something else is needed, an alternative path.

And this might be the second path that, according to Agamben, opens after Heidegger. It is the one he himself, and also Esposito, prefer. Agamben mentions it: "man . . . appropriates his own concealedness, his own animality, which neither remains hidden nor is made an object of mastery, but is thought as such, as pure abandonment" (80). Appropriate his concealedness? To think the pure abandonment of captivation, and to elaborate a practical politics on that basis, is perhaps not to be understood through the notion of appropriation. For man to appropriate his own concealedness means for man to reconstitute himself as a subject, even as a personal subject (since there is no other kind). Resubjectivation is the limit of an affirmative biopolitics, Agamben suggests, which is perhaps the reason why Esposito ends his book with a call for the constitution of a *persona vivente* (living person): "not separated from, or implanted in, life, but coinciding with it as unsplittable conjunction [*sinolo*] of form and force, outside and inside, *bios* and *zoe*" (183–84). Has beatitude not become too much here? Has *homo tantum* not dangerously crossed the border of separation between the infinite production of awakening and the infinite suspension of awakening into, once again, the thematic disawakening of a univocity in being? Can the *persona vivente* do anything but at most offer itself as an ideological banner to ward off the most egregious abuses against disposable human life? I think this is not enough. A curiously regressive humanism seeps into this decisive moment in Agamben's and Esposito's theoretical formulations.

Why define being as force? Force is force. Esposito's vitalism plays a bad trick on him. A politics of the impersonal that can move beyond interhuman relations into the animal and the organic, and vigilant enough to harness the force of technopolitics and to refuse to become one with it, is not necessarily, not in principle, a politics of conjunction or conciliation nor does it need to be. If there is one thing that politics cannot do, it is to be less than political. Attention to the impersonal does not warrant a politics of life. In the affirmation of "life" as the horizon of a philosophy of the future, does life not become yet another transcendental illusion? The historical captivation of the human is a non-cell-based conspiracy, as Thomas Bernhard has put it.[24] Why should the animals' captivation be different? At this point of maximally troubled proximity, a technopolitics commensurate to technoscience should ask itself that question. There is a third path to be opened, beyond Agamben and Esposito, which would be a directly anti-biopolitical path.

An Infrapolitical Solution

It seems to me the dead center of *Da fuori* (2016), where Esposito continues to discuss his own relation to contemporary philosophy, is the presentation of the scission between deconstruction and biopolitics as central and decisive for thought. This is explicitly an interested statement, to the extent Esposito will end up claiming his own position at the mediating point of both perspectives (180). The latter claim is dubious, since, at the same time, he will also claim that an affirmative biopolitics can no longer share the post-Heideggerian paradigm of de(con)struction (171). In any case, Esposito will in effect place the central conflict of his book as a conflict between deconstruction and biopolitics. Deconstruction will have been on the side of "French theory," and biopolitics on the side of "Italian thought." The third contender in this gigantomachy is "German philosophy," a little worse for wear but acknowledged, particularly in its Adornian avatar, as the occupier of the structural site of negativity. German negativity would have been historically vanquished by the impolitical "neutralization" carried out by deconstruction (and by thinkers such as Jean-François Lyotard, and by certain not-too-fruitful aspects, in Esposito's opinion, in the thought of Deleuze or Foucault). An Italian thought of the outside would have come to take over from allegedly failed French neutralization through a radical political affirmation, which is the symbolic position where Esposito sees himself, aided by explicit developments we have already seen of the thought of life in Deleuze and Foucault through an intensification of their Nietzschean genealogy.

Esposito makes his own position in Italian thought complex by finally rejecting the legacy of political theology whose investigation has characterized so much of the best contemporary Italian reflection (Mario Tronti, Cacciari, and Agamben among others). Esposito would be looking, through his affirmative biopolitics, for a destruction of political theology. Esposito asks, and leaves his answer implicit, whether the destruction of political theology would immediately mean the end of politics, that is, the impolitical neutralization of politics. Esposito's wager is not for an end of politics; rather it is for a militant politicity, which is in *Da fuori* exemplified in his proposal for a concrete politics concerning Europe in its present conundrum. He calls it "grand politics": "Never as now, in a present in continuous flight towards an uncertain future, there has been such a vital necessity of what was once defined as 'grand politics'" (226). The attempts at the redefinition of Europe as a "civil power" in Italian jurisprudence are reconducted by Esposito toward the notion of a "popular power," with a basis in the thought of Machiavelli and Gianbattista Vico. If, for Machiavelli, the great seek to oppress and the people seeks not to be oppressed, also for Vico the people, far from forming an undifferentiated and homogeneous set of individuals, is constituted by and through the conflict itself, "a social class opposed to another class" that antagonizes it (237). As a popular power Europe would think of its grand politics as invested in the formation of a people, understood as the formation of a class that refuses to be oppressed and constitutes itself in antagonism to the oppressor class: "Europe's process of political unification . . . will be the result of a real political dialectic. It will no longer respond to the politico-theological machine that imprisons our lives, it will rather work towards its dismantling" (238). Yes, this is a grand-political project for Europe, but at the same time its affirmative-biopolitics component gets diffuse: it is more claimed than showed. In the last instance, as we will see, the notion of the people in Esposito's grand politics dissolves itself into an inevitably reactive neocommunitarianism.

There is no particular nationalist interest in Esposito's claim for Italian thought. Any nationalist interest would be immediately undermined by the thematization of the outside that Esposito posits as the privileged instance of thought in the last century. If biopolitics is today at the center, it is because it can install itself in the outside affirmatively, in view of political efficacy, which is what German philosophy and French theory were never able to reach. Frankfurtian negativity is as politically deluded as French neutralization, which moves toward an impolitical maximization. Affirmative biopolitics would be, according to Esposito, in a position to close successfully, that is, productively, the great crisis of thought intimated by Husserl and Heidegger, Paul Valéry and José Ortega y Gassett, Ludwig Wittgenstein and Oswald Spengler. But this seems too large a claim. In its world avatar (that is, in its importation to Anglo-Saxon universities, and beyond) French theory, which was already a reaction to German philosophy, releases itself into a so-called literaturization of thought that deprives it of the possibility of a practical antagonism to every form of the real. It is a problem that only increases with its North American reception. Literaturization means impoliticization, in a complex way. In reference to Derrida, Esposito says that, on the one hand, "the politics implicit in his texts is born, not so much from a theory of politics, but rather from a kind of resistance in its comparisons and confrontations—from a kind of allergy to any normative philosophy. In that sense it is not possible to speak of the depoliticization of a discourse which, like that of Derrida, is endowed with an immanent politicity, implied in deconstructive practice" (135). On the other hand, he claims "it is not possible . . . to sustain that Derrida's philosophical research carries an effective political gesture" (131). That is, for Esposito, on the one hand, the politicity of deconstruction is immanent to the deconstructive gesture that rejects any normative politicization. On the other hand, it cannot reach true political effectivity. It remains, after all is said and done, merely literature.

One must wonder whether Esposito is passing on to deconstruction a notion of politics that deconstruction will have rejected beforehand. The notion of the impolitical that Esposito uses, referring of course to Esposito's 1988 book *Categorie dell'impolitico*, becomes insufficient: "[Derrida's] more recent works also . . . remain as impolitical as the first. And that, notwithstanding the evident efforts of the author . . . to assume as his object political categories, such as that of democracy" (131). Esposito begins to force his argument in this contradiction in his characterization, which would seem to reduce all politicity to a principle of action, and which can only be solved in the attribution to Derrida, and to the totality of French theory, of a "logic of neutralization" of every practical decision (131). This means, in Esposito's explanation, that deconstruction, and French theory at large, will remain fixed in a logic that excludes conflict and that remains "this side of the line of politics" (131). But with this Esposito engages in a reduction that exceeds his presuppositions. He says that in Derrida or from Derrida "one can no longer distinguish friend from enemy or set into practice any link that is not always already delinked" (131). To the "politics of separation" Derrida invokes in *Politiques de l'amitié* (1994) Esposito responds with the accusation of a "separation from politics" (131), which seems to me an illegitimate gesture that Derrida's writing does not warrant.[25] We must read the gesture retrospectively, from the end of the book and the grand-political approach taken there, as a denunciation of any possibility for deconstruction to establish itself politically within the Machiavellian-Viconian universe of conflict in favor of a "popular power" that could reject oppression. Deconstruction, says Esposito, cannot take sides, and remains suspended in a neutralizing netherworld. But this is an arbitrary accusation, a "political" accusation in a banal sense. Esposito accuses deconstruction of being unable to take sides, thereby remaining suspended in some neutralizing no-man's land.

There is no separation from politics in the Derridean politics of separation. It could also be said that the politics of separation summons forth a hyperpoliticization, repoliticizing in a way that is far removed from any politico-theological presuppositions, including the current substitution of the concept of effective hegemony for that of the general will: that is, the current claim, sustained almost everywhere in the Left, that it is not the general will that should concern us, but rather only hegemonic articulations of the social. A politics of separation is necessarily posthegemonic; and it is so also in its rejection of the singular existent's submission to any particular instance of order and to any communitarian demand, which is, by definition, always already immunitary. In our present, in places where an allegedly new politics makes itself potentially present, the danger is still the same it has always been: the tendential constitution of a militant community attendant to the thought of the leader. But the constitution of a militant community—there is nothing in Esposito's grand politics that allows us to think he has applied to this problem his own understanding of the dangers of any immunitarian approach to politics, surprisingly—places the community in an autoimmunitarian predicament through which community starts to function in the direction of its own destruction. We see it everywhere. In the communitarian closure in favor of a unity of positions, in favor of an alleged new hegemonic constitution of the social, politics is suspended and faith is affirmed. The Derridean politics of separation is against all of that, not only under conditions of constituted power, where silence and conformity are demanded from already formalized institutional sites, but also under constituting conditions, where the unconditional consent to leadership is always already factually premised on the suspension of politics. In those cases, even if power could be redefined as counterhegemonic power, communal power, popular power, power of the multitude, the counterpromise of an effective emancipation from power, from the power of the state and from the power of the state of the situation, is undermined. There is no literature in this critique, but to stand against it, to reject it, is not merely literary either. What is in play in the politics of separation that deconstruction proposes is a non-impolitical hyperpoliticization, subtracted from politico-theological conditions of manifestation; and certainly also subtracted from any affirmative biopolitics that seeks to celebrate communitarian life as such, which amounts to celebrating communion as political procedure. Esposito's position falls into an all-too-well-known contemporary leftist practice that has not ceased to fail in all of its recent avatars and adventures. Interestingly, Esposito himself has given us, in his critique of immunity, the tools to understand how a posited seamless community cannot but destroy itself through autoimmunitarian drifts (which of course so-called cancel culture should make a note of).

Discussing Agamben's "messianic perspective," and comparing it with Tronti's "eschatological perspective" and Cacciari's "*katechontic* perspective," and wondering whether the end of political theology will necessarily imply an end of politics, Esposito alludes to the passages in *L'uso dei corpi* (The Use of Bodies), where Agamben gives up on the constituent-constituted power bipolarity, denouncing it not just as intrinsically politico-theological but as doomed to inefficacy (everything constituent becomes constituted, everything open closes itself, everything liberating will end up oppressing, and this is a function of the call to the constitution of a power in the first place). Agamben says: "for destituent potential it is necessary to think entirely different strategies, whose definition is the task of the coming politics. A power that has only been knocked down with a constituent violence will resurge in another form, in the unceasing, unwinnable, desolate dialectic between constituent power and constituted power, between the violence that puts the juridical order in place and the violence that preserves it" (*Use*, 266). But Agamben is, for Esposito, still looking for "a different figure of politics" (*Da fuori*, 193). Agamben calls it "destituent potential." Esposito's critique is that destituent potential is already internal to the politico-theological *dispositif*: "the 'end' of political theology is [in Agamben] evoked in a politico-theological language, in this case of a messianic character" (193). It is necessary to take another step out of political theology which cannot be taken from the subordinate (that is, still internal to political theology) category of secularization, or from any of its variants (disenchantment, profanation): "the 'resolution,' in the literal sense of the term, of political theology does not go through the category of secularization. Just as it does not go through the categories of 'disenchantment' or 'profanation,' from the moment that the latter place themselves on the reverse side of what they claim to contest. They are, that is, necessarily trapped in the dialectic that joins them, negatively, to enchantment and the sacred" (194). Against the messsianic-secularizing position of Agamben, Esposito calls for a further critical step, in the understanding that transgression, as Georges Bataille made clear in his own work, does not destroy the law but only maintains it and confirms it. It seems difficult to imagine Agamben himself would have been blind to this argument. If it has not escaped him, then we must conclude that Agamben has no particular intention of taking political theology to its end. He needs it. I wonder whether a similar case could be made for Tronti or Cacciari. Esposito affirms his freedom from such a problem, but he does it against the allegedly literaturizing neutralization of allegedly impolitical (now an unwelcome word) deconstruction.

The Pauline *"hos me"* ("as if not"), which is in Agamben the mark of his destituent position, since it unworks the law in faith and opens a new figure of the political in its secularized, profane version, is to my mind effectively deluded as a figure of politics and therefore also as the figure of a new politics. Agamben errs in his insistence on the formation of a new politics on the basis of his critical categories. But is Esposito not doing the same, in a different manner? In the chapter devoted to Italian thought, Esposito proposes as his central thesis the notion that Italian thought is "the attempt to confer political form" on what, in Adorno's negative dialectics, in the "dynamic between power and resistance" Foucault theorized, or in the "dichotomy between the 'molar' and the 'molecular'" in Deleuze, not to mention the allegedly excessive emphasis on death in the Derridean paradigm, for which life is essentially survival, "rests on an inevitably impolitical plane" (170). The "matter" of Italian philosophical discourse will no longer be the social, or writing, or the "neutral circuit of an equivalence between forces" (171), but rather "the political apprehended in its inevitable conflictual dimension" (170). In contemporary Italian reflection, Esposito tells us, there are three conceptual bipolarities that move thought toward its radical politicity and politicization. The first two refer to the early work by Mario Tronti on workers and capital, and to Negri's meditation on constituent power. The third refers to Esposito's own work: to community and immunity. For Esposito, the sense of community registered in his earlier work does not rely on any notion of identity, but rather on a "constitutive alterity" that refers to an "exteriorization" and to a "reciprocal contamination" (179). Esposito's emphasis on *munus*, however, rather than on the *cum* emphasized by the sort of deconstructive expropriation of community apparent in Jean-Luc Nancy, for instance (180), would have enabled Esposito to radicalize the thought of community toward its political valence. *Munus* is common to community and to immunity: "If *communitas* links its members in a reciprocal pursuit, *immunitas* exonerates them from such a duty. In the same way that community remits to something general, immunity remits, on the contrary, to the privileged particularity of a condition subtracted from communitarian obligation" (181). And this latter thing is the problem. Today, for Esposito, we would have amply overtaken the modern immunitarian need, we would have exceeded the limit before which immunity can still be proposed or fought for as effectively political, and we would have reached a stage where immunity, and with it every kind of immunitarian emphasis, would be "no more than a cage where not just freedom consumes itself but also the very sense of existence—that opening to the outside that has been named community" (181).

Esposito is, surprisingly to my mind, arguing that the contemporary auto-immunitarian drift must be rejected in favor of a return to a prudent communitarian shelter that should never have been abandoned. This is, I think, the place where all the previously woven threads of my critique of Esposito's affirmative biopolitics come together. For Esposito—retrospectively, one could perhaps already see him coming in this respect in the last few pages of *Terza persona*—community comes to be understood as the central, essential site of politics for our epoch. Community is even the promise of an epochal overcoming of immunitary nihilism. Today, for Esposito, "the commons has become the real and symbolic form of resistance to the excess of immunization that captures without an end" (181). Italian thought must therefore be defined, in its apex, as communitarian thought, from an understanding of community as the active force in respect of which immunity is reactive—Nietzsche is now probably wanting to turn over in his grave. From here we can understand, according to Esposito, the preceding history of reflection, that is, of modern reflection, as the elaboration and circulation of "a series of narratives oriented to providing increasingly effective immunitarian responses against the risks, real and imagined, of human relations. The modern political is not characterized as such by the norm of the exception, by inclusion or exclusion, but by the immunization of a life deprived from transcendent protection and delivered to itself" (183). Affirmative biopolitics, committed to a reactivation of the commons, must however face the absence of jurisprudence turned toward the institution of the commons, the lexical absence regarding the commons, and the absence of conceptual categories from which to think the commons—since for many centuries the immunitary paradigm and "its politico-theological language" have organized our world. The practice of the outside, if it could in the past have been the very opposite, is today, still according to Esposito, communitarian practice, understood as the search for the deactivation of immunitary practices such as those dependent on the privilege of the upper classes, which can only solve themselves in the oppression of those who would rather not be oppressed. This is Esposito's proposal for a grand affirmative biopolitics, which indeed reformulates and orients the Machiavellian position (the people are a people in search of community, the rich are those who look for immunity), and indeed sets forth, if not a program of action, at least the justification for it.

Returning, however, to the scission between deconstruction and biopolitics that organizes the critical point of departure of *Da fuori*, it remains for us to examine up to what point deconstruction can only be read in an immunitary and countercommunitarian key, since that is finally Esposito's accusation. I suppose Esposito places deconstruction as the favored enemy because he perceives it as the other thought tendency that has also left behind the language of political theology. If deconstruction and affirmative biopolitics were to be, in Esposito's version, the only two visible instances of thought where the politico-theological architecture seems to have been demolished, then it is all the more important for Esposito to eliminate the immunitary and neutralizing residue of deconstruction. But he does this at a great cost to his own thinking.

This is the reason why communitarian thought must take its point of departure in a fundamental rejection of the basic infrapolitical position, which *Da fuori* presents through some words by Nancy: "Thought does not dictate and does not guarantee what must be decided or that it is decided. That is its archi-ethics and its specific responsibility" (133). A non-hostile elaboration of what exists behind those words by Nancy would belie the notion that deconstruction must be thought of as contained in or by the immunitary paradigm. Deconstruction is, rather, a subtraction from what Esposito calls the "logical precedence" of community with respect of immunity. Not that it would prefer to invert the precedence: the subtraction is a subtraction from the very choice between the two, from the very decision and its dictates and guarantees. In the affirmative-biopolitics paradigm, community must rule today over any attempt at immunitary activation. But the obvious question is, then: until when? If modernity can be defined as the history of immunitary excesses against community, at what point of a new effective politics will we feel obliged to state that communitarian excess will overflow, has already overflown, its own conditions and threatens the necessary immunity of the singular existent, without which there would be not just no freedom but also no sense of existence? This is a question that Esposito never bothers with, in spite of its decisive importance. The lack of an answer throws us back into the (vicious) theoretical circle Esposito had wanted to breach.

Da fuori, in spite of its efforts, does not quite ruin deconstruction. On the contrary, deconstruction remains as the effective limit, hyperpolitical and anything but neutralizing, and precisely for those reasons also infrapolitical, in the face of a political appeal that, no matter how grand it means to be, can still not give an adequate account of its own conditions of enunciation. In the book that precedes *Da fuori* in Esposito's production, *Le persone e le cose*, really only a booklet, Esposito ends by sending us off into an unresolved nightmare. If, for Esposito, the fundamental political phenomenon of our time is the fact that "immense masses multiply themselves in the squares of half the world" and "their words incarnate in bodies that move in unison, with the same rhythm, within a single affective wave," if "still deprived of adequate organizational forms, bodies of women and men push the borders of our political systems, asking for transformations irreducible to the dichotomies that have for so long produced the modern political order" (110), that "radical novelty" of the "living body of the multitudes" (111) (remember the notion of *"persona vivente"* that concluded *Terza persona*) is not only asking for a new communitarian lexicon but is also in dire need of a response capable of interrupting the exclusionary link between politics and community. A concluded community is the end of politics. Is it then not the case that affirmative biopolitics, in spite of everything, turns into another theologico-political end? Avoiding that fate is, after all, the function of the politics of separation Derrida once called for. Political theology asks and has always already asked for a construction of politics based on the coextensiveness of life and politics, which is the becoming citizen of the living and the becoming living of the citizen. Infrapolitics prefers Antigone, who marks the (third) path of absolute difference.

7

Infrapolitical Derrida

The Ontic Determination of Politics beyond Empiricism

In the "Fifth Study" of *The Idol and Distance*, Jean-Luc Marion asks what he calls a "brutal question": whether "distance," which in his book refers primarily to the distance between the human and the divine, would come to be "the ontological difference" (200). Marion wants to know whether the very possibility of a new thinking of God and the divine must first come to terms with the Heideggerian presentation of the difference between being and beings, since, from the early texts published by Martin Heidegger, any possible abandonment of the ontotheological structuration of thought (hence, also of the old thinking of God, the divine, and the world) depends on it. Marion quotes *Identity and Difference* (1957) in order to underline two terms in particular, namely, *Unter-Schied*, di-mension or inter-cisssion, and *Austrag*, conciliation or resolution:

> If Being, in the sense of the uncovering Coming-over, and beings as such, in the sense of arrival that keeps itself concealed, realise themselves as different, they do so by virtue of the Same, of the di-mension (*Unter-Schied*). The latter alone grants and holds apart the "between," in which the Coming-over and the Arrival are maintained in relation, separated one from the other and turned one toward the other. The difference of Being and beings, as di-mension (*Unter-Schied*) of the Coming-over and the Arrival, is the uncovering and concealing Conciliation (*entbergend-bergende Austrag*) of the one and the other. (Heidegger quoted by Marion, 200–1)

We may neglect for the moment Marion's theological interests, which will take him toward an understanding of being beyond idolatry and representation but in the direction of "paternal distance." Our interest is to note that di-mension (or inter-cission) and conciliation (or resolution) are also political terms, terms with a certain political valence, or terms that can be read politically if we put them in a political context. We would be talking about a solvable excission, a tendentially conciliatory inter-cission, within a complex game that conceals and unconceals. It would perhaps not be too difficult to propose the transcodification into politics of *Unter-Schied* and *Austrag* in the Heideggerian sentences, but it is far more pressing to wonder whether the thought of ontological difference has already informed any political thought, any conceptualization of politics, over the last century, or whether the satisfied and by now rather willful forgetting of the ontological difference continues to inspire contemporary conceptuality.

The Step Back

Heidegger of course would have recommended a step back from such a forgetting, without which ontotheology would continue its not-so-secret reign in the unthought of contemporary thought: "The step back goes from the unthought—from the difference as such—towards what it is necessary to think. That is, towards the *forgetting* of the difference. The forgetting that it is necessary to think here is the veiling thought on the basis of *lethe* (occultation), a veiling of the difference as such, a veiling that for its part has, from the origin (*anfänglich*), withdrawn itself" (Heidegger quoted by Marion, 206). Heidegger never attempted to formulate any explicit thinking on politics commensurable with the difficulties of the step back, or at least not after the years of his own political and moral catastrophe. But it is fair to say that Heidegger himself was not deaf to the political implications of a thematization of the ontological difference, which amounts to thinking the unthought in the tradition of Western metaphysics. Thinking the ontological difference already had a fundamental political incidence through the "technical" interpretation of contemporary politics it enabled. These are Heidegger's words, and they are frequently glossed over and either dismissed or neglected:

> The step needs a preparation that must be attempted here and now, taking into account being as such in its totality, how it is now and how it begins to show itself in an increasingly clear way. What now is finds itself marked by the mastery of the essence of modern technics, a mastery that is already manifest in all aspects of life through characteristics that receive various names, such as functionalization, perfection, automatization, bureaucratization, information. In the same way we

call biology the representation of what is alive, the representation and formation of the being dominated by the essence of technics can be called technology. The expression can also serve to designate the metaphysics of the Atomic Age. The step back from metaphysics to the essence of metaphysics is, seen from the present and out of the image we have formed of it, the step that goes from technology and the technological description and interpretation of the epoch, to that essence of technics that remains yet to be thought. (*Identidad-Identität*, 114–16)

Marion believes that contemporary thought must think the ontological difference not metaphysically. In the same way as Heidegger, who warns that the step back implies "a duration and a capacity of endurance whose measure we do not know" (*Identidad-Identität*, 114), or following him, Marion insists on the extreme difficulty: "these stakes appear as a task and a test for such thought only inasmuch as, precisely, the passage from the difference toward metaphysics and what it leaves unthought had nothing accidental about it, but came from an historical rigor whose constraints we barely measure" (207). In his own critique regarding the early attempts of Jacques Derrida to deal with the step back through the notion of *différance*, in which Marion acknowledges that Derridian *différance* marginalizes ontological difference "in favor of an 'older' difference" (226) that "enframes it, situates it, and exceeds it" (232), Marion concludes that "Derrida's path . . . leads us further forward, certainly not in the way of an answer, but in the seriousness of the question" (232).

But Marion's critique takes place in the wake of a thought of the divine that Derrida would have kept at a not necessarily paternal distance. What remains to be thought is, then, whether politics could occupy, in the Derridean register, the place of the divine in Marion. This is a barely authorized question, since Derrida never made himself fully explicit in that respect to my knowledge. It would be possible to argue that Derrida never thought of himself primarily as a political thinker, and certainly not the early Derrida, although perhaps, in a secondary or more hidden discursive register, he never thought of himself as anything but a political thinker. But this is a question that in its full reach could be rephrased as the question as to whether the task and the test of contemporary thought could be taken by Derrida to be, in the political terrain, those of attempting to think politically from a nonmetaphysical understanding of the ontological difference. To my mind any attempt regarding a thinking of politics under the general sway of the ontico-ontological difference is always primarily infrapolitical.

Marion refers, accurately enough, to the need for historical rigor. The possibility of a thinking of the political informed by the ontological difference is before anything else a historical possibility, since it can only be a possibility that is opened as such by history itself at the moment of its ontotheological caesura, at the moment of the step back conceived of as a relation with what has been covered over or forgotten by the historical tradition: "Insofar as the step back determines the character of our dialogue with the history of Western thought, it leads in a certain way outside what has been thought in philosophy up until now. Thinking steps back from its business (*Sache*), being, and, with it, it takes what has been thought to a contrary position that allows us to contemplate the totality of that history ... from the source of all thinking. In difference from Hegel, this is not an inherited problem, already formulated, but rather precisely what has never been asked by anybody alongside that history of thought" (*Identidad-Identität*, 113). The difference from Hegel, of course, is absolutely crucial, to the extent it sets the Hegelian thinking of the ontological difference in the realm of the difference between being and the being of beings, whereas the Heideggerian difference refers to something else, and quite otherwise.

Specters of Marx (1994) is the Derridean text where there is a more decisive explicitation of his will to link something like a post-ontotheological political thought to a consideration of history and historicity as such. Speaking about ongoing social transformations, Derrida affirms that they force us to think historicity otherwise: "This is where another thinking of historicity calls us beyond the metaphysical concepts of history and the end of history, whether it be derived from Hegel or from Marx" (*Specters*, 70). And he continues: "in the same place, on the same limit, where history is finished, there where a certain determined concept of history comes to an end, precisely there the historicity of history begins, there finally it has the chance of heralding itself—of promising itself. There where man, a certain determined concept of man, of the *other man* and of man as *other* begins or has finally the chance of heralding itself—of promising itself. In an apparently inhuman or else a-human fashion" (*Specters*, 74).

On the same page Derrida refers to earlier attempts of his to accomplish a rupture with the metaphysical understanding of history in favor of a commitment to the Heideggerian thinking of historicity in the wake of the ontological difference. Derrida presents deconstruction, retrospectively, as always already political, and open from its inception to the promise that other sections of *Specters* will conceptualize as messianicity without messianism, that is, given over to an undetermined future that however keeps the possibility of emancipation and freedom. I would suggest that messianicity without messianism count as an effective recodification of the *Unter-Schied/Austrag* relation, if the messianic is the withdrawing excess that the ontological difference has always already inscribed in the ontic. This new thinking of historicity was certainly already examined by Derrida as early as his 1964–65 Seminar at the Ecole Normale, published as *Heidegger: La question de l'Etre et l'Histoire*.[1] In reference to those years he says:

> Permit me to recall very briefly that a certain deconstructive procedure, at least the one in which I thought I had to engage, consisted from the outset in putting into question the onto-theo- but also archeo-teleological concept of history—in Hegel, Marx, or even in the epochal thinking of Heidegger. Not in order to oppose it with an end of history or an anhistoricity, but, on the contrary, in order to show that this onto-theo-archeo-teleology locks up, neutralizes, and finally cancels historicity. It was then a matter of thinking another historicity—not a new history or still less a "new historicism," but another opening of event-ness as historicity that permitted one not to renounce, but on the contrary to open up access to an affirmative thinking of the messianic and emancipatory promise as promise: as *promise*, and not as onto-theological or teleo-eschatological program or design. Not only must one not renounce the emancipatory desire, it is necessary to insist on it more than ever, it seems, and insist on it, moreover, as the very indestructibility of the "it is necessary." This is the condition of a re-politicization, perhaps of another concept of the political. (74–75)

He could not have been clearer. A liberation of historicity, against its hijacking in the historical thought of Hegel, Marx, "even" Heidegger, is for Derrida a condition of repoliticization and the opening to a non-ontotheological concept of politics—something about which Derrida would have been thinking since, at least, the 1964–65 seminar on Heidegger (which includes, of course, substantial commentary on Hegel and historicity). These are also powerful textual motifs in the essay that Derrida would have written just some months before the beginning of that seminar, "Violence and Metaphysics," where the fundamental theme of his *Auseinandersetzung* with Emmanuel Lévinas can be picked up as a discussion of Heidegger's legacy and the best ways of going about it: historicity and violence, historicity and ontological difference, historicity and errancy or origin. It is therefore not out of line to believe that Derrida's explicitly political reflection in *Specters*, if one has ears to hear, must be referred back to those years. But what is explicitly political, what is sufficiently explicit, and where and why is the line to be drawn, and who draws it?[2]

The Wise Men of Negev

My hypothesis or proposal in what follows does not invoke, however, any explicit politicity in the work of the early Derrida. I do not need to do it, since I think politics is itself crisscrossed by historicity and is nothing but the concretion of historicity: hence the essence of politics is not itself political. I will call the Derridean attempt to find an incipient articulation for his thinking of a new historicity to be revealed in the wake of the ontological difference infrapolitical: not a thinking directly on or of politics, but rather the thinking of that which conditions politics, without which politics could not be thought. For me an infrapolitical perspective, which also seeks to understand the unthought of politics, would be the site from which to pursue the possibility of a new politicity, informed by the ontological difference, and by the attempt to think of it not metaphysically: to think of it, also, or indeed, politically. I want to trace in this chapter a point of entry into Derridean infrapolitics, or the beginning of an infrapolitical perspective, in the very intricate reading by the early Derrida of Emmanuel Lévinas that is rendered in "Violence and Metaphysics: An Essay on the Thought of Emmanuel Lévinas" (included in Derrida's 1967 book *Writing and Difference*, but first published in 1964).

If infrapolitics involves the double solicitation of politics by ethics and of ethics by politics, an infrapolitical perspective will obtain only if either politics or ethics, and particularly given their links in their traditional understanding to old notions of history that Derrida attempts to leave behind, are fundamentally altered in their notion, that is, solicited and destroyed and perhaps reinvented. I agree with Martin Hägglund's critique of the alleged "ethical motivation" in deconstruction insofar as "the logic of deconstruction transforms the fundamental axioms that inform the discussion of ethics" (*Radical Atheism*, 76, 77). If a relationship to the other can only be figured from "the non-ethical opening of ethics," and if "this opening is violent because it entails that everything is exposed to what may corrupt and extinguish it" (88), then there is no nonviolent relationship with the other, and the fact of violence cannot be ethically regulated: it can only be ethically administered. This goes beyond destroying the alleged ethical motivation of deconstruction and leads into an understanding of the latter as ethically destructive. But then it would be equally fair to say that deconstruction can only be defined as political insofar as we allow the traditional concept of politics to waver as well. Political motivations must also be understood, in deconstruction, under the sign of destruction. Or else: deconstruction is political only if the very concept of politics has mutated under its sign. An infrapolitical perspective—this is the risk of its definition—allows us to liberate the nonethical politicity deconstruction harbors as much as its impolitical ethics—both of which the critical tradition has somehow preferred to disavow, or at least to keep mostly silent about. I mean nonethical not in the sense of antiethical, in the same way that infrapolitics (or impolitics) does not refer to any antipoliticity. If there is a nonethical opening to ethics, and if there is a nonpolitical opening to politics, then both ethics and politics, and infrapolitics in its double solicitation, must be placed in deconstruction.[3]

I start off in a double secondarization. The secondariness of ethics does not turn politics into originary and primary and the secondariness of politics does not make ethics primordial. There is also a nonpolitical opening of politics, an embedded and structural, desistent dissimulation of political irruption. I only want to anticipate that infrapolitics is the region of theoretical practice that solicits the constitutive opacity of the ethico-political relation—hence admits, for every practical decision, of no preceding political or ethical light to mark the path. This, far from limiting it, turns infrapolitics into a kind of radical politicity that disavows every limit (without turning it exclusively into a disavowal). We could call it a politics of bad infinity, a shadow politics, and oppose it to any and all heliopolitics of the Good. (I have nothing against the Good, except that those who speak in its name tend to become scoundrels, in my admittedly limited experience.) Derrida would have sought, in a rather *marrano* way, from the very beginning of his itinerary as a thinker, an anti- or nonheliopolitical relationship to politics as a necessary step for the liberation of historicity from politics—that is, for the opening of politics to the ontico-ontological difference, or to the historical unthought of politicity itself. It is not then surprising that his attempt in "Violence and Metaphysics" is to trace the residue of unthought heliocentrism in Lévinas's work.

"Violence and Metaphysics" puts Lévinas' work under a nonresolutive deconstruction. Lévinas remained an important reference for Derrida, but perhaps in the sense that their moment of maximal proximity is at the same time, from Derrida's perspective, also their moment of maximal distance—there is an indifferentiation of proximity and distance, which may also be the case, all in all, for Derrida's relationship to Heidegger. The 1964 essay sketches the figure of that double relation—proximity and distance—in its final pages on eschatology and empiricism. Before getting to it, I would like to dwell briefly on Derrida's *Adieu to Levinas* (1977), an essay written thirty years after the writing of "Violence and Metaphysics." In *Adieu* there is a brief mention of a certain essay by Lévinas on which Derrida chooses not to elaborate. In that reference Derrida hints at the fundamental notion of what I would like to call a Levinasian infrapolitics, which Derrida will always have preferred to deconstruct and then reappropriate. Derrida refers to "Beyond the State in the State," from *Nouvelles lectures talmudiques* (New Talmudic Readings, 1996). Of it Derrida says: "Beyond-in: transcendence in immanence, beyond the political, but in the political" (*Adieu*, 76). Let me do what Derrida does not do but obviously suggests and follow up on Lévinas's "Beyond the State" essay.

Lévinas speaks in it of a certain hatred, not a hatred of democracy, rather a hatred of tyranny, of any and all tyranny: "The response of the ancients of Negev consists in refusing precisely tyranny, even amiable tyranny, and of reserving supreme popularity to the hatred of this irreducible tyranny and of the State that claims it" ("Au-delá," 63). And then he says that it is a hatred that is addressed "to the friends of men in power, a hatred towards this friendship that is made of flattery and *delation*, site of all corruption. But a hatred that can be understood in a more profound manner, as a high degree of critique and control regarding a political power that remains unjustifiable in itself, but to which a human collectivity, through its multiplicity, and while waiting for something better, is pragmatically bound" (64). The *demos* subjected to power is the figure of this hatred which accepts no hierarchy, no *arkhe*, except always in a provisional and revocable manner. Political power is for Lévinas "unjustifiable but inevitable" (64). Its nonjustification is the very condition of democratic government, and the precise power, beyond the state, of the *demos* in the state: the nonjustification of power is, in other words, the very opening for demotic irruption in politics. For Lévinas, "in this refusal of a politics of pure tyranny the lineaments of democracy are designed, that is, of a State open to the best, always on the alert, always to be renewed, always bound towards returning to the free persons that delegate to it, without separating themselves from, their liberty subjected to reason" (64).

There are at least three different sets of problems in the Levinasian fragments I have just quoted. First of all, we have the notion of a "beyond/in," that is, a certain solicitation of the vexing inside/outside structure that we are asked to think not alternately, first in, then beyond, or first beyond, then in, but, if at all possible, simultaneously. Hatred is the term, or the affect, that allows for simultaneity. In the hatred of tyranny—as opposed to, for instance, the love of tyranny—we are simultaneously in and beyond the cause of tyranny, that is, in and beyond state power as such (hatred must have a ground and an object, but it comes from a site that seeks their cancellation, and it is therefore the trace of a beyond, which love, for instance, does not share, since love does not seek the cancellation of its object). Second, hatred is explicitly registered as a hatred of complicity, of the chain of complicity or the chain in complicity that makes tyranny hegemonic through flattery and *delation*, which is a word that does not translate well into English. This radically antihegemonic dimension of Levinasian hatred indicates a desire for a reconstitution of democracy always already on posthegemonic terms. And, third, the demotic hatred of complicity in tyranny has to do with a certain waiting: the sages of Negev are aware that the people only pragmatically accept, while hating, tyranny "while waiting for something better." Insofar as there is waiting, the text says, state power, and the power of the friends of the state, is inevitable: the inevitability is the very function of its pragmatic presence in the face of a certain enabling absence. But it is the absence whose cancellation the waiting awaits that makes tyrannical power also always at the same time unjustifiable, hence unjustified.

In his story of the sages of Negev Lévinas gives us an account of political power always already subjected to its actual negation in the anarchic hatred of those who wait. But the negation is always at the same time merely latent in its irruptive potentiality—it can force an irruption of demotic power against tyranny, or it can also let tyranny be. Even in the latter case, however, the negating hatred persists. This is the "transcendence in immanence" of Derrida's commentary, which signals, I would say, his personal wager for a political position that would be "in politics, beyond politics." And in the state beyond the state. Politics is not simply the possibility or the action of transcending tyranny, and politics does not only occur within the inevitability of and resignation to tyranny. There is a simultaneity of anti-tyrannical political potency that affects both spaces insofar as there is a state always subjected to the possibility of demotic irruption (not tomorrow or in an undeterminable future, but always in every case) and a potency of irruption that cannot be conceptualized as already political as such. It is infrapolitical before the arrival of what must come, but not unconnected to it. The state always subject to the possibility of demotic irruption is therefore not, not quite, messianic democracy, but it is not, as undiluted tyranny, impervious to it either. An elaboration of this thematics through the Levinasian oeuvre would result, I believe, in the elucidation of a Levinasian infrapolitical perspective, that is, not just of his well-known suspension of the political in the name of ethics (in the secondarization of politics to ethics as first philosophy), but also, perhaps surprisingly, in the understanding of the necessary suspension of ethics in the name of a certain politicity that will have become no less fundamental, that is, no lesser aspect of first philosophy: the moment, always possible, when anti-tyrannical hatred ignores the inevitability of power. For that moment there is no previous light, either ethical or political—it happens, at the end of the wait and as end of the wait. If there is here a fundamental agreement between Lévinas and Derrida (Derrida seems to admit that much in his 1977 essay), it is an agreement drawn on the disagreement indicated in the 1964 essay.

Secondary War

The word "politics" does not appear many times in "Violence and Metaphysics," but it makes a crucial appearance toward the beginning of the essay, as part of a compound word. The word is "heliopolitics" (90). Derrida is discussing what Lévinas calls "the break with Parmenides" (89), and a fundamental move toward "a thought of original difference" (90) and away from "the ancient clandestine friendship between light and power, the ancient complicity between theoretical objectivity and technico-political possession" (91). Within the economy of Derrida's essay, such ancient complicity, a spinoff of the alleged identity between thinking and being, which refers to "the entire philosophical tradition, in its meaning and at bottom" as it makes "common cause with oppression and the totalitarianism of the same" (91), must be tested against the Levinasian presentation of the thought of Edmund Husserl and Martin Heidegger, with Hegel in the background. Derrida says on heliopolitics (while quoting Lévinas): "In this heliopolitics 'the social ideal will be sought in an ideal of fusion . . . the subject . . . losing himself in a collective representation, in a common ideal . . . It is the collectivity which says 'us,' and which, turned toward the intelligible sun, toward the truth, experience the other at his side and not face to face with him'" (90). Heliopolitics is therefore the name for an understanding of politics that would mark, in Emmanuel Biset's term, the "co-belonging of philosophy and politics" in the metaphysical tradition through a certain affirmation of a community of subjects, and which must now be vanquished and left behind (*Violencia, justicia y política*, 25).[4] Against heliopolitics the Levinasian term would be "ex-cendence" ("Violence," 85), that is, "a departure from being and from the categories which describe it" following the Platonic notion of an *epekeina tes ousias*, a beyond the substance or beyond being that marks the Levinasian way of positing a radical departure from the philosophical and political tradition of the West and toward the conception of a "community of nonpresence, and therefore of nonphenomenality. Not a community without light, not a blindfolded synagogue, but a community anterior to Platonic light" ("Violence," 91).[5]

As we know, it is the thought of the Other, the "radical priority" of the face of the Other, that organizes for Lévinas the very possibility of ex-cendence, hence of a politics that could not be captured under the name of heliopolitics. This ex-cendence will be described by Derrida toward the end of the essay as "the *dream* of a purely *heterological* thought. . . . A *pure* thought of *pure* difference" whose "true name" is "empiricism," since "the experience of the other . . . is irreducible and is therefore 'the experience par excellence'" (151–52). Through empiricism, says Derrida, Lévinas "is resigned to betraying his own intentions in his philosophical discourse" (151) by opening it to non-philosophy. "Empiricism always has been determined by philosophy, from Plato to Husserl, as *non-philosophy*: as the philosophical pretention to non-philosophy, the inability to justify oneself, to come to one's own aid as speech. But this incapacitation, when resolutely assumed, contests the resolution and coherence of the *logos* (philosophy) at its root, instead of letting itself be questioned by the *logos*. Therefore, nothing can so profoundly *solicit* the Greek logos—philosophy—as this irruption of the totally-other; and nothing can to such an extent reawaken the *logos* to its origin as to its mortality, its other" (152).

The words just quoted mark at the same time the point of maximum proximity and the point of maximum distance between the Levinasian and the Derridean projects (and we can certainly read in this, a bit abysmally, a doubling of Levinasian community, or of the Derridean definition of it: "*eros* in which, within the proximity to the other, distance is integrally maintained; *eros* whose *pathos* is made simultaneously of this proximity and this duality" ["Violence," 90–91]). Throughout his essay Derrida has been at pains to show how Lévinas fundamentally misreads both Husserlian phenomenology and Heideggerian ontology, how Lévinas in fact presupposes both Husserl and Heidegger at the very same time he brings them into question. And yet, Derrida says, "the legitimacy of this putting into question does not seem to us any less radical" (133). We now see the reason: the step into non-philosophy in the wake of a radical empiricism, the "irreducible experience" of the other, sanctions the legitimacy of Lévinas's procedure, which nevertheless Derrida will not follow, or not all the way through. The question is, therefore, why. For me it is also and precisely the question of a specifically Derridean infrapolitics.

I think the answer might be attempted through the second mention of the word "politics" in the Derridean essay. Derrida is arguing that Lévinas gets Heidegger's notion of being wrong, by conceptualizing it as a (part of a) philosophy of power, according to the following words: "To affirm the priority of *Being* over the *existent* is to decide the essence of philosophy; it is to subordinate the relation with *someone*, who is an existent (the ethical relation), to a relation with the *Being of the existent*, which, impersonal, permits the apprehension, the domination of the existent (a relationship of knowing), subordinates justice to freedom" (Lévinas quoted by Derrida, "Violence," 135). Derrida says that there can be, in Heidegger's work, no question of a subordination of any existent to being, therefore no subordination of any ethical relation to any ontological relation, to the extent that "there can be an order of priority only between two determined things, two existents" (136). But being, in Heidegger's determination, "is but the Being-of this existent, and does not exist outside it as a foreign power, or as a hostile or neutral impersonal element.

The neutrality so often denounced by Lévinas can only be the characteristic of an undetermined existent, or an anonymous ontic power, of a conceptual generality, or of a principle" (136), hence it is in no case a neutrality of being. The second mention of "politics" comes, rather unexpectedly, a few pages later, but still in the context of this discussion:

> Being itself commands nothing or no one. As Being is not the lord of the existent, its priority (ontic metaphor) is not an *archia*. The best liberation from violence is a certain putting into question, which makes the search for an *archia* tremble. Only the thought of Being can do so, and not traditional "philosophy" or "metaphysics." The latter are therefore "politics" which can escape ethical violence only by economy: by battling violently against the violences of the *an-archy* whose possibility, in history, is still the accomplice of archism. (141)

The possibility of anarchy is still complicitous with archism. This potential reversal is similar to that which obtains between empiricism and metaphysics, or between non-philosophy and philosophy. Or even between war and its opposite, hence between "politics," in the heliocentric sense Lévinas condemns, and the "eschatology of messianic peace" that is the beyond of war in Lévinas's *Totality and Infinity* (22). This is finally Derrida's objection, and it is not just any objection. It is, as I have already mentioned, the objection that separates both projects of thought at the moment of their maximum proximity.

The waiting position of the Negev wisemen could not exclude a certain ambiguity. In the words of Lévinas already quoted, "the human collectivity" is "pragmatically linked" to a political power "that remains unjustifiable in itself" "while it waits for something better." In the wait, which is a messianic awaiting, Levinasian infrapolitics finds its fullness and its limit. Derrida takes his distance upon positing, even while not making it absolutely clear, an endless politicization without horizon, that is to say, in and through the very absence of that upon which one waits. This is also an interruption of the waiting. He calls it "secondary war:" "This secondary war, as the avowal of violence, is the least possible violence, the only way to repress the worst violence, the violence of primitive and prelogical silence, of an unimaginable night which would not even be the opposite of nonviolence: nothingness, or pure nonsense. Thus discourse chooses itself violently in opposition to nothingness or pure nonsense, and, in philosophy, against nihilism . . . This infinite passage through violence is what is called history" ("Violence," 130). But why would one opt for the lesser violence as opposed to the greater violence? To a certain extent—but let us not take this as a failure in Derrida's essay; there must be reasons for it—no reason is given. Lesser violence is an option for inscription, perhaps even a pragmatic one, a decision in the order of the immemorial, since no one will ever remember having made it: it belongs to the end of the wait and produces itself as the end of the wait, but it follows no previously given ethical or political light. It is, however, precisely and resolutely, the suspension of the wait, and it thus differs from Levinasian infrapolitics. It opposes the wait to the suspension of the wait. It is a decision that takes place in the region of the nonpolitical opening of politics, it is the opening itself, and it is also in the region of the nonethical opening of ethics: against nothingness and pure nonsense, against nihilism. Perhaps this is the ostensible reason, which would then call for a reason of the reason. This is the obscure, infrapolitical site where it becomes possible to say that one would rather be in politics beyond politics, in ethics beyond ethics, or in history, without a beyond, in a history with no wait, beyond wait.

Since this is an important question for later developments in Derridian thought, and specifically for the issue of the messianic-emancipatory promise, let me dwell on it briefly. Martin Hägglund, repeating a Derridean motif already mentioned, speaks about "temporal alterity as the nonethical opening of ethics" (*Radical*, 97). For Hägglund, temporal alterity is not a region but rather a constitutive condition of life that requires what Hägglund calls "originary discrimination" (98, see also 101). He goes on:

> Temporal alterity gives rise to both the desirable *and* the undesirable, to every chance *and* every menace. Hence, alterity cannot answer to someone or something that one ought to "respect" unconditionally. Rather, it precipitates affirmations *and* negations, confirmations *and* resistances, in relation to undecidable events that stem from the "same" infinite finitude. There is thus no opposition between undecidability and decisions in Derrida's thinking. On the contrary, it is the undecidable future that necessitates decisions. One is always forced to confront temporal alterity and engage in decisions that only can be made from time to time, in accordance with essentially corruptible calculations. (97)

Hägglund also says that "In [Derrida's] *Adieu* the nonethical opening of ethics is described as an arche-perjury or arche-betrayal that makes us doubly exposed to violence: 'exposed to undergo it but also to exercise it'" (99). But even all of that cannot appease the question as to why such originary discrimination must submit itself to choosing the lesser violence, even from a flexible definition of 'lesser,' which is obviously always a matter of interested comparison (lesser for whom?). It would be easy to show that the greater violence could in a moment of decision posit itself as apotropaic, engaged in the name of a future diminishing of violence, but then the very notion of a lesser violence becomes moot or unhelpful. A short story by Javier Marías brings the point home: The narrator complains to a friend that he has a business rival who is making his life impossible. The friend tells him he can solve the problem and sets an appointment for him with a fellow. The fellow turns out to be an assassin. The narrator is of course shocked and tells the assassin that he never thought the solution could be murder. The assassin tells the narrator he is sorry about the misunderstanding, but they must now conclude the meeting since he has another appointment. As the narrator exits the Palace Hotel, in one of whose coffee shops the conversation took place, he sees his rival come in and approach the table of the assassin.[6] One must conclude that, within "Violence and Metaphysics," Derrida gives no explicit answer to the question, and the unanswered question takes Derrida, some years later, to his considerations on messianic justice, which is perhaps equally irresolutive. In any case, the option between lesser and greater violence, as a political option, would seem to remain secondary or derived, as it always refers to its conditions, to the region of the nonpolitical opening of politics, which remains enigmatic.

The secondary war of history is the political scene. It is secondary in the face of a hypothetical originary violence, the founding violence of inscription as such, the founding violence of appearance. The co-belonging of philosophy and politics, even as a fallen metaphysical concept, has everything to do with this "economy of war" ("Violence," 148) that assures us there will be no end to conflict as such, there will be no peace but only the negotiated exchange between the inevitability and the unjustifiability of tyrannical power. We are at a junction that can be conceived of, or that Derrida understands, as the crossing of two eschatologies: on the one hand, an epochal, polemological eschatology of erring; on the other hand, an eschatology of messianic peace. The first is associated with Heidegger, and linked to the years immediately following *Being and Time* (1927): " 'Every epoch of world history is an epoch of erring.' . . . If Being is time and history, then erring and the epochal essence of Being are irreducible" ("Violence," 145). The messianic eschatology of peace, the awaiting and the attendant anticipatory move toward a time beyond politics, beyond violence, beyond division and conflict, a time of peace, is Levinasian eschatology. Alluding to right-wing Heideggerian positions, Derrida makes it clear in some brief remarks that it is simply not possible to ascribe an eschatology of the Site to Heidegger, according to which conflict and division could also be finally reconciled through some return to the home. There is an erring through which being dissimulates itself, veils itself through every possible ontic determination that occurs. The veiling of being is history as such, within which "the sacred, it is true, appears. But the god remains distant" (Heidegger quoted in "Violence," 146). The point is that the structure of dissimulation is a counterpoint to the erring that it institutes, which means that erring is precisely not all: and this minimal or maximal not-all is the Heideggerian eschatology. In Heidegger, in a certain Heidegger, it organizes history, as it were, it is history itself, and therefore also the opening and the possibility of a future time not subjected to principle or warranty. In Lévinas, however, history finds its impassable limit in the ahistoricity of the ethical relation, which creates a beyond-history in the timeless time of the traumatic and immemorial encounter with the other. There are two eschatologies, but only the first one is good for Derrida.

Whether politics can be deemed to be unjustifiable but inevitable is to be thought differently from the horizon of history as erring or from the horizon of the immemorial time beyond history. This difference is of course determining for any conception of political practice, but it also marks a different infrapolitical understanding. The ancients of Negev knew that there is a certain irreducible structure of waiting within politics whose tonality now doubles up. The minimal difference is also, opens up into, the maximum difference. This is the way Derrida describes it, in what to my mind is the fundamental point of "Violence and Metaphysics," which opens the very space of a nonheliopolitical infrapolitics that ultimately Lévinas thinks he must abandon in favor of a peculiar sun beyond substance, his *epekeina tes ousias*, the sun beyond the sun of eschatological peace:

> [For Heidegger] Being is . . . the *first dissimulated* . . . For Levinas, on the contrary, Being . . . is the *first dissimulating*, and the ontico-ontological difference thereby would neutralize difference, the infinite alterity of the totally-other. The ontico-ontological difference, moreover, would be conceivable only on the basis of the idea of the Infinite, or the unanticipatable irruption of the totally-other existent. For Levinas, as for Heidegger, language would be at once a coming forth and a holding back; enlightenment and obscurity; and for both, dissimulation would be a conceptual gesture. But for Levinas, the concept is on the plane of Being; for Heidegger it is on the plane of ontic determination. ("Violence," 149)

Derrida proposes an infrapolitics of radically ontic determination, clearly leaning on Heideggerian themes, every time and for the duration of time, that will not let itself be subject to any heliopolitical rescue, and against the Levinasian empirico-messianic infrapolitics—but also, at the same time, against any Husserlian-Heideggerian heliopolitics, and finally against Heideggerian heliopolitics, always latent or otherwise readable in the Heideggerian text.

For the Lévinas of the *Nouvelles lectures talmudiques*, as we saw, democratic politics occurs in the radical solicitation of tyrannical power, understood as unjustified but inevitable at and in the time of waiting. Demotic irruption can always happen in history, within history, that is, until the waiting is over and politics ceases altogether (or until an analogical claim is made that such is already the case, as it will have happened in every hegemonic political regime certain of itself—is this not the only plausible way of interpreting Donald Trump's contention that he can and will only lose reelection if the voting is rigged, and in no other way?). What I am calling Derridean infrapolitics suspends the waiting and posits an endless but in every case imminent political horizon marked both by erring and by the questioning of every dissimulation, where no analogical claims become possible because they are in advance consigned to unjustifiability. If there is, in that double perspective, something like a co-belonging of politics and thought in the shadow of heliopolitics, against all tyranny, and this time without a remainder, then it happens because the subtraction of politics, the difference of politics with itself—the Levinasian hatred of the complicitous friends of the tyrant equals the hatred of the tyrant—refers to its nonpolitical opening: to what subceeds political errancy, which politics guards but also incessantly destroys. If there is a co-belonging of thought and politics, it can be sustained only on the infrapolitical ground that is its constitutive condition. The infrapolitical condition of politics could then in every case be the site of Derrida's "lesser violence."

Coda

Let me offer a brief gloss of what a Derridean option for an eschatology of erring or errancy may mean for infrapolitical reflection but refraining from any attributions to Derrida of things he did not explicitly affirm. They could be implicit, whether in "Violence and Metaphysics" or elsewhere, but the reader will have to decide for herself. In any case, what follows is no longer necessarily interpretation of the Derridean 1964 essay, but rather aims at reading Heidegger's 1930 essay "On the Essence of Truth," the final version of which appeared in *Pathmarks* (1967, but the book was expanded and revised in 1976).[7]

In the Note added to the end of the text, Heidegger says that in the phrase "the truth of essence" (from which the essence of truth must arise, after interpretation) it is important to understand "essence" verbally not nominally, and that such a change in understanding determines that in the phrase "remaining still within metaphysical presentation, Beyng is thought as the difference that holds sway between Being and beings" (153). "Truth" refers to a "sheltering that clears as the fundamental trait of Being" (153). But that truth of essence that still corresponds to metaphysical presentation mutates into "the essence of truth:" "The answer to the question of the essence of truth is the saying of a turning within the history of Beyng. Because the sheltering that clears belongs to it, Beyng appears originarily in the light of concealing withdrawal. The name of this clearing is *aletheia*" (154). This is for Heidegger "a turn within the history of Being" (170).

The turning there named corresponds to "decisive steps" vis-à-vis *Being and Time*, through which we find access to a notion of truth as "ek-sistent freedom" and "as concealing and as errancy" (154). The concealing withdrawal as truth, or the truth as concealing withdrawal, implies a "change in the questioning that belongs to the overcoming of metaphysics" (170). Heidegger claims, therefore, that such a discovery is already the result, or performs in itself, a decisive movement in the recuperation of the ontological difference. "Beyng" (*Seyn*) is now errancy, and with it "every kind of anthropology and all subjectivity of the human being as subject is not merely left behind" (154). Rather, with it we proceed to a "transformed historical position" (154). Errancy is already, Heidegger says not only in 1930 but also through the period of publication and republication of *Pathmarks*, postmetaphysical thought, or a move toward it. Barely three years after *Being and Time*, Heidegger takes a tenuous but clearly stated distance from all politics of being and from the overwhelming metaphorization of being as forgetfulness. In "On the Essence of Truth" there is talk of an opening in comportment, of a freedom, ek-sistent, proper to Dasein, that consists of relating to truth as the letting-be of beings, in both the objective and subjective senses of the genitive. Letting-be must be actively understood, not in the fallen sense of leaving alone: it is a letting be of the thing, letting it be what it is, also as concealing withdrawal and as sheltering that clears. The proposed comportment has to do with a relation with the open region where things can be let be. That open region is truth as *aletheia*. But that also means that the historical human being can participate in the endeavor of distortion and dissimulation: "Because truth is in essence freedom, historical human beings can, in letting beings be, also *not* let beings be the beings that they are and as they are" (146). The mode of relation of the human being to truth moves toward being its relation to untruth. But untruth is not more proper to the human than truth—or less. Untruth also derives from truth as *aletheia*, as unconcealment, but in such a way that what comes into unconcealment is concealment, what is disclosed is closedness: "In the ek-sistent freedom of Da-sein a concealing of beings as a whole comes to pass. Here there *is* concealment" (148).

Concealment is untruth. Every unconcealment comes from concealment, hence untruth is "older even than letting-be itself" (148). Heidegger calls this "the mystery" (148: "The proper non-essence of truth is the mystery"). The mystery is the fact that concealment is the first thing that conceals itself, which means that truth happens first of all as untruth. "This bearing toward concealing conceals itself in letting a forgottenness of the mystery take precedence and disappearing in such forgottenness" (149). In forgottenness the human being holds fast to what is at hand, what is accessible. "This persistence [in holding fast] has its unwitting support in that *bearing* by which Dasein not only ek-sists but also at the same time *in-sists*, i.e., holds fast to what is offered by beings, as if they were open of and in themselves" (150). Heidegger calls the life where mystery as the forgotten essence of truth strongly abides "in-sistent ek-sistence" (150). In-sistent ek-sistence is the state of errancy. It is neither optional nor accidental. It belongs in an irreducible manner to the constitution of Dasein: "The errancy through which human beings stray is not something that, as it were, extends alongside them like a ditch into which they occasionally stumble; rather, errancy belongs to the inner constitution of the Da-sein into which historical human beings are admitted" (150).

If that is the case, what are the political consequences? Not, of course, that in political existence a catastrophic drift is always possible and became actual for Heidegger. But it is conceivable that, from the postulates of "On the Essence of Truth," no Nazi politics of being would have been possible. Heidegger himself says in that text, "By leading them astray, errancy dominates human beings through and through. But, as leading astray, errancy at the same time contributes to a possibility that humans are capable of drawing up from their ek-sistence—the possibility that, by experiencing errancy itself and by not mistaking the mystery of Da-sein, they *not* let themselves be led astray" (151). The latter is an infrapolitical word—perhaps the clearest indication of a Heideggerian infrapolitics: to experience errancy itself as errancy, against every mythical projection, in the nakedness of a traumatic awakening: awakening to forgottenness as forgottenness. In errancy as errancy in-sistent ek-sistence unforgets the forgottenness of the mystery. An eschatology of errancy, which I tried to show earlier becomes Derrida's own wager, is the infrapolitical attempt at an impossible memory that it would be best not to call promise. Its name—Heidegger calls it "freedom" (151)—is the passage to the act of a demotic errancy that understands that its main qualification—nothing else is necessary—is to know no one is qualified, because "*nadie es más que nadie*," nobody is subjected to anybody else's truth, and nobody is trivially a subject to truth.[8]

8
A Negation of the Anarchy Principle

I go out far away from my home, as a hostage, without ever taking up habitation with you, nor ever being your guest, since you have no residence, but I also thereby fulfill my calling, which is to be at home no longer.

—JEAN-FRANÇOIS LYOTARD

Jean-François Lyotard's posthumous book *Logique de Lévinas* (Lévinas's Logic, 2015) brings together some texts on Emmanuel Lévinas or around Levinasian themes that complement the section of Lyotard's *Le différend* (The Differend, 1983) devoted to the French-Lithuanian thinker. In *The Differend* there is a chapter entitled "Obligation," where Lyotard engages with Lévinas and Kant in the fragmented, quasi-aphoristic style that is the hallmark of the book. Lyotard makes some observations that have a bearing on what can conceivably be understood as the ontological difference with a Levinasian twist. Everything has to do with the difference between prescription and description, or with the difference between what Lyotard calls the "ethical phrase (infinity)" and the "speculative phrase (totality)" (*Differend*, 115). Lyotard adds:

> When the universe in which you are the addressee entails an addressor instance that is left empty, and is perhaps "absolutely" not marked, not even by a silence, that is the ethical situation, or the disposition of the universe presented by a phrase of obligation. But that cannot be inscribed into your own experience. For, in this universe, you are presented on the *you* instance, you are called, but experience and cognition take place in the first person, or at least as a self. What you judge

to be the Lord's call is the situation of *you* when *I* is deprived of experience, "estranged," "alienated," "disauthorized." You do not therefore have the experience of the Lord, nor even of alienness. If you were to have that experience, it would not be the Lord, and it would not be ethics. You cannot therefore testify that whatever it is that calls upon you is somebody. And that is precisely the ethical universe. (115–16)

We can suspend for a moment whatever it is that the notion of "ethics" prompts in you. Make no presumptions: Lyotard is pretty fierce in this respect, stating as he does that the "addressor instance is left empty." There is no "somebody" on the other side. There is no one. We have no idea. All we know is that there is a form of discourse, prescriptive, a form of discourse that Reiner Schürmann would have called "imperative" against any notion of merely "indicative" discourse, a form of discourse linked to a "peregrinal ontology" (*Wandering*, 29, 69–73, 87). If *"toute pensée n'est pas savoir"* (not all thought is knowledge; Lyotard, *Logique*, 89), then there is a form of thought whose momentum would be something other than knowledge, nondenotative thought, responsive thought, indeed imperative thought. The reflection is simple: prescription obligates not by referring to truth or falsity. It obligates in terms of what is just. But prescription is not politics, even if politics, in its democratic instantiation, which is the only possible one since nondemocratic politics is merely a game of interests, business not politics, is also about the just. Where is the difference? Democratic politics must universalize its procedures, must turn all decisions into a norm valid for all. Infrapolitics does not universalize, does not normativize. It provides no knowledge. Is it therefore an "ethical praxis" in the Lyotardian sense? I want to explore this problem in the wake of a number of difficulties I have with Schürmann's work. After that I will return to Lyotard's posthumous book—which could in a sense be considered a heartless book, an unfinished book, nothing more than the dream of an editor, since Lyotard himself had no idea such a book would be published under his name.

Four Disagreements

At the end of *Heidegger on Being and Acting: From Principles to Anarchy* (286–89), Schürmann explicates four "Consequences for the Direction of Life." Schürmann suggests that his Heidegger interpretation imposes some obligations on the thinker. I will attempt to describe infrapolitical obligations in disagreement with the alleged "consequences" Schürmann posits regarding Heideggerian thought. My first disagreement has to do with what Schürmann mentions as the no longer "heuristic" function of *Being and Time*'s concentration on "everyday activities" in view of the need to establish a "fundamental ontology." But, beyond the establishment of a fundamental ontology, he says,

> there is another priority of praxis in Heidegger, which appears as early as in *Being and Time* and which remains operative throughout all of his work: to retrieve the being question from the point of view of time, a certain way of life is required. To understand authentic temporality, it is necessary to "exist authentically"; to think being as letting phenomena be, one must oneself "let all things be"; to follow the play without why of presencing, it is necessary "to live without why." Here the priority of praxis is no longer heuristic. . . . According to the mainstream of the metaphysical tradition, acting follows being; for Heidegger, on the other hand, a particular kind of acting appears as the condition for understanding being as time. Here praxis determines thinking. In writings subsequent to *Being and Time*, it is suggested that this praxis is necessarily of a political nature. (287)

There is, then, the call for a certain way of life according to which acting is a precondition of understanding, and praxis determines thinking. This second (nonheuristic, noncognitive) priority of praxis is fundamental to the infrapolitical constellation, which emphasizes it and names it "existential." A praxis of existence—not a politics, not an ethics, certainly not a disciplinarization or institutionalization of existence, which is the reason why infrapolitics breaks and must break with university discourse—opens the way to infrapolitical reflection to the very same extent that infrapolitical thought cannot be premised on anything but a specific relation to existence, a *form* of life.

But Schürmann all too quickly says, "this praxis is necessarily of a political nature." Why is that? Whether Heidegger himself indicated the possible political relevance of this existential understanding of praxis is probably irrelevant one way or another, but it may not be totally irrelevant regarding the fundamental thrust of Schürmann's interpretation. There is, in or behind the attribution to the late Heidegger of a (reluctantly) "anarchic" political drift, an assumption perhaps essential to the work of Schürmann that I would not share: that changes in thinking, in order to be relevant, are necessarily epochal, that is, historical or historial (even if, at a certain point, under the hypothesis of the closure of metaphysics, their epochal or historial stance would mark, according to Schürmann, the end of epochality, the end of epochal history), and, as epochal, they reach and affect and shape and force the compliance of the totality of the political collectivity as such. In other words, the supposition is that the discovery of a nonheuristic, noncognitive praxis of existence must become "political" in order to be hearable or in order to reach the dignity of properly historical presence—that, indeed, there is no historical presence without political relevance, and vice versa.

Schürmann names his own political practice "anarchy." For Schürmann "anarchy," on his terms, is not the singular choice of a thinker but rather the offspring of the contemporary economy of presencing, with which the (contemporary) thinker should comply. Anarchy would be a paradoxical *nomos* at the end of principial (metaphysical) epochs, that is, at the end of the time of metaphysical epochs. "The *nomos* or injunction always and everywhere determines the *oikos*, the abode of man" (235). But I would like to argue that there is a certain incoherence in claiming both that thinking presupposes a particular *exercitium* that belongs to the thinker's singular existence (a change in the direction of life, the obligation of a nonheuristic, noncognitive praxis before understanding, an existential immersion in existence) and claiming at the same time that thinking only lives through attunement to a nomic or temporal presencing that affects everyone. I would say, rather, that changes in the direction of life do not have to become historical or epochal, do not have to become "political" and bind everyone, in order to appear as obligations, hence already dramatically relevant for the singular endeavor of thought.

The second problem I would like to point out in Schürmann's Heidegger interpretation follows from the first. Schürmann says:

> Being can be understood as time only through its difference from history. The investigation into the concrete epochs and their regulation is what binds the later Heidegger's phenomenology to experience. Since this is, however, not an individual's experience, the issue of phenomenology proves to be political in a broad sense. An economy of presence is the way in which, for a given age, the totality of what becomes phenomenal arranges itself in mutual relations. Any economy is therefore necessarily public. (287)

The politicity of epochs has to do with the fact that epochs force an order of the visible (things, words, actions) into an order of domination. Principial epochs—all epochs are based and even founded on principial rule—guarantee the domination of the principle as hegemonic domination: at the time of modernity, for instance, subjectivism dominates hegemonically, and it dominates all orders of existence: politically as well as philosophically or artistically, and in any other register of cognition. But Schürmann's distinction between history and time prepares his affirmation of an end of epochal history that opens the visibility of presencing as nondomination.

At the end of the cycle of principial epochality, where we hypothetically are (this is what is called "the closure of metaphysics," as the mark of our time), the thinker can move or prepare the way for anarchy as nondomination, that is, as principial de-nomination. But the politicity of the thinker is then either prophetic or it has the character of a historical vanguard. In both cases it appears as messianic, as it incorporates and enables a promise: the "early" correspondence of the thinker, as a response to an incipient unconcealing presencing of historical time, is a commitment to and an announcement of a general dispensation to come, a dispensation that, on becoming general, becomes political as well. The thinker appears in this account as the vanguard of history, as a preparer, as a harbinger. The thinker is still, in this account, a worldhistorical figure, a hero in a sense that becomes hardly distinguishable from the Hegelian determination of the hero. Infrapolitics must take exception. Infrapolitics prefers to consider its own time, which is the time of posthegemony, as the deconstruction of all political legitimation, including therefore the preparatory, anticipatory, or transitional legitimation of a purported, posthistorical economy of presencing of universal reach. Infrapolitics gives up on preparatory thinking (it is, in that sense, a nonmessianic thinking of the nowtime) as it refuses to countenance the distinction between history and time.

This is the third problem: "The hypothesis of closure results from the reduplication 'will to will' substituting itself for the difference 'being and entities.' Enframing, then, is not like any other principle. It is transcendence abolished. Total mechanization and administration are only the most striking features of this abolition and reduplication, of this loss of every epochal principle; a loss that, as Heidegger suggests, is happening before our eyes" (288). For Schürmann technology would be "the age without a beyond" (285) that terminates the epochal cycle, the history of being. He claims that, at the end of the epochs, "originary time" resurfaces into a presencing no longer to be understood as the constant presence of the metaphysical dispensation. Responding to originary time—the worlding of the world, the thinging of the thing—is what the thinker today prepares: "to think is to follow the event of presencing, without recourse to principial representations" (286). But the withering away of epochs need not be thought of as the welcoming of an unepochal dispensation, about which we know nothing and we experience nothing others may not have also known and experienced in any of the previous transitional times. Infrapolitics does not pretend that its claim is a claim about the end of history as such, the end of epochality, it makes no claim about the singular experience of time it enables, it makes no claim that others, our ancestors, in their epochal perplexity and delusion, were stuck in a dead end the will to will has now cleared by opening up, through its very intensification, an inaugural glimpse into an entirely other time, the time of non-epochal or nonhistorial history. Infrapolitics remains content with its affirmation of a "simple dwelling" in the here and now, instead of thinking of itself as the promoter of a "step into the blue" (284) at the abyssal end of the history of being. Another way of putting this, maybe, would be to say that the time of infrapolitics is always the time of what Schürmann refers to as "the legislative-transgressive fracture" or double bind (*Broken*, 25), a posthegemonic time that refuses legislation and refrains from transgressing it into an alternative one.

And, as to the fourth problem, Schürmann says: "*Poiein kata phusin*. . . . Thinking is essentially compliant with the flux of coming-to-presence, with constellations that form and undo themselves. To think is to follow the event of appropriation, to follow *phuein*" (289). Schürmann proposes two master terms for such compliance: nonattachment and releasement, both taken from Heidegger in specific reference to Meister Eckhart. There is certainly a difference between submitting to ordering principles and "acting according to presencing," in compliance with the worlding of the world and the thinging of the thing. But who guarantees the public, collective, universal compliance with the second under the guise of the (transitional and paradoxical) principle according to which there are no principles? A second-order hegemony, in this case presumably guaranteed by the thinkers and the poets to come, would be no better than the pedestrian economy of the principle. Infrapolitics prefers the suspension of compliance, not out of any fundamental suspicion toward the mysterious dispensations of the fourfold, rather out of a fundamental suspicion of its interpreters. Letting-be is infrapolitically to be thought of as, indeed, existential releasement for the sake of a radical attachment to the free singularity of existence, which is therefore also an unattachment to everything else. Letting-be is not to be thought of, infrapolitically, as the secret hegemony of the thinkers and the poets to come. It is only what singular existents do if they would.

Let me sum up the four disagreements, which are disagreements regarding Schürmann's drawing of consequences after his otherwise admirable interpretation of Heideggerian thought. They all amount not to a rupture with Schürmann's thought, but rather to its infrapoliticization. Schürmann's Heidegger interpretation remains all too political—that is in a sense both its strength, celebrated as such when the book was published, as it was a radically revisionist interpretation of Heidegger's politicity, and its weakness, to the extent things can be seen otherwise. All of the disagreements also have to do with the structure of obligation. Against Schürmann, first disagreement, the obligation of thought is not an obligation of a historico-political nature; the obligation of infrapolitical thought, second disagreement, is not of the order of the heroic, and it cannot be, as it does not found itself on a difference between time and history that necessarily turns history into a site of cognitive dispensation as opposed to the mere existentiality of the time of life; infrapolitical obligation, third disagreement, does not depend upon the final catastrophe of the principle that kills all principles, technology or the will to will as the unintentional provider of originary time, and infrapolitical obligation does not respond to the event of post-technological presencing, it is fond of no steps into the blue, and it does not like to fall into any unthinkable abyss of the "not-beyond"; finally, infrapolitical obligation, fourth disagreement, does not claim to breach the path for universal compliance with the presencing of the fourfold, the worlding of the world, or the thinging of the thing. Infrapolitical obligation, through those disagreements which are perhaps better to be understood as a negation of the premise, appears as a much more modest endeavor. We could sum them all up into the negation of the principle of anarchy as exposed by Schürmann, to which I now turn.

The Principle of Anarchy

The original French title of *Heidegger on Being and Acting: From Principles to Anarchy* is *Le principe d'anarchie* (1982), that is, the principle of anarchy. The admittedly complicated conjunction between "principle" and "anarchy" is motivated, for Schürmann, on the alleged or suspected fact that the "hypothesis of metaphysical closure," and the consequent loss of any recourse to principles or principial thought, do not immediately condemn us to an aprincipial world, since, on the "transitional" line, at the line but not beyond the line, we can only think, our language can only offer us to think, the lack of a recourse to principles through the painful enunciation of the principle of anarchy, the principle of nonprinciples. The principle of anarchy would necessarily be a precarious phrase—no principle if anarchy, no anarchy if principles; and yet, there is a principle of anarchy as a placeholder for an unthinkable time to come where anarchy would (have) dissolve(d) the principiality of any principle, including itself as principle. This is not a trivial affair. If, as Schürmann establishes at the end of *Broken Hegemonies*, a hubristic insistence on the maintenance of principles as constant presence equals something like (nonethical, nonmoral, but nevertheless overwhelming) evil, the principle of anarchy might also be considered historical evil—is it not after all a reluctant recourse to principles in the last instance, in the very face of the absence of principles? Is it not a desperate clinging to the principle—an irremediable and yet radically bogus extension of its presence—under the ruse of anarchy? How are we to preempt the hypothesis of closure from being hijacked by the ultimate catastrophe—its falsity? Would the principle of anarchy still be a bite into evil, apotropaic or not, but in any case fundamentally a most serious kind of bite, to the extent that it knows itself as evil even if it is committed to minimizing its growth and expansion? This cannot be what Derrida meant with his "lesser violence."

Lévinas, whose work could be considered committed to the awakening of goodness in his sense, published *Otherwise Than Being* in 1974. Chapter 4 opens with a section on "Principle and Anarchy" (99–102). It could have been expected that any posterior attempt at dealing with the "and" in Lévinas's phrase would refer back to that work and those pages—and to the rest of the Levinasian chapter those pages initiate. And yet Schürmann's *Heidegger on Being and Acting* devotes only one footnote to Lévinas (see 346, on the difference between originary and original Parmenidism, which will not concern us), and, let us say, half of another one, whose main thrust is intended as a sharp critique of Derrida. That section of the second footnote states:

> Among the company of writers, notably in France, who today herald the Nietzschean discovery that the origin as one was a fiction, there are those who espouse the multiple origin with jubilation, and this is apparently the case with Deleuze. There are others who barely conceal their regret over the loss of the One, and this may indeed be the case with Derrida. It suffices to listen to him express his debt to Lévinas: "I relate this concept of trace to what is at the center of the latest work of Emmanuel Lévinas," Jacques Derrida, *Of Grammatology*, p. 70. The article by Emmanuel Lévinas to which he refers announces in its very title—"*La trace de l'autre*," the Other's trace—how far Derrida has traveled from his mentor. For Derrida, the discovery that the "trace" does not refer back to an Other whose trace it would be is like a bad awakening: "arch-violence, loss of the proper, of absolute proximity, of self-presence, in truth the loss of what has never taken place, of a self-presence which has never been given but only dreamed of," ibid., p. 112. (Schürmann, *Heidegger*, 321–22n44)

It is a strange and not easily understandable note. There is no mention in it of Lévinas's take on "principle" and "anarchy," or on "principle and anarchy," unless we extend the intended critique of Derrida into an indirect critique of Lévinas's notion of the trace (which refers to an Other understood as neighbor), as always already nostalgic of the pure presence of the One. If so, there would be a terminal disagreement at the level of conceptualization. But the footnote does not really warrant it. In fact, the footnote might on equal or even hermeneutically superior grounds be taken to be an endorsement of the Levinasian position against the Derridean "bad awakening." In that case

Schürmann would be approving, or at least not disapproving, of the Levinasian notion of the trace as strictly the trace of the Other. But what about Schürmann's relation with "principle and anarchy" as Lévinas discusses it?

For Lévinas, "consciousness" does not exhaust the horizon of being and should not be, against modernity, considered the name of the being of beings. Or perhaps it can be considered precisely that, but then the positing of a non- or meontological region (from the Greek *"me,"* meaning "non"), beyond being, certainly beyond consciousness, becomes obligatory. Within that structure, "principle" is very much on the side of consciousness: in fact, subjectivity is the principle invoked in the phrase "principle and anarchy," as the following quotation attests:

> Being a theme, being intelligible or open, possessing oneself, losing itself and finding itself out of an ideal principle, an *arche*, in its thematic exposition, being thus carries on its affair of being. The detour of ideality [Lévinas has just said that "even an empirical, individual being is broached across the ideality of logos," 99] leads to coinciding with oneself, that is, to certainty, which remains the guide and guarantee of the whole spiritual adventure of being. But this is why this adventure is no adventure. It is never dangerous: it is self-possession, sovereignty, *arche*. (*Otherwise*, 99)

If there were to be a "spirituality" beyond "the philosophical tradition of the West," it would have to be found beyond the sovereign consciousness, that is, beyond always already archic being. It would be the place of "anarchy." Of a dangerous and adventurous anarchy. Anarchy is presented by Lévinas as a persecution and an obsession. "The subject is affected without the source of the affection becoming a theme of representation" (101); "Anarchy is persecution. Obsession is a persecution where the persecution does not make up the content of a consciousness gone mad; it designates the form in which the ego is affected, a form which is a defecting from consciousness. This inversion of consciousness is no doubt a passivity—but it is a passivity beneath all passivity" (101). Far from being a hypertrophy of consciousness, it hits us as irremediable and always unwelcome trouble. It comes from outside. It is not domesticable, tamable, it admits of no reduction to *arche*. It is an absolute passion: "This passion is absolute in that it takes hold without any a priori" (102). Do we want it? But that question is only a question posited to consciousness, to the archic. Beyond consciousness, Lévinas says, we cannot resist it, and that is all there is to it.

Anarchy is therefore for Lévinas the unconditional call that befalls us from the Other, or the other, whomever that may be, and thus it is the dismantling of any archic certainty, the dismantling of the principle of consciousness or consciousness as principle. What is it, specifically? Lévinas calls it "a relationship with a singularity" (100). It therefore irrupts from a "proximity" we cannot organize or measure, and it is a proximity beneath all distances ("it cannot be reduced to any modality of distance or geometrical contiguity," 100–101). It is the "trace": "This way of passing, disturbing the present without allowing itself to be invested by the *arche* of consciousness, striating with its furrows the clarity of the ostensible, is what we have called a trace" (100).

Is this in any way commensurate to Schürmann's thought of the principle of anarchy? Does it come under the possible indirect critique in Schürmann's footnote? Yes, without a doubt, the Levinasian anarchy is "arch-violence, loss of the proper, of absolute proximity, of self-presence, in truth the loss of what has never taken place, of a self-presence which has never been given but only dreamed of" (100). Schürmann's critique may hint at the notion that any surprise in this regard, such as the Derridean one, would be always naïve or feigned. It is true that Lévinas makes it dependent on the encounter with the other as neighbor ("What concretely corresponds to this description is my relationship with my neighbor," 100). This is what Derrida is said to depart from, and what Schürmann seems perhaps, in our second reading, to take for granted as correct. But it is difficult to judge here whether Schürmann's acceptance of the notion of the trace as necessarily the trace of the face of the other in me, as face, that is, as human referent, is exclusive, in the sense that it would preempt an expansion of the trace referent. In fact, it does not seem it could be so. The irruption of anarchy would not for Schürmann, any more than for Derrida, be reducible to an encounter with human otherness, even if the encounter with human otherness could trigger it every time, or sometimes, also as a persecution and also as an obsession. In Lévinas the persecutory obsession of relational anarchy does not seem to be triggered by unspecified being, by being in general, or by being as difference, it would not seem to be triggered by, for instance, the "legislative-transgressive predicament" of a transitional time—it is always, it seems, a relationship with a singularity that does it, with an entity—the widow, the orphan, the neighbor—that poses a demand and imposes an obligation. We have already seen Lyotard's intended correction to the restrictive interpretation of ethical otherness in *The Differend*—for Lyotard the addressor may not be "somebody," may be absolutely unmarked.

But, leaving Lévinas's ultimate position aside, there is something else in Schürmann's gesture of (non)citation that should be questioned. Schürmann, by invoking the principle of anarchy as the political response in transitional times to the absence of metaphysical principles after the metaphysical closure, seems to naturalize, hence disavow, the persecutory aspect of meontological anarchy by positing (displeased) surprise at Derrida's feigned surprise and celebrating Deleuze's jubilation in the face of it. As if there were nothing particularly painful in being thrown over to an anarchic relation as radical obligation. As if, therefore, the resources of subjectivity—the subjectivity of the thinker—were or could be enough to keep the dangerous adventure of anarchy at bay, under control. The Schürmannian principle of anarchy could then be thought to be still the subjective reaction to the epochal dismantling of ontology (as metaphysics). But, if so, the principle of anarchy emerges, plainly, as principle, and principle of consciousness. Anarchy runs the risk of becoming yet another form of mastery, or rather: anarchy, as principle, is the last form of mastery. At the transitional time, posited as such by the hypothesis of metaphysical closure, metaphysics still runs the show as consolation and consolidation. But this may not be good enough. It is not exposure but counterexposure. It is reaction, taming, and reenclosure. Let us now see if Lyotard's unfinished work on Lévinas can help us deal with it.

Neither Norm nor Duty

Against the "Hegelian persecution" (*Logique*, 19), Lyotard finds in Lévinas the claim "the self does not proceed from the other; the other befalls the self" (24). The ethical phrase depends on the radical exteriority that Hegel's phenomenology must dismiss: "the demand of the exteriority of the exterior-interior relation is no less required for ethical discourse than the demand of the interiority of the same relation is required for phenomenological deployment" (27). In Hegelian terms, the speculative approach would concern the true and the false, whereas the nonspeculative engagement—discourses on justice, on aesthetics—would be relegated to "discursive arts" such as morals or politics, literature or rhetoric. But Lévinas inverts the terms and wants to claim that philosophy, as first philosophy, "does not consist in describing the rules that determine the truth or falsity of statements, but rather those that determine their justice or injustice" (29). The game is served. It has to do with establishing a philosophical procedure on prescriptions not descriptions. And it is prescriptions that introduce the anarchy that, without them, would be merely whimsical, another toy of principial consciousness. Lyotard says:

> An expression like "Welcome the stranger!" . . . must be valid not because it can be inferred from previously accepted statements, or because it would conform to more archaic propositions, rather from the only fact that it is an order that has its authority in itself. It is there-

fore in some way a command of command. In particular the considerable importance Lévinas attaches to the idea of anarchy resides in the refusal to infer normative statements. And it is also there where his attacks on ontology, not just Heideggerian but also for instance Spinozist, find their strength: ontology would only be another word for a metalanguage of descriptive statements. (37–38)

The thinker who made the most of the attempt to deal with prescriptions rather than descriptions in the philosophical tradition was Kant, whose notion of the categorical imperative in the second *Critique*, the *Critique of Practical Reason*, is ostensibly conceived of as an imperative. But Lyotard shows how the Kantian second *Critique* guts the anarchy of the Kantian imperative by referring it on the one hand to a causality (freedom) and on the other hand by referring it to the need for universal consensus, for normativization (40–60). Lévinas, against all of that, would have attempted to pursue the thought of an obligation never convertible into a norm, hence a savage obligation.

Norms pass through the understanding before they can force action, whereas obligations prompt action before understanding. In the latter case, obligations follow the Schürmannian specification of the nonheuristic, noncognitive praxis, and bring the issue into the region of existential infrapolitics. Infrapolitics must reject what Lyotard terms, following Lévinas, "the infatuation of the Self in knowledge" (65). The interruption of the domination of knowledge, that is, of the infatuation of the descriptive statement, is a precondition for infrapolitical exercise. Does it turn infrapolitics into an "ethical phrase"? "Do not let 'you' ever become 'I'" (73) is the prescription that Lyotard pragmatically extracts from his analysis: a prescription cannot be tamed into description. For Lyotard, the incommensurability between obligation and enunciation is also the incommensurability between the freedom of the sovereign subject and becoming-a-hostage to the addressor. And Lyotard says, "but the ethical and political question does not begin with the question of liberty where the I plays, it begins with the obligation that seizes the you. Not with the power to announce . . . but with the other power, which is in the West an impotence, which is to-be-required-for" (73).

Infrapolitics is a praxis outside the universe of knowledge. This characterization, seized by the power of unconditional obligation to no known addressor, is consistent with the four disagreements indicated earlier with Schürmann's Heidegger interpretation. There is no anarchy principle that does not turn anarchic persecution into a norm, that does not turn anarchic obsession into a universalizable duty. But norm and duty do not belong in the infrapolitical region. It is indeed possible that the universe of politics and ethics, that the universe of ethics and politics, begins in the obligation imposed by an unknown exteriority on the you. But it is also possible, if not necessary, that, before ethics and politics, another discursive instance is interposed—that which refers to the infrapolitical acknowledgment of an addressor without referent that replaces every possible solipsism and every possible infatuation with a practice of existence that could then be conceptualized only as a kind of savage moralism, subtracted from every norm.

9

On the Illegal Condition in the State of Extraction

How Not to Be an Informant

Glenn Greenwald, one of the journalists who helped Edward Snowden in his whistle-blowing tasks, titled his account of that story *No Place to Hide: Edward Snowden, the NSA, and the US Surveillance State*. The fact that we live in a surveillance state, that the state is surveillant today, that it thrives on information, that information is its currency and content, should not obscure the obvious corollary that information is us, and we are the referent of information. Think National Security Agency, yes, but think also of Google and Facebook, of Twitter and Instagram, of your email, of your annual reviews, of your post-tenure reviews, of your citations or lack thereof. You might find yourself trying to prove again and again that you have not smoked a single cigarette in the last ten years or that you are suffering from no preexisting condition, an impossible task of course, and then you will have to surrender your iPhone and laptop, together with their passwords, to the competent or incompetent airport authorities, and then to the highway patrol. And this is just the beginning. Your body temperature may be recorded from now on, as well as the history of all your associations with the sick and diseased. You may not be able to spend a dime without being examined at Central Computing. We become information, we are nothing but information—we are quantified, and our bodies are now, insofar as the state (or the workplace) is concerned, the primary site for information extraction and information use: information glorifies or abjects bodies. We are good or bad information, and we will be rewarded, or punished, accordingly.

For a surveillance state—surveillance is the state of the situation, not just the institutional state—the extraction of information becomes the primary modus operandi, and extraction, the task of extraction, develops and is developing a logic of its own that immediately becomes ideology. Think about how weird it is that your mood may be so dependent on a given weekend on how many likes you received on the picture of your ailing cat with happy mother, ailing mother with happy cat. Or on whether you had more or less than, say, twenty visits to your latest blog entry. Or on the fact that nobody has retweeted your last five Twitter posts, even though you were as sincere as you could have been in them. In the meantime, your screen time is consuming more and more of your day, as your iPhone is telling you even though you have not asked, and you spend most of the time waiting and waiting for some form of recognition, for a witnessing of your existence, without which you are nothing. And all of this, trivial or painful as it may be, in spite of the fact that you are still a citizen in legal condition, that is, a citizen within the democratic law that can still find shelter in the Kantian notion of freedom as autonomy. Imagine if you were illegal: the illegal condition would be a form of radical servitude, a form of contemporary radical servitude, just one among others, but perhaps also something more than just one, to the extent that it could be said that contemporary legal conditions push us all toward the illegal.

We live, increasingly, in a state of extraction, but we have not yet figured out the implications of a primary or fundamental logic of state extraction. We have not yet registered the fact that it will change our lives, a little at first, then a little more. We have not figured out its implications for our own predicament—for the predicament, that is, not of state functionaries as such, not of extractors and surveyors, which is a predicament of domination, but the predicament of those who would rather not be dominated, and who understand that giving up on their own domination of others, on their own efforts at extraction, is the logical price to be paid. These latter figures, those who refuse domination, those who prefer not to be dominated, hence not to dominate and not to extract—they might in fact constitute a border of the human, between the legal and the illegal, even a border of the border. They are the possible dwellers of a hyperborder behind which information will not be shared—an opaque site of silence and secrecy, a place of radical reticence concerning unconcealment.

Another book on these issues, Bernard Harcourt's *Exposed: Desire and Disobedience in the Digital Age*, goes beyond the notion of a surveillance state to claim that we live today in what Harcourt calls an "expository society," which is itself a function of the fact that the surveillance state feeds on what it produces, thrives on a social desire for exposition, for so-called transparency, for exhibition and shameless publicity. If the expository society has come to replace earlier figures of late modernity—the disciplinary society, the control society, the securitarian society—even while it retains most of the features of those earlier models, it is because exposition can encompass them all. For Harcourt, the triumph of the expository society is a dialectical triumph. It marks the moment in which the infinite desires of the population are successfully channeled by the state's primary interests in information extraction: in fact, they are put at the very service of information extraction. Nobody forces us voluntarily to reveal everything we give away in an earnest Facebook discussion: but it will be used. With a caveat: the "state" in the expository society is not only the state of governance, the governing state, it is also the state of exchange, the economic state: we are all participants, willingly or not, and we are all exposed. Only infrapolitical or protopolitical life remains outside the expository society, to the precise extent that it does; only that in us which is infrapolitical or protopolitical escapes the state of surveillance. Which therefore merits some consideration.

What is it, in us, within us, that exceeds or subceeds the position of participant, that is, the position of informant, which is the direct counterpart to the surveillance state, the surveillance economy, the surveillance or expository society? If there is surveillance, there are informants, willing or unwilling, or both. No surveillance without informants, no informants without surveillance. But what, specifically, is an informant? If we are all informants, how are we so? We might want to start developing this question through a minimal phenomenology of the informant—I say "minimal" because it will be unsatisfying, and there would be much more to bring up about this. I think it will be useful to develop this minimal phenomenology of the informant in connection with the phenomenology of evil developed by Immanuel Kant in his book *Religion within the Limits of Reason Alone*. My interest is not to denounce as evil any and every informant, that is, any and every denizen of our expository society. Yes, that would enable us perhaps better to reserve the place of goodness for that theoretical position of the hyperborder dweller, always a temptation, always a moralistic temptation. But it would also be simplistic and wrong. It is not a matter of good versus evil—it is more a matter of how to isolate a kernel in the human that is resistant to the demands and satisfactions of expository life, which belong in the death drive, from which kernel, therefore, it could perhaps be possible to preserve the promise of another present, hence of another future.

Evil is for Kant in every case "illegal," to the very extent that it is always outside the law, and not just outside but also disobedient to the moral or unconditional law that ciphers the freedom of the human. The subject of evil is in every case a subject to evil: "We call a man evil . . . not because he performs actions that are evil (contrary to law) but because these actions are of such a nature that we may infer from them the presence in him of evil maxims"

(*Religion*, 16). The evil may rise out of or in connection with so-called propensities, of which Kant selects three, linked to "predispositions" defined as "elements in the fixed character and destiny of man" (21). The latter are (1), the predisposition to *animality*, (2) the predisposition to *humanity*, and (3) the predisposition to *personality*. The first one can be grafted with "beastly vices" (22), which are in every case the vices of a "purely mechanical self-love" (22), namely, "gluttony," "lasciviousness," "drunkenness," and the like. A propensity for "frailty" (24), where inclination is stronger than the heart, explains this first form of evil, which we may call *beastly evil*. The second one—the predisposition to rational humanity, which means that we all want "to acquire worth in the opinion of others" (22)—can be corrupted through "wickedness" (24) into "jealousy" and "rivalry," and it gives rise to "diabolical" evil (22), as in "envy, ingratitude, spitefulness." And the third one, the predisposition to *personality*, is probably the most interesting one: here there is an almost insurmountable and undecidable impurity that, at the limit, keeps us from deciding whether any of our actions can be properly registered as a free action, solely conditioned by the moral law, which is the law of freedom. The propensity here, which is to act as if we were acting morally, is *radical evil*, to the extent that it distorts the moral principle by overdetermining it with intentions that do not themselves conform to duty: pathological "vices concealed under the appearance of virtue" (29), a universal pathology, only rarely escapable.

Three kinds of evil: beastly, diabolical, and radical. How do we map these different forms of evil onto a (minimal) phenomenology of the informant? Let us take, for instance, the example given to us by Salvadoran journalist Oscar Martínez in his *History of Violence*. He will tell us the story of a fellow called Abeja, an informant to the Salvadoran police. He prefaces it by saying:

> Without these murderers, hundreds more murderers would be walking the streets. Without these rapists, hundreds more rapists would be stalking the nights. The plea-bargain witness: criminals the state pardons in exchange for their testimony. Their lives in grave peril, many of these women are battling the most dangerous gangs of the continent. Nobody but the state backs them up, and often the state becomes their enemy. (Martínez, 109)

A gang member, himself or herself having indulged in violent criminal activity many times, gets arrested and plea-bargains with the Salvadoran state to become a witness against other gang members. It is his or her way out of permanent jail time, but at the same time he or she risks becoming a target for the gangs themselves. If there is anything like a witness protection program in El Salvador, it is haphazard, thoroughly precarious, incompetent, and certainly never to be taken for granted or relied upon. These gangbangers, Abeja for instance, are taking their lives into their own hands. They have become informants. God knows, they will die for it sooner or later, and sooner rather than later. How do we understand that? Coercion may be an explanation: they do not have a choice, the police have threatened to kill them unless they cooperate (in truth, given the state of affairs in El Salvador and other Central American countries, if there is successful prosecution of gang crimes, which happens rarely, it is usually through plea-bargain witnesses, not through proper police investigations) or to leak that they are traitors and give them no protection, expose them; so our gangbanger, take Abeja, must comply and hope for the best, which can be some additional days or weeks or months of life. This is mere opportunism on the part of the gangbanger—it does not rise to the level of evil behavior, but it is not necessarily moral behavior either. An informant has accepted to become an informant. At the moment, we cannot know what kind of an informant he or she is—just an undifferentiated one, like most of us in the surveillance state.

But Martínez, in his story "The Most Miserable of Traitors," does not speak of coercion. He says: "In late 2011, Abeja, a twenty-something-year-old kid, sat in front of prosecutors from Chalatenango and, for an undisclosed reason, admitted to being a member of the Fulton Locos Salvatrucha. He said that his clique dedicated itself to extortion, murder, and drug trafficking in the states of San Miguel, Santa Ana, Sonsonate and Chalatenango. He told them many secrets, secrets that spanned sixty-three typed pages" (Martínez, 113–14). This was not a trivial case, since Abeja's testimony could be decisive for the Salvadoran state's prosecution of José Misael "Medio Millón" Cisneros, one of the top Mara Salvatrucha leaders deemed to be "the mastermind behind the country's cocaine exports" (112). The Salvadoran police imprisoned Abeja in the tiny municipal police station of Agua Caliente and had him there for fifteen months of quasi-starvation (apparently the Salvadoran police feel no obligation to feed their prisoners) and neglect, until Abeja decided to escape the prison and forfeit his plea-bargain witness status. No wonder. As Martínez puts it, "Plea-bargain witnesses, especially former gang members, have to deal with the fact that their cliques have committed many crimes against the police. In other words, their guardians will often have a profound hate for them. Sometimes they're even forced to testify about the complicity of the police. Abeja did exactly that in Medio Millón's trial" (119).

We should not feel too sympathetic for the police or indeed for the witness. They are all bad, most of them anyway, and indifferently so. They simply fulfill their roles: some are police, some are gangbangers. Israel Ticas, "the only forensic investigator in all of El Salvador" (117), appreciates the importance of the gangbangers turned witnesses, since they enable him to find and exhume bodies that would otherwise remain disappeared. But Ticas also tells us that the witnesses are not devils turned angels. When Martínez asks him whether the witnesses feel sorry for their actions, Ticas says: "No. They're totally calm. I admire that about those fuckers. They're not even embarrassed" (118). And Ticas continues: "One time I pulled out a boy about five years old and a girl about eight. The witness said they promised the girl that they wouldn't kill her little brother if she let herself be raped by fifteen men. They raped her and killed them both. It was in Ateos, in 2006. I found the two little bodies hugging" (118).

The informants are participants in what they inform about. Their information is testimonial. They speak up, risking their lives, but not because they are embarrassed about what they did, or others did. The reason for their informing, as Martínez puts it, remains "undisclosed" (113). We do not know, we cannot know. Is the informant himself or herself a subject of radical evil, diabolical evil, beastly evil? Or is the informant, to the contrary, after all a subject to the surveillance state, to the state of extraction, fulfilling the moral law, the unconditional law, the categorical imperative? Under what conditions is it fair to say that the informant is, in fact, in truth, doing the right thing? Does it matter? For the surveillance state, it does not. Undifferentiated informants are good enough, since only the information as such counts. That is why the state has no compunctions at the level of extracting it from anybody. A few years ago I read in the *New York Times* an article about how the Mexican state very likely "targeted with sophisticated surveillance technology sold to the Mexican government to spy on criminals and terrorists" a team of international investigators appointed by the Inter-American Commission on Human Rights to investigate the forced disappearance of forty-three students in Ayotzinapa in September 2014.[1] This happened a few weeks before the investigators published their final report, but certainly after the Mexican authorities had become aware that the commission's report rejected the government's version, which was lying and incompetent, of what had taken place. According to the *Times*, the investigators, all of them endowed with diplomatic immunity but still targets of the cyberweapon known as Pegasus, which renders all antisurveillance encryption useless in smartphones at the same time it turns the same smartphones—through their microphones and cameras—into surveillance tools against their owners, had complained that the Mexican "government essentially obstructed their inquiry and then cast them out by refusing to extend their mandate." At the same time, "an investigation by The New York Times and forensic cyberanalysts in recent weeks determined that the software had been used against some of the country's most influential academics, lawyers, journalists and their family members, including a teenage boy" (Ahmed). Surveillance runs amok, in excess of every law, in excess of every legal justification, just because it can. The surveillance state is itself a state in the "illegal" condition, certainly in the Kantian sense.

So perhaps we should alter the question and ask, not about varieties of evil in the informant himself or herself, but about varieties of evil in the surveillance state. Is the state of extraction not the one who, through their many agents, indulges in antimoral behavior, in evil behavior, in illegal behavior? Would the surveillance state be a state of beastly evil, diabolical evil, or radical evil? Is the extraction of information a symptom of the frailty of the state, of the wickedness of the state, or of the impurity of the state? Or is the state, de facto, following its own merely opportunistic drive to do all it can do in its effort to fulfill its own mandate so as better to protect its citizens: "if we must inform, let us inform; if we must extract, let us extract; if we must expose, let us expose"? The expository state, like the computer program that analyzes whether you are entitled to receive health insurance or life insurance, rather than take advantage of an opportunity, is obliged to fulfill state functions to the most extreme possibility in the deployment of its own logic understood as categorically imperative. Performance means you must go all the way. Is the surveillance state in fact, for the most part, and in general, a moral state?

Let me invoke one more example, this time Roberto Rangel's 2015 memoir *Me decían mexicano frijolero* (They Called Me a Bean-Eating Mexican), as told to Ana Luisa Calvillo. It could in fact be a place where to identify the primary features of a degree-zero informant—that is, within the phenomenology of the informant, an undifferentiated, unwilling informant who could not be subject to any moral judgment either to adjudicate evil or goodness. Roberto Rangel would have been or be entitled to the atrocious honor of configuring the most extreme type of informant, the informant who informs against his will, against his life, against his libidinal satisfaction, against anything that could be considered an aspect of his happiness; a slave informant, or informant slave, whose performance follows a deconstituent imperative. Rangel is told by the California police, "inform, it is your law, you signed a contract, you have no option, and if you fail to do it we will disembowel your girlfriends, we will kill your children, and then we will get rid of you after torturing you." Rangel does not have a life, although he seeks it. But it has been stolen. He knows he is serving rogues, he knows that the system surrounding him also serves those rogues, he has no resources, and the miracle is always the miracle of a precarious survival, after he fails as informant, in jail for fifty-seven years for an imagined murder, fifty-seven fake years, because Rangel cannot count, cannot serve, cannot be, or he can be only cannon fodder, that is, someone doomed just because he is a bean-eating Mexican, nothing else would be consistent, truth and justice are not part of the procedure. Only derision, only monumental mockery.

Sadistic mockery comes from the police officer than runs him as an informant and turns him into a sexual slave and humiliates and degrades him in every visit, the police officer that calls him *"mexicano frijolero"* at the moment of rape, that is, every time he rapes him, and makes him eat meat that has been spat on the floor because beaner Mexicans who think they can come to the United States and expect to eat meat deserve nothing else. They are themselves meat, usable sexually or economically, usable for extraction, but beyond that they are nothing. They are only transcripts, screens for the deployment of a predatory drive that is ultimately owned by the surveillance state, the corps of police, all the corps of police, all the force of the state. Roberto Rangel falls into a machine for crushing bodies and spirits, after information has been extracted from them, whatever meager information they are able to provide, and he will not get out of it. Paradoxically, only jail brings on a certain measure of peace, and the possibility of learning how to read, learning how to write, how to give a *testimonio* that nobody will ever be able to believe, not really, it is probably a fiction, one cannot give it proper credit lest one enters the psychotic night: it is not just Officer Rivas or María from Immigration Services, it is also all the other agents who must disbelieve every word from Rangel, and also the lawyer, the state attorney, the judge, no one can stick to the *testimonio*, to Rangel's simple word, but what simple word, everything is a lie, it has to be, the truth of Rangel's story can only show itself through its own impossibility, which means it never will, it does not. It is the psychotic night of the world. From its depth—but it is the depth of the state of extraction, of the surveillance state—Rangel hears that he is a bitch, nothing but a bitch, I will make you my bitch, you will become a bitch, I will give you proper existence as a bitch, your being must match your worth, your name is the name of a bitch, proper name, *mexicano frijolero*, suck my cock or I will gut your son. This was Rangel's *testimonio*, as told to Ana Luisa Calvillo.

Mutatis mutandis, at the level of structure, is that so essentially different from our former US president when he demanded that Mexican President Peña Nieto pay for the wall, pay for my wall, I know it is absurd but you must or you will suffer the consequences, you have no option, and if you fail to comply I will gut your children, I will kill your girlfriends, I will make you my bitch, you already are my bitch: this is also the psychotic night in international politics, of which Kant would have spoken many years ago when he mentioned "the international situation, where civilized nations stand towards each other in the relation obtaining in the barbarous state of nature (a state of continuous readiness for war), a state, moreover, from which they have taken fixedly into their heads never to depart. We then become aware of the fundamental principles of the great societies called states—principles which flatly contradict their public pronouncements but can never be laid aside, and which no philosopher has yet been able to bring into agreement with morality" (*Religion*, 29).

The surveillance state can and will always function in view of the maximization of its own libidinal cathexes, its own libidinal release, and its agents will take opportunistic advantage of it every time. This is the impurity of the state, of every state, its ongoing and ceaseless radical evil, which matches or mimics that of Officer Rivas, the Fresno, California, detective who has or can purchase the trust of his people, of the Drug Enforcement Administration, of the California Highway Patrol, of the district attorney, of the lawyers, the judges. Frankly, after all, Officer Rivas can access all the cocaine in the world, and the money, which is the reason he can use and uses informants.

There are other kinds of informants. We could appeal to the fictional example of Butcher's Boy, the protagonist of Thomas Perry's *The Informant*, who informs a Justice Department agent because that information serves his own interests, his own calculations, his cold plan for revenge, or perhaps not revenge, just caution, those fellows should be in jail or dead as far as I am concerned. He, Butcher's Boy, is an assassin, a cool one, but he still cannot assassinate everyone, there are too many of them, so he helps himself, as an assassin, by becoming an informant, through calculation: this type is of course the radical informant, or the radical evil informant, since his informing actions do denounce criminals who deserve it but for opportunistic and immoral reasons. In Officer Rivas's case, his informant was the site of diabolical evil, not as agent but as patient. Butcher's Boy is an agent of radical evil.

There is a moment in Don Winslow's *The Force* (2017), a novel, when the protagonist, Denny Malone, a very reluctant informer who is forced to betray his friends, becomes a different kind of informer. We can imagine a serious informant, a professional informant, the informant who informs out of duty, the informant who accepts a life of risk and constant betrayal, a life lived in infinite distance, because there is a law that must be fulfilled, a law that must be made fulfilled, so that to become an informant means to affirm freedom, to be totally within the law, hence totally free, no matter the price. This would be the moral informant, the radical opposite of Roberto Rangel, a full-degree informant, perhaps the type that Robert Mazur's *The Infiltrator* presents or would like to present if we could take his self-presentation at face value—he performs the perfectly professional, the perfectly nonpathological actions of an undercover police officer who befriends and then betrays any number of people at the service of the law. So we would have three primary types of informants: the zero-degree informant, Roberto Rangel; the undercover officer serving the true interests of the law, Robert Mazur maybe, full-degree informer, moral informer; and the radical-evil informant represented by Butcher's Boy in Thomas Perry's novel. This is to say that a typology or phenomenology of the informant can absorb the Kantian analysis of varieties of evil: there is diabolical evil, there is radical evil, and there is moral freedom, and perhaps all kinds of beastly evil in between. And there is nothing else.

But it is still a very precarious typology that settles nothing. We know little, we can only imagine, about those "undisclosed" reasons that marked Abeja's intentions, for instance. Why should one become an informant? Why should one give his or her life over to the machinations of an extractive state? Why should one do it, really? Or in the best of cases, when one is not bound by duty, like the undercover officer, when one is not bound by diabolical wickedness, like it is the case for Roberto Rangel, and when one is not coerced by opportunistic calculations having to do with self-interest? Why is it the case that most informants in the surveillance state, or Facebook users, you yourself, for instance, give freely of their own bodies through a production of *jouissance* that, as we know, is far from being always pleasant? Perhaps because we want something back: the informant, any informant, is always in the position of Tobias, Tobit's son, the youth whose angel fled and who spent the rest of his life, until he died at 107 years of age, missing him, awaiting his return. It is perhaps not possible to live without an angel, or we can only do so in nostalgia for the angel. For Rangel the angel is perhaps the son he has never met and will never meet, the second daughter of his other girlfriend he also loses, the children that come and go and from whom he cannot expect any returns, no longer, and then, if no longer, then when? Rangel wants to cross the border, wants to return after his deportation, he has a son, he wants to be received by his son, and he falls into the hands of a diabolical police force. Without proper papers, he becomes a slave, soon addicted to his very slavery, and he loses his very capacity to inform, since it requires a distance that is now lost.

One would think we are lost in the illegal condition, outside the law that is the law of freedom. One would think that the surveillance state has no respect for freedom's law. Informants—the subjects of the surveillance state are all informants, that is what they are, what we are, willing or unwilling, some of us innocent enough, some of us mired in the evil about which we are or are not embarrassed—informants cannot make a claim to freedom, unless they find themselves in the improbable predicament of informing on the side of the categorical imperative, informing as a function of a universalizable maxim of behavior. Or, on the contrary, we might ask, is it, could it be, that, since the state is the only constituted authority, only being and becoming an informant to the state will give us our freedom? Informing defines, in fact, our very legitimacy as citizens, even if we were to be informing an illegal state, whose illegality would not be our responsibility. Could it be that, today, the categorical imperative is best served by informing on ourselves and others as well we might, unconditionally, for the sake of coming into the law, for the sake of abandoning the abjection of the illegal condition? It is not less Facebook that we need, it is more Facebook, more sincerity, more exposure, more confession, and, yes, we should encourage university authorities to read all our emails, until, finally, we would have said it all, they would know it all, and there would be nothing left to say.

But I can think of a place, the border of the border, the hyperborder, where information would not have to be shared, where language and politics would not come together under the form of the imperative to inform, an opaque site of silence and secrecy, a place of radical reticence concerning unconcealment. Such a place, if it exists at all, would be protopolitical or infrapolitical, would be directly outside politics, outside the expository society, in exodus from the state of extraction, the state of surveillance. We can use here Werner Hamacher's very rich 2014 essay "On the Right to Have Rights." Let us assume that the right to secrecy, which in the North American tradition, following US Supreme Court decisions, is frequently referred to as the right to privacy, is a human right. The surveillance state demonstrates once again what Hamacher, following Hannah Arendt's famous analysis in *The Origins of Totalitarianism*, says about the state in general: "it is left to the 'good will,' and that is to say to political opportunism and, more precisely, to property, security, and private interests masquerading as interests of the state, to either adopt human rights as the measure of political decisions or to reject them altogether: human rights themselves could always legitimate any of their arbitrary manipulations" (183).[2] The universalization of the surveillance state, however, immediately means that there is no room for the right to secrecy. To be deprived of the right to privacy is to be deprived of a human right that is also a citizen right. Once this process starts, Arendt says and Hamacher agrees, the human will be produced as "structurally worldless" (184), the human being will have become, from the perspective of the state, a hyperborder dweller, naked life as such.

Arendt's postulate of a "right to have rights," as is well known, is the demand of a right to politics, that is, a right to regulate human and public life through language, not violence. But the right to politics, which points to public life, is only the mirror side of the right to secrecy, the right to a private life. If the right to politics, as Arendt says, can be experienced only through its loss, the same is the case for the right to secrecy: the right to secrecy is the secret right to have rights, which the opportunism of the surveillance state will want to take away. Let me then propose that the right to secrecy is the same as the right to politics. Hamacher says that this right that grounds all rights and can only be perceived in its very loss is a "protopolitical right" (191), that is, a condition of politics, the very possibility of political determinability and determination. This, in Hamacher's words, is what takes place when the right to politics/secrecy, which is the right to rights, is lost at the hands of a rogue state (or of a rogue institution):

> Politics [is] not any more a lingual process of searching for a common form of life but instead the mere form of the self-reproduction of an established procedural schema that must have negated its provenance out of linguistic processes of deliberation, reduced language to acts of judgment, and eliminated its political relevance. If the *polis*—as Arendt assumes with Aristotle—was ever the place, free of definition, of the *being-human* in the sense of the speaking-being, politics became the procedure of grasping precisely this being as an already-spoken- and decided-being, as a fact and a fate, and the procedure for immobilizing its generative, redefining, and indefinite movement. Human existence is henceforth not anymore graspable as an *a priori* partaking in a political world through language but instead only as an existence at the threshold of politics. (193–94)

But an existence at the threshold of politics, even before it becomes understandable as a protopolitical existence, is an infrapolitical existence. Hamacher talks about it as an existence constituted by "a law without right" (197), "unqualified, mere existence" (197). Hamacher's extraordinary conclusion follows:

> The language of those who have no world can only be the language of the liberation of a world that is other than the world from which they were exiled: it can only be a language for such a world that is not meant, intended, and defined through intentions; not an already known world that is appropriated in its knowledge but rather a world released from aims and securities, a world let free by anyone who relates to it, and only for this reason, it is absolutely a world—free from all concepts of the world. (203)

The protopolitical position is indeed, for Hamacher, the beginning of another politics, a new beginning, but a beginning "that cannot be traced back to any other and that can be surpassed by none, since it is a beginning merely for further beginnings and is offered to them without commanding them. The beginning of language and law in the claim is an *arche an-arche*" (204). An anarchic beginning, a new politics after the destruction of politics that is the general consequence of the consummation of the state into a state of extraction—such is, maybe, the promise of protopolitics. In the temporal gap of the promise, neither believing nor disbelieving it, dwells infrapolitics.

Notes

Preface to the English-Language Edition

1. First, *Marranismo e inscripción* (2016), which appeared in English as *Against Abstraction: Notes from an (Ex)Latin Americanist* (2019). *Tercer espacio y otros relatos*, which is a vast revision of a previous book of mine, was published in 2021. *Sosiego siniestro*, which is a continuation of the present book on infrapolitics, appeared in Madrid in 2020.

**Exergue. On Jacques Derrida's *Glas*:
A Possible Second Moment in Deconstruction**

1. I think the difference with Hartman's position, which was fairly common among the old guard of deconstruction in the 1980s, is clear. Many people formed in deconstruction have since developed their own positions, and they could not be simply assimilated to Hartman's—they have evolved into their own understanding of things. What I am claiming as a "second" moment of deconstruction has a specific sense, however, in that it requires a shift of focus from the text of *écriture* to existence. A possible redefinition, then, of deconstruction as an infrapolitical thought of existence could be accepted or denigrated, but it does claim a turn in thought, which of course no one is obliged to undertake.

2. The enigmatic and immense issue of the death drive that Sigmund Freud presented in his metapsychology is not alien to Antigone's situation. I must leave this issue—the death drive in its intimate and extimate deployment, and its possible connection to infrapolitical practice—out of consideration in this book, but I will come back to it in subsequent texts.

1. The Last God: María Zambrano's Life without Texture

1. There have been attempts to understand the mostly silent or nonexplicit interest Zambrano had for Heidegger's work. Certainly Jesús Moreno Sanz, perhaps the best-informed Zambranian scholar, has insisted that Zambrano's oeuvre is in a constant dialogue with Heidegger's, and also with Nietzsche. See Moreno Sanz, ed., *María Zambrano*, 25, 27–28. But there are other contributions to a discussion of this critical confrontation, among which I should mention Sergio Sevilla, Oscar Adán, and Massimo Cacciari's *"Investigación."*

2. The reader should consider the possible relation between Zambrano's concept of degrounded relation and Heidegger's ontico-ontological difference.

3. I must point out the untranslatability of *hace nacer* here, since nothing could be more wrong than the obvious translation, "brings into being."

2. The Wolf's Hide: Ontotheological Militancies

1. See Spivak, "Subaltern," 16.

2. Badiou devotes a full essay to the study of the political configuration of the theological virtues, faith, hope, and charity: *Saint Paul*.

3. On the notion of ontotheology, perhaps more properly onto-theo-logy, see Heidegger's essay "The Onto-theo-logical Constitution of Metaphysics" in *Identidad*, 99–157.

4. See Leyte, *Epocas*, 61 and following for a wider characterization of Schelling's "positive philosophy" within the axiomatic affirmation that reason is "the historical itself."

5. See in particular Deleuze, *Nietzsche*, 39–72.

6. This chapter's genesis had to do with two perplexities: that many of the demands of subaltern sectors in any society have an objectively reactionary character, and that the "glory" of a subject understood as a subject of the hegemonic articulation cannot exhaust politics. To go beyond a progressive-reactionary conceptualization is for me a necessary part of the endeavor of de-teleologizing Marxism.

7. Was the second Iraq war progressive or reactionary? Was the war against Al-Qaeda, or later DAESH, progressive or reactionary? No matter what one thinks about the military-political doctrine of preemptive attack, or of unilateralism, or of the occupation of one country by another country's military forces in general terms, it seems obvious that for those recent events the adjective "reactionary" does not quite work in the historical context, even if some of its ideologues are straightforward reactionaries.

8. Quoting Plato, Donoso states that religion has always been considered "the indestructible foundation of human societies" (*Ensayo*, 6). That is the real reason why "at the same time faith diminishes, truths in the world diminish as well" (6), and error proliferates. Such errors can only be a fallen and false version of eternal

truth: "In every region, in every historical time, and among all the human races, an immortal faith in a future transformation has been kept, so radical and sovereign that it would bring together for ever the Creator and its creatures, human nature and divine nature.... The difference between the most pure dogma of Catholic theology and the dogma that has been altered by human traditions is in the way of reaching that supreme transformation and that sovereign goal" (38). Donoso is obviously desperate to keep alive the function of the master as supreme creator and transformer of the world.

9. Re "aura," see Benjamin, "Work of Art," 103 and following. Benjamin acknowledges the relation of aura to the religious to the extent that he says that artistic production has its origins in ceremonial objects destined to serve the divine (105). See also Benjamin, "The Storyteller." With regard to Schmitt, see *Political Theology*: "All the significant concepts of the modern theory of the State are secularized theological concepts" (36). But Schmitt is perhaps simply quoting Donoso, who will have said in the first page of his *Essay* that "in every political question there is always involved a great theological question" (5). Given Benjamin's interest in Schmitt's political theology, we could think about the unexpected and unexplored connection between Benjamin and Donoso.

10. "The Wolf's Hide" was for a time a preliminary title for this book, certainly in homage to Valle-Inclán, but also to underline the fact that an apotropaic strategy—to take from evil a bit of evil to protect from evil and transform it into effective action— is an essential infrapolitical tactic, perhaps even *the* essential strategy.

11. An almost paradigmatic example of subalternist recoil is to be found in Dipesh Chakrabarty's *Provincializing Europe*. The epigraph to the first publication of the essay titled "Postcoloniality and the Artifice of History," included in the book, was a phrase from Louis Althusser, "Push thought to extremes." The book retains the epigraph, but it also includes a 1999 postscript where Chakrabarty renounces what he calls his "politics of despair," to which he was committed in 1992, when he wrote the essay in its original version. This is recoil. Is it a simple withdrawal, a subtraction, therefore in this case a disavowal of the extreme of thought, its limit? Clearly there is no recoil without a limit-experience.

3. Infrapolitical Distance: A Second Note on the Concept of Distance in Felipe Martínez Marzoa

1. But see the mention of *to deinon* in the 1933–34 seminar *Being and Truth* (76). Generally speaking, *Being and Truth* is very close to the dominant pathos in *Introduction to Metaphysics* and confirms an unequivocal nearness to Nazism or hyper-Nazism.

2. Clare Pearson Geiman and Richard Capobianco have insisted on the difference between the Heideggerian interpretation of Sophocles's *Antigone* in *Introduction to Metaphysics* and the interpretation in *Hölderlin's Hymn "The Ister."* Here I am only interested in focusing on the second one, which is more consonant

with what the chapter tries to say regarding Martínez Marzoa's position vis-à-vis distance and its infrapolitical import. The 1935 interpretation, I think it is fair to say, was still exegetic or apologetic regarding National Socialism. Toward the end of the book, but in a way that is consistent with the totality of it, Heidegger states that he wants to defend "the inner truth and greatness of National-Socialism," and he adds between parentheses in the 1953 revision "(the encounter between technology and modern humanity)" (*Introduction*, 213). In the 1942 analysis it is no longer possible to deduce such allegiances, even though some of the sentences in that seminar are still a bit ambiguous—but not those in the interpretation of Antigone and her destiny.

4. Infrapolitics and the Politics of Infrapolitics

1. One of the participants at the conference went so far as to say that it seemed inappropriate to him to speak of *infrapolitics*, since, in his opinion, nothing was thinkable previous to politics. My response was to tell him that such a "nothing" was precisely what was at stake: the "nothing" that politics declares and at the same time kills. His reaction was stunned perplexity (and disagreement, of course).

2. See Scott, *Two Cheers*, xx, for a quick definition. Scott started using the term in *Domination* (1990). See also Robin Kelley, *Race Rebels*, for a use that follows and develops Scott's. Infrapolitics in my sense is not incompatible or even alien to Scott or Kelly, but it seeks to move into other sites and other regions of existence.

3. See Alvarez Yáguez, "Límites," for a revised version of the contribution to the University of Madrid Workshop on Posthegemony, Literature, Infrapolitics organized by José Luis Villacañas (June 2014).

4. I am referring to an important thread in Heidegger's "Dialogue." See, for instance, 49–52.

5. It is probably not necessary to say that my interest in posthegemony does not refer to the rendering of it Jorge Alemán naturalizes: "The 'posthegemonic' moment cannot not be a fantasy imagining an acephalic world exclusively given over to the cultivation of its drives." See "Apuntes," 2.

6. Although Emmanuel Lévinas's *Totality and Infinity* must be first credited, Schürmann's proposal regarding aprincipial thought in *Heidegger on Being and Acting* made it thematic for post-Heideggerian philosophy: "It is through a historical deduction of the categories of 'the other beginning' that action deprived of a unifying *pros hen* will become thinkable" (9). This is explicitly associated by Schürmann to an anarchic political project connected to "a cessation of principles, a deposing of the very principle of epochal principles, and the beginning of an economy of passage, that is, of anarchy" (9).

7. Malabou thematized the fantastic in her book on Heidegger: "The fantastic, far from designating a simple logic of the phantasm or an intrusion of the phantasm into the real, characterizes precisely the real of the phantasm. Ontological difference, the convertibility between the two (ex)changes [this is Malabou's way of referring to the Heideggerian "beginnings"], the new ontological gift, and the

new exchangeability are not pure abstractions. They constitute our real, the way the real registers the impact of its deconstruction and change" (182).

8. There was a conversation between Benjamín Mayer and Jaime Rodríguez Matos, two members of the Infrapolitical Deconstruction Collective, on the subject of Jacques Lacan's seminar *Le sinthome*. It happened in April 2015, during the same day I was translating this text into Spanish. Let me transcribe a few segments of it: "Can Lacan's teaching be considered post-university? You make me think that the answer is yes, of course, to the extent in which the status of knowledge in psychoanalysis implies the possibility of assimilating the *object a* Lacan thematized. This is the abyss of university discourse, since the latter can only momentarily but at the same time tragically assume that knowledge (S2) can assimilate *jouissance* (a). If we read it in that way, then psychoanalysis is indeed essentially post-university. Infrapolitically, I could remember here the response Freud gave in an interview done by Eastman, which has been mentioned in the course of several polemics. Eastman: 'What are you politically?' Freud: 'Nothing.' We can imagine the range of positions concerning what Freud said on that occasion. On the one hand, we are before the fact that the analyst's discourse, which is the reverse of the discourse of the master, must necessarily constrain itself to an "active neutrality," as I would call the positing of the impossibility to assimilate *jouissance* to knowledge or to any principle of authority (S1). But, on the other hand, we are before the fact of the necessary 'politicity' in any psychoanalytic intervention, although it is often referred to in ethical terms. I believe infrapolitics opens up a new range of approximations concerning this kind of Freudian *koan*, which I could gloss as: politically, Freudianism is nothing; infrapolitically, it is everything. To that extent psychoanalysis would be infrapolitical from beginning to end, to the same extent it is post-university. Which suggests to me a definition of infrapolitics, following this thread, in the following terms: infrapolitics refers to the inassimilabilty of *jouissance* by any master signifier. Infrapolitics is to the field of power what a post-university position is to the field of knowledge. Even taking into account or precisely taking into account that power and knowledge imply each other always already. As far as the later Lacan goes, his 'madness' could always be read as the post-university interpellation of his previous teaching. But, inherently, it does not seem to me more post-university than the previous teaching. What is at stake is a clearer orientation toward an analytic dismantling of things. Two additional comments: when Lacan turns prosopopeic and says 'I, the Truth, speak,' we should not understand in the dogmatic sense it seems to suggest, because what speaks here is precisely the (negative) truth that knowledge lacks. At the same time, responding from one's own beliefs or symptoms, as you, Jaime, suggest the later Lacan does, is not more humble, we could say, since the Truth cannot speak except from its beliefs and symptoms to the extent that Truth does not become manifest except in the form of the impresentable" (Benjamín Mayer Foulkes, in Infrapolitical Deconstruction, Private Facebook Group, April 18, 2015). Rodríguez Matos replied: "I am not looking for anything humble. I am not interested in identifying a dogmatic or dictatorial Lacan to contrast him with a

humbler one or anything like that. What I am interested in, if it can be done, if it is possible to do it, is to point out the move in Lacan from an emphasis on the symbolic to an emphasis on something else, which is not that. So: I do not want either to accuse or to defend the Master! The Real attracts my attention for reasons that are perhaps not very important from a clinical perspective. The Real, it seems to me, takes us to think Lacan in relation to the Heideggerian ontico-ontological difference, except that from a much more immediate or pedestrian site. [Somebody else] has already said he does not agree with this, and I can go along with the disagreement to a certain extent, but the connection seems more important to me than fixing on the difference—yes, the Real is still a category of the 'subject,' but it is also a direct reference to being outside beings. I will leave it there. I don't want to complicate or manipulate things, but there is something in this much more relevant than any accusation of dogmatism, and I do not want to be put in the position of one of those reactionaries that negate Lacan in such a way" (Jaime Rodríguez Matos, same conversation, April 21, 2015).

9. See on this the devastating reading of Cacciari's 1976 book in Mandarini, "Beyond Nihilism," 1–7.

10. See the two volumes of *No matar* (edited by Belzagui and García, respectively) for a compilation of some of the most significant contributions to the polemic.

11. See, however, the fascinating essay by Luis García, "No matar," where he associates Del Barco's "revolutionary practice" to Walter Benjamin's notion of divine violence. See also Villalobos's essay on Del Barco's critique of Marxism as "liberationist discourse."

12. See Graff Zivin, 14–17, on the ethics/politics discussion in the wake of Del Barco's letter, which she places within a phantom intellectual history of their mutual substitution and finally the suspension of any possible substitutional paradigm.

13. See, on Rozitchner, Sztulwark's essay "Poema y política," which is an attempt at interpreting Rozitchner's work in a manner quite different from the one I have just summarized.

14. See Viveiros's short essay, probably the best account of Amazon Basin metaphysics ever produced.

15. See Deleuze and Guattari, *What Is Philosophy?* and Derrida, *The Right to Philosophy*.

16. I am sure the expression could be documented in Ingold's work, but I am referring to private conversations when he was my colleague at the University of Aberdeen.

17. See in particular García Linera, *Forma*, chapters 5 and 6, 229–365.

5. The Absolute Difference between Life and Politics

1. Nancy had referred to general equivalence in *La communauté affrontée* (2001), where he says, "what reaches us is an exhaustion of the thought of the One and of

a unique destiny of the world, which ends in a unique absence of destiny, in the unlimited expansion of the principle of general equivalence or rather, through a counter-blow, in the violent convulsions that reaffirm what is all-powerful and omnipresent of a One that has become, or has become again, its own monstrosity" (12). The theme of general equivalence is also crucial in *Verité de la democratie* (2008), where Nancy suggests a reinvention of democracy through the abandonment of the principle of general equivalence. Nancy proposes a democracy without figure, which presupposes a certain rupture between democracy and politics. If democracy must, in Rousseau's terms, "re-engender the human" and "opens the destiny of the human and the world to new gestures," then politics can no longer offer, Nancy says, "the measure or the site of such a destiny" (*Verité*, 60). Hence a democratic politics will have to be defined as a politics in retreat, which is what I am calling infrapolitics, having understood its incapacity to assume the totality of the human destiny. For Nancy democracy cannot be subsumed by politics, which liberates it from its obsolete characterization as a politics of ends. Democracy in Nancy is only the means for an infrapolitical deployment.

2. See Martin Heidegger, *Contributions*, 106–9 and 348–49, for an early conceptualization; see also his "Age of the World Picture," 135 and following.

3. On hegemony theory, let me make the following remarks. Toward the end of *En la frontera: Sujeto y capitalismo* (2014), Jorge Alemán offers an abbreviated description of his intellectual and existential project: "analytic discourse can contribute to highlighting what structural aspects in the constitution of a mortal, sexuated, and speaking existence are not available, for ontological reasons, for absorption by the circular and unlimited movement of Capital" (124–25). Alemán's understands that his wager for analytic discourse against capitalist discourse is a wager at the limit, and it is a wager for another beginning and for another form of existence. Alemán rereads Marxian surplus value from the Lacanian *plus-de-jouir* and the Freudian unconscious from the subversion of the subject in Heidegger and Lacan. His explicitly political wager is to suspend the principle of equivalence from which capital produces subjectivity, hence predicting an exit, which is both an exit from capitalism and an exit from metaphysics. The exit, Alemán says, would have to be understood as "another discourse of the master" (121), where the master is either the unconscious or philosophy itself, now fully homologous. Who anchors this new discourse of the master? It is here that Alemán's position become controversial to my mind. Alemán says: hegemony, in the Laclauian version, or rather, in Alemán's version of the Laclauian version, grounds the discourse of the master. Hegemony stands in, in Alemán, in every case, although there are, he says, few cases, as hegemony is for him the new irruption of an emancipatory politics, as the aporetic or impossible configuration of a solitude and a commonality that, upon articulation, subvert the subject of will to power, the modern subject, the Cartesian-Hegelian subject that sits at the center of capitalist discourse or is capitalist discourse as such. Alemán says: "the discourse of the master can be interpreted as the concept of hegemony in Laclau. And this is because if . . . no collective will exists *a priori*,

if there is no people that is already constituted in its field and its being, then only hegemony, when it appears, permits the retroactive translation into a collective will" (*En la frontera*, 121). In other words, only hegemony, in every case not a social power formation, not the consolidation of uses and habits that mark the materiality of power at a given time, but rather the precarious and even contingent articulation of a set of singular demands that come together in an equivalential chain, has a political chance. For him, hegemony is the new name of politics. Only hegemony accedes politics. Only hegemony—hegemony theory—is left standing from the collapse of modern categories, or the categories of political modernity. Hegemony counters domination precisely because hegemony articulates multiple singularities in their demands against domination, and because the articulation of singularities is ceaseless and never reaches the point of identification with a leader—it always transcends it. This is, of course, Alemán's version of a new egalitarian symbolization, which only the Left can accomplish, he claims, in its material search for an exit from capitalist discourse against every "conservative and nostalgic dream of a return to the symbolic Father" (*En la frontera*, 107). But here is the problem, to my mind. The fact that political praxis can or may open the possibility of a new social bond does not necessarily mean that political praxis will do so. Yes, hegemony theory, in Laclau's theorization, does affirm that every hegemonic articulation is always already punctual and contingent, finite, never given beforehand, never eternal, radically open, and only sustained and sustainable in and through its very cathexis, which depends on the articulation of social singularities. The result is that the social bond is precarious and always partial. But this is no guarantee that the very hegemonic process does not, therefore, and in virtue of its very precariousness, articulate a conversion that will suture singularity into equivalence every time. The articulation of equivalential chains is no defense against a radical reassertion of the principle of general equivalence in hegemony theory—on the contrary, I would say: it sets its very ground, its very plausibility. The articulation of chains of equivalence and their suture into any particular leadership is only the first step of the plausible, which is in every case a hegemonic closure in the wager for power of whatever group may rise as the winner in a state of the situation. No matter how precariously and contingently (nothing is eternal). But in their very precariousness, rationalized as merely transitional in every case, hegemonies in power will have ruined the very possibility of an exit from the situation that demanded emancipatory practices.

4. Could we change our lives in favor of the incommensurable? For Nancy, the incommensurable "opens onto the absolute distance and difference of what is other—not only the other human person but also what is other than human: animal, vegetable, mineral, divine" (*After Fukushima*, 27). And yet it is perhaps not necessary to bring these reflections into the sphere of the thought of the totally other, of the other of the other, or of otherness in general. Whatever is incommensurable is also nonappropriable, it resists capture, and it embodies a remainder of signification that we probably should not push into any radical beyond, where, by definition, it would remain out of reach, hence also out of any possible relationality.

5. See for all this Heidegger, *Heraclitus*, 10 and following. The first part of the seminar is an extended commentary on the knucklebones fragment. Let me add that I do not refer to this seminar casually—a lot of what goes on in it is consistent with what I will later thematize as infrapolitics. Following it up in the Heideggerian text will have to wait for another occasion.

6. Up until the late 1930s Heidegger had only spoken about a "destructive repetition" of the history of thought understood as the history of metaphysics. The series of notebooks started in 1936 that would later form *Contributions* and other volumes and would only end in the 1940s insist forcefully on the notion of "another beginning" of thought, another "inception," but this is a history whose reach remains opaque and radically enigmatic. It is interesting that Friedrich Nietzsche also announced, toward the end of his life, a splitting of history into two, and the necessity of a new beginning for thinking. The point I wish to make here, anticipating developments in the main text, is that Heidegger's "other beginning" has a lot to do with his attempts to leave behind the residues of "transcendental anthropology" that still clung to *Being and Time*'s *Dasein*: entirely to leave behind an understanding of the human as *animal rationale* and to proceed, through transitional thinking, to the production of a notion of *Da-sein* would mean to leave metaphysics behind. For people like Jorge Alemán (but there aren't many) leaving metaphysics behind is a necessary condition of finding an exit to capitalist discourse. See Heidegger, *Contributions*, 139–47.

7. Possible alternative routes for Marxism could be glimpsed in Sergio Villalobos's *La desarticulación* and Gareth Wiilliams's *Infrapolitical Passages*, and those are understandings produced from within the Infrapolitical Deconstruction Collective. Outside the group, but like the previous two books, Jacques Lezra's *Nature of Things* renews the materialist tradition and opens theoretico-critical pathways. See also Carlos Casanova's *Estética y producción*.

8. At the end of the seminars conducted in Le Thor and Zähringen in the 1960s and 1970s, the editors note that Heidegger referred, in relationship to certain Parmenidean fragments, and especially fragment 1, verse 28, "it is necessary to experiment, to make the experience (*pithesthai*) of all things," to a "tautological thought" that would be the "primordial sense of phenomenology." This is the movement that Heidegger describes: "phenomenology is a path that leads away to come before . . . , and it lets that before which it is led show itself" (*Four Seminars*, 80). That tautology of the inapparent is the decisive infrapolitical experience that makes it distinct from any form of "inner experience." Infrapolitics is very much an attempt at letting things be in their unconcealed concealment.

9. I am also borrowing from Alemán the notion in this chapter that, in order to think that difference, we cannot appeal to experts.

10. I must refer here to Zambrano's notion of "life without texture," explained in Chapter 1.

11. An example of infrapolitics would be the one associated with Antigone, a crucial figure of the Western tradition whose infrapolitical drift, a condition of its

tragicity, has been denied and disavowed over and over again. For an infrapolitical Antigone see Moreiras, "Infrapolítica marrana," which expands on Chapter 4 of this book. But a wider consideration would have to take on several recent texts, particularly feminist readings of Antigone, from Luce Irigaray to Judith Butler, from Adriana Cavarero to Moira Fradinger, from Bonnie Honig to Fanny Söderback. See particularly Butler's *Antigone's Claim*, Honig's *Antigone, Interrupted*, and Söderback, ed., *Feminist Readings*. See also Philippe Lacoue-Labarthe's "De l'éthique."

12. There are many places in Heidegger's work that mention the Parmenidean identification of being and thinking (*einai-noein*). See for instance *Identidad*, 68–69 and following. But see Daniel Dahlstrom, "Heidegger's Initial Interpretation," which is a tracing, starting in the seminar on Aristotle from 1922, of how Heidegger read Parmenides's Fragment 3 both positively and also from the point of view of its "recuperative destruction." Dahlstrom shows how the fragment begins to figure, in Heidegger's reading, as one of the decisive deviations in metaphysics toward the interpretation of Being as mere presence. To break the metaphysical identification of being and thinking implies the opening of the temporal-historical horizon in infrapolitical experience.

13. The extraordinary link that Badiou posits between feminism (if that is the word) and communism in this text is consistent with the Lacanian determination of female enunciation and the Not-All. Infrapolitics endorses it. Gabriela Méndez Cota, in "Feminismo," has begun to study it in reference to the work of Claire Colebrook. See Colebrook, *Death of the Posthuman* and *Sex after Life*.

14. On the imperative form of thought see Reiner Schürmann, *Wandering Joy*: "Two forms of thought confront each other. The type of thought that urges a path upon existence can be called 'imperative' thought; this is opposed to 'indicative' thought, which apprehends the real and establishes a noetics of it" (29).

15. See Schürmann, *Wandering*, in particular 29, 69–73, 83.

16. The discussion concerning "the history of being" and its potential end fills entire shelves in the Heideggerianist library. A fundamental book on metaphysical epochality, which is in no way merely exegetic, as some other books are, is Schürmann's *Broken Hegemonies*.

6. A Politics of Separation: An Alternative Politicity

1. See my book *Against Abstraction*, 125–51.

2. I am referring to Bosteels's essays "El otro Marx" and "De Marx a Heidegger."

3. On the notion that the essence of politics is not political see Heidegger, *Hölderlin*, 82–86, on which I already commented in Chapter 3 of this book. That the *polis* has a prepolitical essence supplements the notion, attributed by Heidegger to Aristotle, according to which what the human being is cannot be politically determined. It is because the human being is a "political animal," in Aristotle's definition, that the human being can belong to or in the *polis*, but belonging in the *polis* concerns the essence of the human rather than its political subdetermination.

"If 'the political' is what belongs to the *polis*, and therefore is essentially dependent upon the *polis*, then the essence of the *polis* can never be determined in terms of the political, just as the ground can never be explained or derived from the consequence" (*Hölderlin*, 85).

4. See Alemán, *Soledad*. The notion of "soledad: común" is for Alemán the point of departure for any plausible theorization of political community.

5. On Heidegger's notion of "mere life" (*Nur-Lebenden*), which Derrida must have associated with Agamben's work, this is what Derrida says: "I think I understand what that means, this 'nothing more' (*nur*), I can understand it on the surface, in terms of what it would like to mean, but at the same time I understand nothing. I'll always be wondering whether this fiction, this simulacrum, this myth, this legend, this phantasm, which is offered as a pure concept (life in its pure state—Benjamin also has confidence in what can probably be no more than a pseudo-concept), is not precisely pure philosophy become a symptom of the history that concerns us here" (*Animal*, 22). A reading of *The Animal That Therefore I Am*, Derrida's posthumous and unfinished book on subjects that are very close to Esposito's and Agamben's, would be advisable.

6. As Deleuze glosses it, "a scoundrel, a bad apple, held in contempt by everyone, is found on the point of death, and suddenly those charged with his care display an urgency, respect, and even love for the dying man's least sign of life. Everyone makes it his business to save him. As a result, the wicked man himself, in the depths of his coma, feels something soft and sweet penetrate his soul. But as he progresses back towards life, his benefactors turn cold, and he himself rediscovers his old vulgarity and meanness. Between his life and his death, there is a moment where *a life* is merely playing with death" (Deleuze, "Immanence," 386).

7. Agamben, "Absolute," 233. Re necessary illusions, Agamben says: "This illusion [of transcendence] is . . . something like a necessary illusion in Kant's sense, which immanence itself produces on its own and to which every philosopher falls prey even as he tries to adhere as closely as possible to the plane of immanence" (227).

8. Agamben refer to the Sartrean *il y'a* as developed in "La transcendence de l'ego," which Deleuze studies in *Logic of Sense* (Agamben, "Absolute," 224); and Esposito refers to the importance of the alternative Levinasian *il y'a* for Blanchot in *Terza*, 158.

9. There is of course a lot to argue here if Agamben implies that Heidegger, Levinas, or Derrida fall into transcendental subjectivity as victims of the Kantian "necessary illusion."

10. The notions of "active and reactive forces" are of course major interpretive categories in Deleuze's *Nietzsche and Philosophy*. See in particular chapter 2 (39–72). I have always felt that the attribution of those categories as ultimate ontological categories to Nietzsche is excessive, although they show up in many guises in Deleuze's thought—they belong more to Deleuze than they do to Nietzsche.

11. It is arguable, however, that the ontotheological primacy of the concept of the person did suffer a great challenge precisely through the history that Esposito

retraces in the first chapter of *Terza persona*, namely, the period between the development of modern biology in the early nineteenth century and the end of World War II.

12. Esposito makes it clear that for the long tradition of civil law the human body is juridically not to be confused with the thing. The body is not what one has, but rather what one is. See *Terza*, 114–18.

13. The essay in question is "La nature des pronoms" (1956), published in *Problèmes de linguistique générale* (1966).

14. Esposito refers to Agamben's *The Open* punctually, to state that "through different paths, it reaches the same conclusions" (*Terza*, 140n19). My purpose will be to expand on those conclusions.

15. Hiu Lui Ng was a New Yorker of Chinese nationality married to an American citizen and with two American-born sons who was arrested in the process of his final interview for a green card on the basis of having overstayed his visa years earlier. He was detained and shuttled through jails and detention centers for many months and denied urgently necessary medical care until he died in custody after tremendous physical suffering. The withholding of medical care is another aspect of the technopolitical administration of life, especially for people deemed to be nonpersons or quasi-persons or less-than-persons. See Bernstein.

16. For "immunitarian drift" and in general for the notion of immunity see, Esposito, *Immunitas*.

17. About the nonsubject, see Moreiras, *Línea de sombra*.

18. Agamben links Deleuzian beatitude with the Gnostics, and then with Benjamin, as part of the underlying eschatological frame of his book. See *Open*, 81–84. The notion of "the whatever" refers to Agamben's *The Coming Community*.

19. "When the difference vanishes and the two terms collapse upon each other — as seems to be happening today — the difference between being and the nothing, licit and illicit, divine and demonic also fades away, and in its place something appears for which we seem to lack even a name" (*Open*, 22).

20. It is interesting that the restitution of the notion of human nature in a substantive sense is for conservative thought in general the best defense against technoscientific threat. See Fukuyama, 29–47.

21. And as I would have liked to have shown also for Derrida, whose book on "the autobiographical animal," mentioned in note 5, is a radical critique of the separation human/animals in the philosophical tradition and down to the very same Heideggerian text on which Agamben focuses his analysis.

22. The awakening of captured closedness to its own captivity, rather than the beginning of politics, is for me a necessary condition of the second or reflective infrapolitics — and the enigmatic region of the absolute difference between life and politics.

23. Among the many possible books on these subjects, see Habermas, Fukuyama, and Rajan.

24. "The way you might investigate a conspiracy, say. And it is perfectly possible that the non-flesh-related, by which I don't mean the soul—that what is non-flesh-related, without being the soul, of which I can't say for certain whether it exists, though I must say I assume it does, that this thousand-year-old working assumption is a thousand-year-old truth—but it is perfectly possible that the non-flesh-related, which is to say, the non-cell-based, is the thing from which everything takes its being, and not the other way round, nor yet some sort of interdependence" (Bernhard, 4).

25. The notion of a "politics of separation" in Derrida deserves serious study, but from its mention in *Politics of Friendship* it is simply not possible in any way to suggest that it wants to be "a separation from politics." This is the relevant passage: "How can a politics of separation be founded? Nietzsche dares to recommend separation, he dares to prescribe distancing in the code excluding distance, in this very distance, and as if were provoking it, in the language that remains as much that of friendship as that of politics, of state, of family" (55). The emphasis on distance as an internal moment in the political relation—let me remind you of my references to "distance" in Chapters 2 and 3 of this book—is to my mind a reference to an infrapolitical fold in the very structure of politics, which is very much present in Nietzsche as well as in Derrida's thought.

7. Infrapolitical Derrida: The Ontic Determination of Politics beyond Empiricism

1. In "Violence and Historicity," which is a meditation on Derrida's "Violence and Metaphysics" (1964) carried over to a study of the 1964–65 seminar, Michael Naas notes that we are far from having understood the complexity of the early Derrida's relations with Heidegger's work, and that we will not be in a better position until many other seminars have been published: "Philosophy of History" and "Silence," from 1959–60, "The Present (Heidegger, Aristotle, Kant, Hegel, Bergson)," from 1960–61, "The World in Heidegger," from 1961–62, and "Error and Errancy: Heidegger" and "History and Truth," from 1963–64.

2. Fredric Jameson's *Specters of Marx* includes some elaboration on several of the problems of the reception of Derrida's most explicitly political thought in the hands of the guardians of political correctness. That Western Marxism continues to be singular reluctant to abandon its own presuppositions is not a surprise, but Jameson puts his finger wrongly on the wound a couple of times: "Derrida's reserves about Marx, and even more strongly about the various Marxisms, all turn very specifically on this point, namely the illicit development of this or that Marxism, or even this or that argument, of Marx himself, in the direction of what he calls an ontology, that is to say, a form of the philosophical system (or of all metaphysics) specifically oriented around the conviction that it is some basic identity of being which can serve as a grounding or foundational reassurance for thought" (37). This type of irony, which consists in refusing in advance the critical charge coming from

any non-Marxist presupposition, thus defamiliarizing it, which turns that critical charge into something at best whimsical, continues with Jameson's observations on the relationship between Heidegger and Derrida (Derrida would have gotten under Heidegger's skirt in order to vindicate Heidegger's alleged grandiosity and then better and more effectively throw him to the winds as himself still trapped by metaphysics [28, 34]). But the most equivocal moment in Jameson's essay comes with his reading of Derrida's reading of the Heideggerian essay "The Fragment of Anaximander." Jameson comes very close to a rightist reading of Heidegger but is aware that he cannot simply blame Derrida for taking that kind of reading upon himself. He then proceeds to reduce the project of rethinking historicity beyond Hegel as a mere mourning process that motivates the apparition of ghosts and specters, hence disavowing everything that is relevant and original and should be taken seriously by Jameson himself in Derrida's reading.

3. Derrida refers to the "non-ethical opening of ethics" in *Grammatology* 140. I thank Erin Graff Zivin for reminding me of this passage.

4. Biset's point throughout his book is that there is the possibility of an alternative conceptualization of the belonging together of philosophy and politics that deconstruction enacts. On my part, I would use alternative terms to talk about the co-belonging: thought and infrapolitics, as opposed to philosophy and politics. The co-belonging of philosophy and politics is too close to the Balibarian philosophical anthropology for my taste and brings us to the neighborhood of the Parmenidean or pseudo-Parmenidean identity of being and thinking.

5. This would be a community not subject to the autoinmmutarian drift mentioned in Chapter 6: a community fully open to a politics of separation, therefore.

6. See "Un inmenso favor," in *Mala índole*, 325–35.

7. See Peter Trawny, *Freedom to Fail* (2015), in which the notion of errancy in Heidegger occupies center stage. See also his *Heidegger et l'antisémitisme* (2014). See also Jean-Luc Nancy's *Banalité de Heidegger*, which is a provocative and thought-provoking book written in a certain dialogue with Trawny's reflections.

8. In a conversation that took place before the writing of this essay, Arturo Leyte comments on the notion of "experiencing errancy as errancy" as an exception to mythical projections: "I think it may well be, provided one does not lose sight of the fact that with it one can also fall into a mythical projection—precisely by raising errancy to the level of category (or error as foundation)—since there is no position that can find itself permanently free from falling into a mythical projection, a projection that infrapolitics should definitely steer clear of. After all, from Heidegger's perspective, even logic was mythically projected into the exceptional position that defines itself as 'the position that does not result from a mythical projection.' Heidegger never stopped denouncing, in the wake of Nietzsche, the concept as an expression of error, but then it is a matter of not letting that 'otherwise than concept' (and what would it be?) simply replace 'truth.' The issue is complicated, and Heidegger's little essay is a permanent challenge."

9. On the Illegal Condition in the State of Extraction: How Not to Be an Informant

1. On "forced disappearance" in Mexico, including important considerations on the Ayotzinapa events, see Federico Mastrogiovanni.

2. Hamacher refers of course to the chapter in *Origins* entitled "The Decline of the Nation-State and the End of the Rights of Man."

Works Cited

Adán, Oscar. "María Zambrano y la pregunta por el Ser." *Aurora* 1 (1999): 59–79.
Agamben, Giorgio. "Absolute Immanence." In *Potentialities: Collected Essays in Philosophy*. Edited and translated by Daniel Heller-Roazen. Stanford, CA: Stanford University Press, 1999. 220–39.
———. *The Kingdom and the Glory: For a Theological Genealogy of Economy and Government (Homo Sacer II, 2)*. Translated by Lorenzo Chiesa (with Matteo Mandarini). Stanford, CA: Stanford University Press, 2011.
———. *The Open: Man and Animal*. Translated by Kevin Attell. Stanford, CA: Stanford University Press, 2004.
———. *The Use of Bodies (Homo Sacer IV, 2)*. Translated by Adam Kotsko. Stanford, CA: Stanford University Press, 2016.
Ahmed, Azam. "Spyware Trailed Investigators in Mexico." *New York Times*, July 10, 2017.
Alemán, Jorge. "Apuntes sobre la emancipación." *Eldiario.es*, March 28, 2015. http://www.eldiario.es/zonacritica/Apuntes-Emancipacion_6_369623060.html
———. *En la frontera: Sujeto y capitalismo—Conversaciones con María Victoria Gimbel*. Barcelona: Gedisa, 2014.
———. *Lacan y el capitalismo*. Granada: Universidad de Granada, 2018.
———. *Soledad: Común—Políticas en Lacan*. Madrid: Clave Intelectual, 2012.
Althusser, Louis. "Ideology and Ideological State Apparatuses (Notes Towards an Investigation)." In *Lenin and Philosophy and Other Essays*. Translated by Ben Brewster. New York: Monthly Review Press, 1971.
Alvarez Yágüez, Jorge. "Límites y potencial crítico de dos categorías políticas: Infrapolítica e impolítica." *Política común* 6 (2014). https://doi.org/10.3998/pc.12322227.0006.013.
Arendt, Hannah. *The Origins of Totalitarianism*. New York: Schocken, 2004.

Badiou, Alain. *Ethics: An Essay on the Understanding of Evil*. Translated by Peter Hallward. New York: Verso, 2001.
———. *La vraie vie*. Paris: Fayard, 2016.
———. *On a raison de se révolter*. Paris: Fayard, 2018.
———. *Saint Paul: La fondation de l'universalisme*. Paris: Presses Universitaires de France, 1997.
Balibar, Etienne. *Citizen Subject: Foundations for Philosophical Anthropology*. New York: Fordham University Press, 2017.
Belzagui, Pablo René, ed. *No matar: Sobre la responsabilidad*. Córdoba, Argentina: Ediciones del Cíclope, 2007.
Benjamin, Walter. "The Storyteller: Observations on the Works of Nikolai Leskov." In *Selected Writings, Volume 3: 1935–38*. Edited by Howard Eiland and Michael W. Jennings. Translated by Edmund Jephcott, Howard Eiland, et al. Cambridge, MA: Belknap Press of Harvard University Press, 2002. 143–66.
———. "The Work of Art in the Age of Its Technological Reproducibility: Second Version." In ibid. 101–33.
Bensaïd, Daniel. *Marx for Our Times: Adventures and Misadventures of a Critique*. Translated by Gregory Elliott. New York: Verso, 2002.
Benveniste, Emile. *Problèmes de linguistique générale*. Paris: Gallimard, 1976.
Bernhard, Thomas. *Frost*. Translated by Michael Hoffman. New York: Vintage, 2008.
Bernstein, Nina. "Ill and in Pain, Detainee Dies in U.S. Hands." *New York Times*, August 13, 2008.
Biset, Emmanuel. *Violencia, justicia y política: Una lectura de Jacques Derrida*. Villa María, Argentina: Eduvim, 2012.
Bosteels, Bruno. *The Actuality of Communism*. London: Verso, 2011.
———. "De Marx a Heidegger: Un itinerario paradigmático (El caso de Oscar del Barco)." *Revista latinoamericana del Colegio Internacional de Filosofía* 5 (2018): 79–119.
———. "El otro Marx." In *Sujeto, transmodernidad, descolonización: Debates filosóficos latinoamericanos*. Edited by Mabel Moraña. Frankfurt and Madrid: Iberoamericana/Vervuert, 2018. 39–68.
———. "Politics, Infrapolitics, and the Impolitical: Notes on the Thought of Roberto Esposito and Alberto Moreiras." *New Centennial Review* 10.2 (2010): 2015–238.
Butler, Judith. *Antigone's Claim: Kinship between Life and Death*. New York: Columbia University Press, 2000.
Cacciari, Massimo. *Krisis: Saggio sulla crisi del pensiero negativo da Nietzsche and Wittgenstein*. Milan: Feltrinelli, 1976.
———. "Nietzsche and the Unpolitical." In *The Unpolitical: On the Radical Critique of Political Reason*. Edited by Alessandro Carrera. Translated by Massimo Verdicchio. New York: Fordham University Press, 2009. 92–103.
———. "Para una investigación sobre la relación entre Zambrano y Heidegger." *Archipiélago* 59 (December 2003): 47–52.

Calvillo, Ana Luisa. *Me decían mexicano frijolero (El caso Rangel)*. Mexico: Ficticia, 2015.
Capobianco, Richard. *Engaging Heidegger*. Toronto: University of Toronto Press, 2010.
———. "Heidegger's Turn Toward Home: On Dasein's Primordial Relation to Being." *Epoché* 10–11 (Fall 2005): 155–73.
———. *Heidegger's Way of Being*. Toronto: University of Toronto Press, 2014.
Casanova, Carlos. *Estética y producción en Karl Marx*. Santiago, Chile: Metales Pesados, 2016.
Chakrabarty, Dipesh. *Provincializing Europe: Postcolonial Thought and Historical Difference*. Princeton, NJ: Princeton University Press, 2000.
Clastres, Pierre. *Society against the State*. Translated by Robert Hurley and Abe Stein. New York: Zone Books, 1989.
Colebrook, Claire. *Death of the Posthuman: Essays on Extinction, Vol. 1*. Ann Arbor: Open Humanities Press, 2014.
———. *Sex after Life: Essays on Extinction, Vol. 2*. Ann Arbor: Open Humanities Press, 2014.
Dahlstrom, Daniel O. "Heidegger's Initial Interpretation of Parmenides: An Excursus in the 1922 Lectures on Aristotelian Texts." *Review of Metaphysics* 70 (2017): 507–27.
Del Barco, Oscar. "Comments on the Articles by Jorge Jinkis, Juan Ritvo, and Eduardo Grüner in *Conjetural*." *Journal of Latin American Cultural Studies* 16.2 (2007): 155–82.
———. "No matarás: Thou Shalt Not Kill." *Journal of Latin American Cultural Studies* 16.2 (2007): 115–17.
Deleuze, Gilles. "Immanence: A Life . . ." In *Two Regimes of Madness: Texts and Interviews 1975–1995*. Edited by David Lapoujade. Translated by Ames Hodges and Mike Taormina. New York: Semiotext(e), 2006. 384–89.
———. *Nietzsche and Philosophy*. Translated by Hugh Tomlinson. New York: Columbia University Press, 1986.
Deleuze, Gilles, and Felix Guattari. *What Is Philosophy?* Translated by Hugh Tomlinson and Graham Burnell. New York: Columbia University Press, 1994.
Derrida, Jacques. *Adieu a Levinas*. Translated by Michael Naas and Pascale-Anne Brault. Stanford, CA: Stanford University Press, 1999.
———. *The Animal That Therefore I Am*. Edited by Marie-Louise Mallet. Translated by David Wills. New York: Fordham University Press, 2008.
———. *The Beast and the Sovereign, Volume 1*. Edited by Michel Lisse, Marie-Louise Mallet, and Ginette Michaud. Translated by Geoffrey Bennington. Chicago: University of Chicago Press, 2009.
———. *The Beast and the Sovereign, Volume 2*. Edited by Michel Lisse, Marie-Louise Mallet, and Ginette Michaud. Translated by Geoffrey Bennington. Chicago: University of Chicago Press, 2011.

———. *Clamor*. Translated by Cristina de Peretti, Luis Ferrero Carracedo, et al. Madrid: La Oficina, 2016.

———. *Glas: Que reste-t-il du savoir absolu?* Paris: Denoël-Gonthier, 1981.

———. *Heidegger: La question de l'Etre et l'Histoire—Cours de l'ENS-ULM 1964–1965*. Edited by Thomas Dutoit and Marguerite Derrida. Paris: Galilée, 2013.

———. "Letter to a Japanese Friend." In *Derrida and Différance*. Edited by David Wood and Robert Bernasconi. Evanston, IL: Northwestern University Press, 1998. 1–5.

———. *Of Grammatology*. Translated by Gayatri Spivak. Baltimore, MD: Johns Hopkins University Press, 1974.

———. "*Ousia* and *Grammé*: Note on a Note from *Being and Time*." In *Margins of Philosophy*. Translated by Alan Bass. Chicago: Harvester Press, 1982. 29–68.

———. *Politics of Friendship*. Translated by George Collins. London: Verso, 1997.

———. "The Right to Philosophy from the Cosmopolitical Point of View. (The Example of an International Institution)." *Ethics, Institutions, and the Right to Philosophy*. Edited by Peter Pericles Trifonas. Lanham, MD: Rowman and Littlefield, 2002.

———. *Specters of Marx: The State of the Debt, the Work of Mourning & the New International*. Translated by Peggy Kamuf. New York: Routledge, 1994.

———. "Violence and Metaphysics. An Essay on the Thought of Emmanuel Levinas." In *Writing and Difference*. Translated by Alan Bass. Chicago: University of Chicago Press, 1978. 79–153.

Donoso Cortés, Juan. *Ensayo sobre el catolicismo, el liberalismo y el socialismo*. Edited by José Luis Gómez. Barcelona: Planeta, 1985.

Dove, Patrick. "Memory between Politics and Ethics: Del Barco's Letter." *Journal of Latin American Cultural Studies* 17.3 (2008): 279–297.

Esposito, Roberto. *Categories of the Impolitical*. Translated by Connal Parsley. New York: Fordham University Press, 2015.

———. *Da fuori: Una filosofia per l'Europa*. Turin: Einaudi, 2016.

———. *Immunitas: Protezione e negazione della vita*. Turin: Einaudi, 2002.

———. *Le persone e le cose*. Turin: Einaudi, 2014.

———. *The Origin of the Political: Hannah Arendt or Simone Weil?* Translated by Vincenzo Binetti and Gareth Williams. New York: Fordham University Press, 2017.

———. *Terza persona: Politica della vita e filosofia dell'impersonale*. Turin: Einaudi, 2007.

Fukuyama, Francis. *Our Posthuman Future: Consequences of the Biotechnology Revolution*. New York: Picador, 2002.

García, Luis Ignacio. "No matar: Una botella arrojada al mar." *Papel Máquina* 9 (2015): 33–62.

García, Luis Ignacio, ed. *No matar: Sobre la responsabilidad—Segunda compilación de intervenciones*. Córdoba, Argentina: Universidad Nacional de Córdoba, 2010.

García Linera, Alvaro. *Forma valor y forma comunidad: Aproximación teórico-abstracta a los fundamentos civilizatorios que preceden al Ayllu universal*. Buenos Aires: Prometeo, 2010.

Geiman, Clare Pearson. "Heidegger's Antigones." In *A Companion to Heidegger's Introduction to Metaphysics*. Edited by Richard Polt and Gregory Fried. New Haven, CT: Yale University Press, 2001. 161–82.

Graff Zivin, Erin. "El giro ético o Lévinas en Latinoamérica." *Pléyade* 19 (January–June 2017): 91–111.

Greenwald, Glenn. *No Place to Hide: Edward Snowden, the NSA, and the US Surveillance State*. New York: Picador, 2014.

Guha, Ranajit. *History at the Limits of World History*. New York: Columbia University Press, 2002.

Habermas, Juergen. *The Future of Human Nature*. Cambridge: Polity Press, 2003.

Hägglund, Martin. *Radical Atheism: Derrida and the Time of Life*. Stanford, CA: Stanford University Press, 2008.

Hamacher, Werner. "On the Right to Have Rights." *CR: The New Centennial Review* 14.2 (2014): 169–214.

Harcourt, Bernard. *Exposed: Desire and Disobedience in the Digital Age*. Cambridge, MA: Harvard University Press, 2015.

Hartman, Geoffrey. "Homage to Glas." *Critical Inquiry* 33 (Winter 2007): 344–61.

Head, Simon. *Mindless: Why Smarter Machines Are Making Dumber Humans*. New York: Basic Books, 2014.

Heidegger, Martin. "The Age of the World Picture." In *Off the Beaten Track*. Edited and translated by Julian Young and Kenneth Haynes. Cambridge: Cambridge University Press, 2002. 57–85.

———. "The Anaximander Fragment." In *Early Greek Thinking: The Dawn of Western Philosophy*. Translated by David Farrell Krell and Frank A. Capuzzi. San Francisco: Harper & Row, 1984. 13–58.

———. *Basic Principles of Thinking*. Freiburg Lectures 1957. In *Bremen and Freiburg Lectures*. Translated by Andrew J. Mitchell. Bloomington: Indiana University Press, 2012. 77–166.

———. *Being and Time*. Translated by Joan Stambaugh. Albany: State University of New York Press, 1996.

———. *Being and Truth*. Translated by Gregory Fried and Richard Polt. Bloomington: Indiana University Press, 2010.

———. *Contributions to Philosophy (Of the Event)*. Translated by Richard Rojcewicz and Daniela Vallega-Neu. Bloomington: Indiana University Press, 2012.

———. "A Dialogue on Language between a Japanese and an Inquirer." In *On the Way to Language*. Translated by Peter D. Hertz. San Francisco: Harper & Row, 1971. 1–54.

———. *Elucidations of Hölderlin's Poetry*. Edited and translated by Keith Hoeller. Amherst, MA: Humanities Books, 2000.

———. *Four Seminars*. Translated by Andrew Mitchell and François Raffoul. Bloomington: Indiana University Press, 2003.

———. *Heraclitus: The Inception of Universal Thinking and Logic—Heraclitus's Doctrine of the Logos*. Translated by Julia Goessner Assaiante and S. Montgomery Ewegen. London: Athlone, 2018.

———. *Hölderlin's Hymn "The Ister."* Translated by William McNeill and Julia Davis. Bloomington: Indiana University Press, 1996.

———. *Identidad y diferencia/Identität und Differenz*. Edited by Arturo Leyte. Translated by Helena Cortés and Arturo Leyte. Barcelona: Anthropos, 1988.

———. *Introduction to Metaphysics*. Translated by Gregory Fried and Richard Polt. New Haven, CT: Yale University Press, 2000.

———. *Kant and the Problem of Metaphysics*. Translated by Richard Taft. Bloomington: Indiana University Press, 1997.

———. "Letter on Humanism." In *Basic Writings*. Edited by David Farrell Krell. New York: Harper & Row, 1977. 189–242.

———. "Messkirch's Seventh Centennial." Translated by Thomas J. Sheehan. *Listening*, 8.1–3 (1973): 40–57.

———. "On the Essence of Truth." In *Pathmarks*. Edited by William McNeill. Cambridge: Cambridge University Press, 1998. 136–54.

———. "On the Question Concerning the Determination of the Matter for Thinking." Translated by Richard Capobianco and Marie Göbel. *Epoché* 14.2 (2010): 213–23.

———. "On the Question of Being." In *Pathmarks*. Translated by William McNeill. Cambridge: Cambridge University Press, 1998. 291–322.

———. "Overcoming Metaphysics." In *The End of Philosophy*. Translated by Joan Stambaugh. Chicago: University of Chicago Press, 2003. 84–110.

———. *Parmenides*. Translated by André Schuwer and Richard Rojcewicz. Bloomington: Indiana University Press, 1998.

———. "The Pathway." *Listening: Journal of Religion and Culture* 8.1–3 (1973): 32–39.

———. "Phenomenological Interpretations with Respect to Aristotle: Indication of the Hermeneutic Situation by Martin Heidegger." Translated by Michael Baur. *Man and World* 25 (1992): 355–93.

———. *The Question Concerning Technology and Other Essays*. Translated by William Lovitt. New York: Harper & Row, 1977.

Honig, Bonnie. *Antigone, Interrupted*. New York: Cambridge University Press, 2013.

Jameson, Fredric. "The End of Temporality." *Critical Inquiry* 29.4 (Summer 2003): 695–718.

———. "Marx's Purloined Letter." In *Ghostly Demarcations: A Symposium on Jacques Derrida's Specters of Marx*. Edited by Michael Sprinker. New York: Verso, 1995. 26–67.

Kant, Immanuel. *Religion within the Limits of Reason Alone*. Edited and translated by Theodore Greene and Hoyt H. Hudson. New York: Harper One, 2008.

Kelley, Robin. *Race Rebels: Culture, Politics, and the Black Working Class*. New York: Free Press, 1994.
Kirk, G. S. J., E. Raven, and M. Schofield. *The Presocratic Philosophers*. Cambridge: Cambridge University Press, 1983.
Krell, David Farrell. "*Das Unheimliche*: Architectural Sections of Heidegger and Freud." *Research in Phenomenology* 22 (1992): 43–61.
Lacan, Jacques. "Du discours psychoanalytique." http://ecole-lacanienne.net/wp-content/uploads/2016/04/1972-05-12.pdf.
———. *The Seminar of Jacques Lacan, Book II: The Ego in Freud's Theory and in the Technique of Psychoanalysis, 1954–1955*. Edited by Jacques-Alain Miller. Translated by Sylvana Tomaselli. New York: Norton, 1991.
———. *The Seminar of Jacques Lacan, Book VII: The Ethics of Psychoanalysis, 1959–1960*. Edited by Jacques Alain Miller. Translated by Dennis Potter. New York: Norton, 1992.
———. *The Seminar of Jacques Lacan, Book XVII: The Other Side of Psychoanalysis*. Edited by Jacques-Alain Miller. Translated by Russell Grigg. New York: Norton, 2007.
Laclau, Ernesto. "Identity and Hegemony: The Role of Universality in the Constitution of Political Logics." In Judith Butler, Ernesto Laclau, and Slavoj Žižek, *Contingency, Hegemony, Universality: Contemporary Dialogues on the Left*. London: Verso, 2000.
Lacoue-Labarthe, Philippe. "De l'ethique: A propos d'Antigone." In *Lacan avec les philosophes*. Paris: Albin Michel, 1990. 19–37.
Laertius, Diogenes. *Lives of Eminent Philosophers*. Volume 2. Translated by R.D. Hicks. Cambridge, MA: Harvard University Press, 1995.
Lévinas, Emmanuel. "Au-delá de l'Etat dans l'Etat." In *Nouvelles lectures talmudiques*. Paris: Minuit, 2005. 45–76.
———. *Otherwise Than Being, or Beyond Essence*. Translated by Alphonso Lingis. Boston: Kluwer Academic, 1991.
———. *Totality and Infinity. An Essay on Exteriority*. Translated by Alphonso Lingis. Pittsburgh: Duquesne University Press, 1969.
Leyte, Arturo. "La naturaleza *reaccionaria* de la filosofía." *Res publica* 13–14 (2004): 165–80.
———. *Las épocas de Schelling*. Madrid: Akal, 1998.
Lezra, Jacques. *On the Nature of Marx's Things: Translation as Necrophilology*. New York: Fordham University Press, 2018.
Loraux, Nicole. "Notes sur l'un, le deux et le multiple." In *L'Esprit des lois sauvages: Pierre Clastres ou une nouvelle anthropologie politique*. Edited by Miguel Abensour. Paris: Seuil, 1987. 155–70.
Lyotard, Jean-François. *The Differend: Phrases in Dispute*. Translated by Georges Van den Abbeele. Manchester: Manchester University Press, 1988.
———. *Logique de Levinas*. Edited by Paul Audi. Paris: Verdier, 2015.

Malabou, Cathérine. *The Heidegger Change: On the Fantastic in Philosophy.* Translated by Peter Skafish. Albany: State University of New York Press, 2011.

Mallon, Florencia. *Courage Tastes of Blood: The Mapuche Community of Nicolás Ailío and the Chilean State, 1906–2001.* Durham, NC: Duke University Press, 2005.

Mandarini, Matteo. "Beyond Nihilism: Notes Towards a Critique of Left-Heideggerianism in Italian Philosophy of the 1970s." *Cosmos and History: The Journal of Natural and Social Philosophy* 5.1 (2009): 1–16.

Marías, Javier. "Un inmenso favor." In *Mala índole: Cuentos aceptados y aceptables.* Madrid: Alfaguara, 2012. 325–35.

Marion, Jean-Luc. *The Idol and Distance: Five Studies.* Edited and translated by Thomas A. Carlson. New York: Fordham University Press, 2001.

Martínez, Oscar. *A History of Violence: Living and Dying in Central America.* London: Verso, 2016.

Martínez Marzoa, Felipe. *El concepto de lo civil.* Santiago, Chile: Metales Pesados, 2008.

———. "Estado y legitimidad." In *Los filósofos y la política.* Edited by Manuel Cruz. Mexico: Fondo de cultura económica, 1999. 85–101.

———. "Estado y *pólis*." In ibid. 101–15.

———. *Heidegger y su tiempo.* Madrid: Akal, 1999.

———. *La filosofía de "El capital."* Madrid: Taurus, 1983.

Mastrogiovanni, Federico. *La desaparición forzada en México como estrategia de terror.* Mexico City: Penguin Random House, 2016.

Mazur, Robert. *The Infiltrator: The True Story of One Man against the Biggest Drug Cartel in History.* New York: Back Bay, 2016.

McCarthy, Cormac. *The Crossing.* New York: Knopf, 1994.

Méndez Cota, Gabriela. "Feminismo, infrapolítica, extinción." *Pensamiento al margen.* Special issue of *Infrapolítica y Democracia.* 2018. http://pensamientoalmargen.com.

Moreiras, Alberto. *Against Abstraction: Notes from an Ex-Latin Americanist.* Austin: University of Texas Press, 2020.

———. *Infrapolítica: Instrucciones de uso.* Madrid: La Oficina, 2020.

———. *Infrapolítica: La diferencia absoluta (entre vida y política) de la que ningún experto puede hablar.* Santiago, Chile: Palinodia, 2019.

———. *Línea de sombra: El no sujeto de lo político.* Santiago, Chile: Palinodia, 2006.

———. *Sosiego siniestro.* Madrid: Guillermo Escolar, 2020.

———. *Tercer espacio y otros relatos.* Nottingham: SPLASH, 2021.

Moreno Sanz, Jesús, ed. *María Zambrano: La razón en la sombra—Antología crítica.* Madrid: Siruela, 2004.

Naas, Michael. "Violence and Historicity: Derrida's Early Reading of Heidegger." *Research in Phenomenology* 45.2 (2015): 191–213.

Nancy, Jean-Luc. *After Fukushima: The Equivalence of Catastrophes.* Translated by Charlotte Mandel. Stanford, CA: Stanford University Press, 2014.

———. *Banalité de Heidegger*. Paris: Galilée, 2015.
———. "The Decision of Existence." In *Birth to Presence*. Translated by Brian Holmes. Stanford, CA: Stanford University Press, 1993. 82–109.
———. *La communauté affrontée*. Paris: Galilée, 2001.
———. *La communauté désavouée*. Paris: Galilée, 2014.
———. *Verité de la democratie*. Paris: Galilée, 2008.
Perry, Thomas. *The Informant: Butcher's Boy, Book 3*. New York: Mariner, 2012.
Preston, Paul. *Comrades! Portraits from the Spanish Civil War*. London: HarperCollins, 1999.
Rajan, Kaushik Sunder. *Biocapital: The Constitution of Postgenomic Life*. Durham, NC: Duke University Press, 2006.
Rancière, Jacques. *Disagreements: Politics and Philosophy*. Translated by Julie Rose. Minneapolis: University of Minnesota Press, 1999.
Rozitchner, León. *Levinas o la filosofía de la consolación*. Buenos Aires: Biblioteca Nacional, 2013.
Schmitt, Carl. *Political Theology: Four Chapters on the Question of Sovereignty*. Translated by George Schwab. Cambridge, MA: MIT Press, 1985.
Schürmann, Reiner. *Broken Hegemonies*. Translated by Reginald Lilly. Bloomington: Indiana University Press, 2003.
———. *Heidegger on Being and Acting: From Principles to Anarchy*. Translated by Christine Marie-Gros and Reiner Schürmann. Bloomington: Indiana University Press, 1990.
———. *Wandering Joy: Meister Eckhart's Mystical Philosophy*. Grand Barrington MA: Lindisfarne Books, 2001.
Scott, James C. *Domination and the Arts of Resistance: Hidden Transcripts*. New Haven, CT: Yale University Press, 1990.
———. *Two Cheers for Anarchism: Six Easy Pieces on Autonomy, Dignity, and Meaningful Work and Play*. Princeton, NJ: Princeton University Press, 2012.
Sevilla, Sergio. "La razón poética: Mirada, melodía y metáfora—María Zambrano y la hermenéutica." In *María Zambrano: La razón poética y la filosofía*. Edited by Teresa Rocha Barco. Madrid: Tecnos, 1997. 87–108.
Sheehan, Thomas. "But What Comes before the After?" In *After Heidegger?* Edited by Richard Polt and Greg Fried. London: Rowman & Littlefield International, 2018. 41–55.
Söderback, Fanny, ed. *Feminist Readings of Antigone*. Albany: State University of New York Press, 2010.
Sophocles. *Antigone*. In *Antigone, Women of Trachis, Philoctetes, Oedipus at Colonus*. Edited and translated by Hugh Lloyd-Jones. Cambridge, MA: Harvard University Press, 1994.
Spivak, Gayatri Chakravorty. "Subaltern Studies: Deconstructing Historiography." In Ranajit Guha and Gayatri Chakravorty Spivak, *Selected Subaltern Studies*. New York: Oxford University Press, 1988. 3–32.
Sztulwark, Diego. "Poema y política en León Rozitchner." Typescript.

Tarizzo, Davide. "Political Grammars: The Unconscious Foundations of Modern Democracy." Unpublished prospectus.
Trawny, Peter. *Freedom to Fail: Heidegger's Anarchy*. Translated by Ian Alexander Moore and Christopher Turner. Cambridge: Polity, 2015.
———. *Heidegger et l'antisémitisme: Sur les "Cahiers noirs."* Translated by Julia Christ and Jean-Claude Monod. Paris: Editions du Seuil, 2014.
Valle-Inclán, Ramón María del. *Obra completa, I: Prosa*. Madrid: Espasa, 2002.
Villalobos-Ruminott, Sergio. *La desarticulación: Epocalidad, hegemonía e historicidad*. Santiago, Chile: Macul, 2019.
———. "Notas al Seminario sobre Infrapolítica." (February 19, 2015). Unpublished.
———. "Oscar del Barco: La crítica del marxismo como técnica liberacionista." *Papel Máquina* 9 (August 2015): 133–53.
Viveiros de Castro, Eduardo. *The Inconstancy of the Indian Soul: The Encounter of Catholics and Cannibals in 16th Century Brazil*. Translated by Gregory Duff Morton. Chicago: Prickly Paradigm Press, 2011.
Wachtel, Nathan. *The Faith of Remembrance: Marrano Labyrinths*. Translated by Nikki Halpern. Philadelphia: University of Pennsylvania Press, 2013.
Williams, Gareth. *Infrapolitical Passages: Decontainment, Narco-Accumulation and Populism*. New York: Fordham University Press, 2020.
Winslow, Don. *The Force*. New York: HarperCollins, 2017.
Zambrano, María. *El hombre y lo divino*. Madrid: Siruela, 1991.
———. *Persona y democracia: La historia sacrificial*. 1958. Barcelona: Anthropos, 1988.

Index

Abensour, Miguel, 69
Adorno, Theodor, 148
Agamben, Giorgio, 28, 69, 122–24, 126–27, 136–44, 147–48
Alemán, Jorge, 69, 96–97, 121, 200n5, 203n3
aletheia, 140, 168
Althusser, Louis, 37
Alvarez Yáguez, Jorge, 64
anarchy, 51, 71, 112, 160, 163, 172–74, 178–81, 195, 200n6; principle of, 176–81
Anaximander, 107–9
Antigone, 7–8, 50, 53, 55–59, 151, 205–6n11
Arendt, Hannah, 105, 129, 193–94
Aufhebung 3–6, 8

Badiou, Alain, 11, 27, 43, 86, 91–92, 95, 97–104, 198n2
Balibar, Etienne, 93–95
Bataille, Georges, 148
Benjamin, Walter, 11, 40, 122
Bensaïd, Daniel, 40
Bentham, Jeremy, 37
Benveniste, Emile, 126, 133
Bernhard, Thomas, 143
Bhabha, Homi, 28
Bichat, Xavier, 127–28
bioethics, 126, 131
biopolitics, 86, 116, 122–28, 135, 137, 141–45, 147, 149–51
Biset, Emmanuel, 161
Blanchot, Maurice, 134, 136
Borges, Jorge Luis, 60

Bosteels, Bruno, 114–17
Brown, Wendy, 28
Butler, Judith, 28

Cacciari, Massimo, 69, 71, 119–20, 147–48
Calvillo, Ana Luis, 189–90
Clastres, Pierre, 80–81, 83
communism, 16, 33, 36, 89–91, 98–99, 102, 104, 114; communist politics, 100, 114
communitarianism/communitarian thought 17–18, 20, 24, 132–37, 144, 146–47, 149–51; countercomunitarian politics, 69, 133–34, 136, 150
community, 7, 18, 51–53, 60, 69, 83–84, 116, 118, 132–35, 137, 141, 146–51, 161–62; political; 18, 51, 129. *See also* immunity
Comte, Auguste, 128
cultural studies, x, 67
cybernetics, 61–62

Dasein, 17–18, 54–55, 111, 140–41, 168–69, 205n6
death drive, 96–98, 100, 102, 185, 197n2
deconstruction, xi, 1–5, 7, 64–65, 127, 142–48, 150, 155–59, 174, 197n1
degrounded relation, 9–10, 13, 15, 17, 19–20, 22–24, 34
del Barco, Oscar, 69, 72–79, 115
Deleuze, Gilles, 27, 30, 82, 122–24, 126–27, 136–37, 139, 144, 148, 177, 179–80
democracy, 9–13, 15, 61–62, 67, 80, 82, 90, 99, 117–18, 128–29, 159–60, 202–3n1;

democracy (*continued*)
  democratic politics, 9–13, 21, 67, 118, 167, 171; posthegemonic, 67, 80–82
Derrida, Jacques, 1–8, 11, 28, 64–65, 69, 82, 107–9, 116, 123, 139, 145–46, 151, 154–69, 177, 179–80
différance, 108–10, 154
disinheritance, 18, 20. *See also* legacy
dispositif, 127, 130–31, 147, 135, 140, 147
divine, the, 13, 14, 19, 154
Donoso Cortés, Juan, 10, 33–34, 35–38, 49, 198–99n8
Dove, Patrick, 78
Dussel, Enrique, 28

Eckhart, Meister, 175
egalitarian symbolization, 97–99, 102, 104
Engelhardt, Hugo, 131
epoch/epochal, 9, 13, 19, 36, 50, 61, 66–67, 70–71, 112, 116, 119–20, 124–25, 149, 154, 156, 165, 172–74, 180
errancy, 38, 55–56, 98, 104, 156, 167–69
Esposito, Roberto, 69, 105, 107, 114–17, 120–39, 142–51
ethics, 76–77, 79, 117, 136, 157–58, 164, 171, 182; ethical relation, 135–36, 162, 166

Foucault, Michel, 27–28, 122, 126–27, 136–37, 139, 144, 148
freedom, 38–39, 42, 44, 96, 106–7, 110, 125, 128, 132–33, 150, 155, 162, 168–69, 181, 184, 185–86, 191–93
Freud, Sigmund, 35, 69, 99, 130, 197n2

García Calvo, Agustín, 29
García Linera, Alvaro, 84
gender, 13, 99, 102
general equivalence, 52, 60–62, 71, 73–74, 86–91, 98–100, 102
Gianbattista, Vico, 144
Gracián, Baltasar, 107
Greenwald, Glenn, 183
Guattari, Felix, 27, 82, 123
Guha, Ranajit, 44–49

Hägglund, Martin, 157, 164
Hall, Stuart, 28
Hamacher, Werner, 193–94
Harcourt, Bernard, 184–85
Hartman, Geoffrey, 2–5, 7, 197n1
Hegel, Georg, 3–7, 16, 28, 30, 34, 45–50, 77, 94–95, 155–56, 161, 180

hegemony, xi, 14–15, 32, 37, 46–48, 70–72, 74, 78, 81, 82–83, 89, 103, 108, 112, 121, 146, 159, 173, 175; counterhegemony, xi, 47, 59, 62, 66, 77, 146–47; hegemonic power, 71–72, 78; hegemonic subalternism, 48–49; posthegemony, 61, 63, 67–68, 70, 74, 77, 80–83, 120, 146, 160, 174–75. *See also* democracy: posthegemonic
Heidegger, Martin, 9, 13–18, 20–22, 47–48, 50–59, 62, 69–72, 87, 91, 103, 107–9, 111–12, 116, 123, 139–42, 145, 152–54, 156, 158, 161–62, 165–69, 171–75, 181
Heraclitus, 83, 91–92, 97–99
historicity, 17, 20–21, 27, 31, 40–41, 44–49, 155–58
Hobbes, Thomas, 130
Hölderlin, Friedrich, 56–57, 116
Husserl, Edmund, 28, 123, 139, 145, 161–62

ideology, 37–38; of the person, 121, 125, 131, 139
immunity, 147–50, 208n16
impersonal, the, 105–6, 123, 126–27, 131–34, 136–39, 142–43, 162. *See also* person
impolitical, 67, 97, 105, 114–21, 144–45, 147–48, 158. *See also* unpolitical
infrapolitics, ix, 5, 7–8, 10, 22, 24–25, 27, 29, 31, 39, 44, 50, 53, 59–72, 74, 77–79, 83, 85–87, 90, 96–97, 104–22, 124, 127, 131, 150–51, 154, 157–58, 160, 162–64, 166–69, 171–72, 174–76, 181–82, 185, 193–95; Infrapolitical Deconstruction Collective, xi, 67; infrapolitical distance, 53, 59; infrapolitical obligation, 171, 176; infrapolitical region, 29, 65–66, 69, 97, 104, 158, 164, 181–82, 193; infrapolitical site, 119, 157, 164
Irigaray, Luce, 28, 69, 107

Jameson, Fredric, 27–28, 209–10n2
jouissance, 6–7, 96, 98, 192, 201–2n8

Kant, Immanuel, 35, 47–48, 139, 170, 181, 185–86, 190
Kojève, Alexandre, 138

Lacan, Jacques, 33–35, 37–38, 69, 92–93, 96, 104, 107, 116, 118
Lacoue-Labarthe, Philippe, 116
Laclau, Ernesto, 28, 45, 70, 203–4n3
Latin American studies, x, 64, 67–68
legacy, 18, 20–25; un-legacy, 18–24, 71

INDEX

Lévinas, Emmanuel, 10, 13, 71, 116, 123, 134–36, 138–39, 156–63, 166–67, 170, 177–81, 200n6
Leyte, Arturo, 29–30, 69, 198n4
life without a texture, 9, 13, 21–24
Loraux, Nicole, 80
Lyotard, Jean-François, 144, 170–71, 179–81

Machiavelli, Niccolò, 144
Malabou, Cathérine, 68–69
Mallon, Florencia, 79–81, 83–84
Marías, Javier, 165
Marion, Jean-Luc, 152–54
marranismo, 68, 70, 158
Martínez, Oscar, 186–88
Martínez Marzoa, Felipe, 22, 25–27, 29–31, 49–53, 56, 58, 60–61, 69, 73–74
Marx, Karl, 39–40, 48, 73, 75, 89, 98, 155–56; Marxism, 32, 74–75, 89–90, 95, 198n6, 209–10n2
Mazur, Robert, 191–92
Merleau-Ponty, Maurice, 123
metaphysical closure, 62, 172, 174, 174, 180
militancy: militant subject, 28, 44, 115–16; political, 76; progressive, 21–22, 28–29, 31–32, 34–35, 39–40, 42–45, 47–49; reactionary, 21–22, 28–29, 31–32, 34, 39–40, 42–45, 49; revolutionary, 72, 76; subjective/ontotheological, 10, 21–26, 28–31, 34–35, 74, 98. *See also* progressivism; reaction
modernity, 10, 13–14, 21, 25–30, 33–34, 36, 40, 49, 60–61, 66–68, 73–74, 86, 94–95, 98, 100, 104, 121, 130, 150, 173, 178
Moreno Sanz, Jesús, 198n1

Nancy, Jean-Luc, 28, 69, 86–90, 99, 103, 107, 109–11, 116, 148, 150
Nazism, 15, 57, 71–72, 126, 128–30, 135, 169, 199n1, 199–200n2
Negri, Antonio, 27, 148
Nietzsche, Friedrich, 11, 16, 19, 30–31, 50, 107, 119–20, 137, 139, 149, 205n6

Oedipus, 54–55
ontico-ontological difference, 108, 154, 166, 198n2
ontological difference, 53, 59, 70, 108–9, 111, 152–58, 168, 170, 200–1n7
ontotheology, 4, 17, 19, 25, 31, 66, 71, 73, 125, 128, 139, 152, 153, 155, 198n3
Ortega y Gasset, José, 145

Parmenides, 10, 14, 25, 49, 161
Peña Nieto, Enrique, 190
Perry, Thomas, 191–92
person, 115–16, 121, 125–37, 139, 142; third-person, 126–27, 133–36, 138. *See also* impersonal, the
Pessoa, Fernando, 107
philosophical anthropology, 47, 90, 93–94, 96–97, 100, 103
Plato, 58, 162, 198–99n8
polis, 50–53, 56–60, 91, 141, 194, 206–7n3
political, the, xiii, 10–15, 18, 20–22, 24, 27–28, 32–33, 37, 42, 49, 52–53, 58, 60, 66, 68–69, 72, 90, 92, 94, 119–20, 128, 133, 136, 139, 141, 148–49, 155, 159–60
political theology, 19, 115–17, 119, 127–28, 144, 147–48, 150–51; politico-theological, 144, 146–47, 149–50; post-theological, 35, 37–38; theologico-political, 33, 116, 151
politics, 10–14, 18, 24, 52–53, 59–60, 62–63, 66–67, 69–70, 73–74, 76–79, 83, 85–87, 90–97, 99, 103–7, 110–21, 124, 126–28, 132–39, 141–51, 153–69, 171–73, 182, 190, 193–95; heliopolitics, 67, 158, 161, 166–67; political thought, 10, 15, 19, 47, 104, 153, 155; revolutionary, 73–74
postmodernity, 41
Primo de Rivera, Pilar, 132–33
progressivism, 22, 29–32, 34, 39, 42–43, 45–49. *See also* reaction

Ranciére, Jacques, 12, 117
Rangel, Roberto, 189–92
reaction, 22, 29–31, 32–34, 36–37, 39–46, 48–49, 94, 198n7
Rozitchner, León, 77–78

sacred, the/sacredness, 13, 14, 19, 23–24, 77–78, 132
sacrificial history, 10–13, 18, 21, 24, 71
Sartre, Jean-Paul, 105
Schelling, Friedrich, 30
Schmitt, Carl, 10, 12, 16, 32, 40
Schopenhauer, Arthur, 128
Schürmann, Reiner, ix, 50, 61, 69, 71, 106, 171–79, 181, 200n6
Scott, James C., 64
Sheehan, Thomas 107, 109, 111–12
Singer, Peter, 131
Snowden, Edward, 183
Sophocles, 57, 107, 199–200n2
Spengler, Oswald, 145

Spinoza, Baruch, 139
Spivak, Gayatri, 28, 44, 46, 48
state of extraction, 184, 188–90. *See also* surveillance state
subaltern studies, x
subalternity, 13, 19, 20–21, 24, 28, 32, 44, 46–49, 68, 79
subjectivity, 10, 13, 15–16, 18–19, 21–24, 27–28, 30–31, 43, 48, 62, 74–75, 105, 111, 115, 122–27, 168, 178, 180
surveillance state, 183–85, 187–94

Tarizzo, Davide, 69, 118
technology, 60, 87, 96, 102, 141–42, 154, 174, 176
technopolitics, 121–24, 126–28, 134, 138, 141–43
technoscience, 121–22, 126, 130, 143

Teresa of Ávila, 107
Tronti, Mario, 69, 144, 147–48
Trump, Donald, 120, 167, 190

unpolitical, 119–20

Valéry, Paul, 145
Valle-Inclán, Ramón, 41–42
Villalobos-Ruminott, Sergio, 68
violence, 55–57, 76–77, 147, 163–67, 177, 179

Weil, Simone, 69, 105–7, 116, 132
Winslow, Don, 191
Wittgenstein, Ludwig, 145

Zambrano, María, 9–11, 13–22, 69, 71
Žižek, Slavoj, 28

Alberto Moreiras is Professor of Hispanic Studies at Texas A&M University. He is the author of *The Exhaustion of Difference: The Politics of Latin American Cultural Studies* (Duke University Press, 2001), *Against Abstraction: Notes from an Ex–Latin Americanist* (University of Texas Press, 2020), *Sosiego siniestro* (Guillermo Escolar, 2020), and *Tercer espacio y otros relatos* (SPLASH, 2021).

www.ingramcontent.com/pod-product-compliance
Lightning Source LLC
Chambersburg PA
CBHW030528010526
44110CB00048B/781